GENEALOGIES OF THE SECULAR

SUNY SERIES IN THEOLOGY AND CONTINENTAL THOUGHT
Douglas L. Donkel, editor

# GENEALOGIES *of the* SECULAR

## The Making of Modern German Thought

*Edited by* WILLEM STYFHALS & STÉPHANE SYMONS

Cover: Thierry de Cordier, *Iconotextures (10,000 Definitions of God), no. 12*, detail, 2014–2016. Ink on paper. Courtesy of the artist Thierry de Cordier and Xavier Hufkens, Brussels. Photograph by Dirk Pauwels.

Published by State University of New York Press, Albany

© 2019 State University of New York

All rights reserved

No part of this book may be used or reproduced in any manner whatsoever without written permission. No part of this book may be stored in a retrieval system or transmitted in any form or by any means including electronic, electrostatic, magnetic tape, mechanical, photocopying, recording, or otherwise without the prior permission in writing of the publisher.

For information, contact State University of New York Press, Albany, NY
www.sunypress.edu

Library of Congress Cataloging-in-Publication Data

Names: Styfhals, Willem, 1988– editor. | Symons, Stéphane (Philosopher), editor.
Title: Genealogies of the secular : the making of modern German thought / edited by Willem Styfhals and Stéphane Symons.
Description: Albany : State University of New York Press, [2019] | Series: SUNY series in theology and continental thought | Includes bibliographical references and index.
Identifiers: LCCN 2018052659 | ISBN 9781438476391 (hardcover) ISBN 9781438476414 (ebk.) | ISBN 9781438476407 (paperback)
Subjects: LCSH: Secularization (Theology)—History. | Secularism—Germany—History. | Postsecularism—Germany—History.
Classification: LCC BT83.7 .G46 2019 | DDC 211/.6—dc23
LC record available at https://lccn.loc.gov/2018052659

10 9 8 7 6 5 4 3 2 1

CONTENTS

Introduction     1
*Willem Styfhals
& Stéphane Symons*

*Part I*    GENEALOGY AND SECULARIZATION:
CONCEPTUAL PERSPECTIVES

Genealogy Trouble: Secularization and
the Leveling of Theory     21
*Kirk Wetters*

"The God of Myth Is Not Dead"—
Modernity and Its Cryptotheologies:
A Jewish Perspective     51
*Agata Bielik-Robson*

*Part II*    PHILOSOPHY AND THE SECULAR:
AN ALTERNATIVE HISTORY OF THE GERMAN
SECULARIZATION DEBATE

83    The "Distance to Revelation" and
the Difference between Divine and Worldly
Order: Walter Benjamin's Critique of
Secularization as Historical Development
*Sigrid Weigel*

101    Theology and Politics: Ernst Cassirer and Martin
Heidegger before, in, and after the Davos Debate
*Jeffrey Andrew Barash*

| | |
|---|---|
| 119 | Is Progress a Category of Consolation? Kant, Blumenberg, and the Politics of the Moderns<br>*Michaël Foessel* |
| 131 | Hannah Arendt, Secularization Theory, and the Politics of Secularism<br>*Samuel Moyn* |

*Part III* JACOB TAUBES: SECULARIZATION, HERESY, AND DEMOCRACY

| | |
|---|---|
| Secularization and the Symbols of Democracy: Jacob Taubes's Critique of Carl Schmitt<br>*Martin Treml* | 159 |
| On the Symbolic Order of Modern Democracy<br>*Jacob Taubes* | 179 |
| In Paul's Mask: Jacob Taubes Reads Walter Benjamin<br>*Sigrid Weigel* | 193 |

*Part IV* JAN ASSMANN: A LATE VOICE IN THE GERMAN SECULARIZATION DEBATE

| | |
|---|---|
| 219 | Secularization and Theologization: Introduction to Jan Assmann's Monotheism<br>*Daniel Steinmetz-Jenkins* |
| 231 | Monotheism<br>*Jan Assmann* |

| | |
|---|---|
| Contributors | 243 |
| Index | 247 |

# Introduction

WILLEM STYFHALS & STÉPHANE SYMONS

In his book *The Kingdom and the Glory*, the Italian philosopher Giorgio Agamben coins the notion "theological genealogy" to trace the modern concept of power back to theological speculations between the second and the fifth centuries. Agamben is particularly interested in "locating government in its theological locus in the Trinitarian *oikonomia*."[1] Thus describing a structural kinship between modern political concepts and premodern theology, Agamben explicitly holds on to the presuppositions of the project of political theology. Political theology, a concept famously introduced by the German philosopher and jurist Carl Schmitt in a book of that name (1922), points to the various continuities and even identities of theology and (modern) politics.[2] Agamben's interest in theological genealogy remains essentially political but opens up toward a wider approach as well, supplementing Schmitt's notion with his own views on an "economic theology."[3]

When extricated from the specific politico-economic context in which Agamben introduced the concept of theological genealogy, his genealogical project is ultimately a quest to expose a nonsecular core behind the overall drive for secularization and modernization. On this point, Agamben, as well as many other contemporary theorists, are indebted to genealogical readings of secular modernity that were first developed in twentieth-century German thought and in the German debates on secularization. This German discourse on religion and modernity is the object of study of this book. Many decades before the contemporary debates on political theology and postsecularism, German philosophers as diverse as Karl Löwith, Carl Schmitt, Hans Blumenberg, or Jacob Taubes, and even Walter Benjamin, Martin Heidegger, Ernst Cassirer or Hannah Arendt, already exposed, assessed, and discussed the theological origins of secular modernity. These thinkers not only addressed the carryover of theological concepts into the modern discourse on politics and economics but also conceptualized the various ways in which theological forces had implications for a wider range of modern cultural manifestations and, according to some, even constituted the essence of modernity as such.

## SECULARIZATION AND GENEALOGY

Traditionally, the genealogical relations between theology and modernity were understood through the concept of secularization. This concept was used most famously by Carl Schmitt in his renowned *Political Theology* to trace modern secular concepts back to their premodern theological origins.

> All significant concepts of the modern theory of the state are secularized theological concepts not only because of their historical development—in which they are transferred from theology to the theory of the state, whereby, for example the omnipotent God became the omnipotent lawgiver—but also because of their systematic structure, the recognition of which is necessary for a sociological consideration of these concepts. The exception in jurisprudence is analogous to the miracle in theology.[4]

Insofar as secularization is, for Schmitt, a historical process that connects modern concepts back to their theological origins, secularization is essentially a genealogical concept. Although neither Schmitt nor any of the other thinkers discussed in this book explicitly identified their intellectual project as genealogical, the concept of secularization is ultimately used to give insights into the *genealogy of the secular*.[5] Nonetheless, the concept of secularization is hardly exhaustive of the possible genealogical relations between the modern and the premodern or between the secular and the theological. Going beyond the concept of secularization proper, this book takes into account the heterogeneity and conceptual variety of genealogical readings of modernity that were conceived in twentieth-century German thought. While the notion of secularization played an undeniably central role in twentieth-century German intellectual history, its conceptual limitations make it unsuitable for representing the German discussions on the relation between religion and modernity in general. These conceptual limitations are twofold: on the one hand, the notion of secularization is too general and vague to be conceptually useful; on the other hand, secularization designates a too-specific relation between theology and modernity.

The conceptual scope of secularization is initially so wide that it ultimately has to incorporate contradictory meanings. In its most common and straightforward meaning, secularization designates the modern decline of religious authority that concretely takes shape in the separation between church and state or in a decreasing number of believers. In relation to these aspects, Charles Taylor understands secularization as "a move from a society where belief in God is unchallenged and indeed, unproblematic to one in which it is understood to be one option among others."[6] In addition to this intuitive historical and sociopolitical interpretation, the concept of secularization can also have a second meaning in many respects is opposed to its first meaning. Secularization, in this sense, designates the transformation of religious practices and theological ideas into secular forms. This is the meaning of secularization that Schmitt appealed to. German philosopher Hans Blumenberg was probably the first to point to this ambiguity in the concept of secularization in his renowned *The Legitimacy of the Modern Age* (1966).

> There is after all a difference between, on the one hand, saying that in a particular state the "secularization of the countryside" is very advanced, and that this is indicated by the empirical decline of obligations owed by the village communities to the church, and, on the other hand, formulating the thesis that the capitalist valuation of success in business is the secularization of 'certainty of salvation' in the context of the reformation doctrine of predestination.[7]

The scope of these two discourses on secularization could hardly be more divergent. In the first instance, secularization is an empirical category that describes certain sociological, historical, and political (r)evolutions; in the second instance, where Blumenberg made an implied reference to Max Weber's *The Protestant Ethic and the Spirit of Capitalism*, secularization becomes a theoretical or philosophical concept that is used to make sense of modern intellectual history.[8] Instead of describing the supposed disappearance of religion in the modern age, this second meaning of secularization designates the hidden survival of structural religious contents in modern culture.

Uncovering the tacit continuation of religion within the secular, the second meaning of secularization problematizes the first. It conceptualizes not so much the decline but the changed nature and possible continuation of religion in modernity. What is at play is not the *death* of religion but its *afterlife*. This specific interpretation of secularization has been discussed most explicitly in the German secularization debates of the 1950s, '60s, and '70s that find their origins in ways of thinking that were influential in Germany during and even before the interwar period. As such, these theoretical and philosophical debates constitute a major focal point of this book.

However, since secularization is but one way to conceive the transformations, transfers, ramifications, and survivals of religious motives in modern or secular phenomena, its meaning has become too narrow to account for the richness of the debate in twentieth-century German thought. Many authors have analyzed the genealogical connections between religion and modernity without making use of the concept of secularization. Max Weber, for instance, traced the logic of capitalism back to the Calvinist doctrine of predestination but he did not frame this issue as a theory of secularization—as Blumenberg's statement that was quoted above might seem to suggest. For Weber, the modern politico-economical system and the human practices that are defined as capitalism were at their point of origin conditioned by assumptions and beliefs that can only be termed religious, but he does not label this relation as one of "secularization." Generally, Weber conceived of the relation between religion and modern society as one of *rationalization* and *disenchantment* instead of secularization.

In highlighting the connection between religion and capitalism, Walter Benjamin's genealogy of modern economy shared some of Weber's insights. Moreover, Benjamin similarly studied the relation between economy and religion without appealing to the notion of secularization. However, Benjamin goes much further than Weber in that, in his view, capitalism is an "essentially religious phenomenon" because it "serves essentially to allay the same anxieties, torments, and disturbances to which the so-called religions offered answers."[9] Both capitalism and religion, that is to say, are to be understood as a "cult" driven by a "vast sense of guilt that is unable to find relief."[10] Benjamin argued against the mere opposition between religious or cultic forces and a supposedly secularized society, emphasizing that capitalism's religious core will not be simply annihilated by the "reformation of this religion ... or even from the complete renouncement of this religion."[11]

From a very different perspective, Aby Warburg equally dropped the category of secularization, preferring instead the *afterlife* (*Nachleben*) of religion. In many of his essays, the German art-historian Warburg outlined how the belief in pagan gods and the ritual practices that come along with it have survived the Christian dominance of the Middle Ages and preserved a strong influence well into the age of Reformation. Warburg's genealogical project focuses on the *survival* (*Fortleben*) of religious essences and ultimately analyzed how the accompanying feelings made possible the modern quest to carve out the central position of humanity. In his analysis of Albrecht Dürer's engraving *Melencolia I*, for instance, Warburg interpreted the newly found confidence in the powers of human intellect as originating from the endeavor to ward off the deep threat that is posed by planet-gods. In his view, contemplative activity and the individual mental efforts of thinking arose from the attempt to neutralize the spirit of Saturn. "Here," wrote Warburg, "the cosmic conflict is echoed in a process that takes place within man himself. The daemonic grotesques have disappeared; and saturnine gloom has been spiritualized into human, humanistic contemplation."[12] As such, Warburg argued that modern reason and the supplementary method of meticulous observation and calculation cannot be simply opposed to irrational beliefs and pagan anxieties since the latter are in many ways the driving force behind the former.

As opposed to Weber, Benjamin, and Warburg, the German theories of secularization in the strict sense only described the modern *immanentization* of theology. The classic example of such a secularization thesis is Karl Löwith's claim that the modern ideal of progress is a secularized form of eschatology. According to Löwith, both the faith in divine providence and the theological concept of a redemptive end of time (*Eschaton*) secretly structure the modern belief in the progressive meaning of history. As such, a theological content is understood as living on under the guise of a distinctly modern concept. In his book *Meaning in History*, Löwith shows how the modern philosophy of history repeats the Christian history of salvation but wrongfully applies its transcendent content to the immanent course of profane history: "the moderns elaborate a philosophy of history by secularizing theological principles and applying them to an ever increasing number of empirical facts."[13] For Löwith, as well as for his contemporaries such as Eric Voegelin or Odo Marquard, this transposition of theological contents to historical phenomena is not just an innocent category mistake. Rather, their immanentization creates the dangerous illusion that immanent history and our actions within it pertain to an absolute meaning, thus potentially resulting in totalitarian politics. In general, these theories of secularization as immanentization are indeed predominantly pessimistic about modernity.

According to Blumenberg, secularization's implied rejection of the "legitimacy of the modern age," as well as its narrative of continuity, finds its origin in the metaphorical history of the concept. Secularization first came into being as a juridical concept around the end of the seventeenth century, designating the expropriation of ecclesiastical goods and territories by lay political authorities. In a later stage, this specific juridical concept was used as a metaphor for the relation between Christian ideas and modern culture, more generally. Because of this metaphorical background, Blumenberg argues, secularization has certain connotations that simply cannot be dismissed. For one, the connotation of identity and continuity is fundamentally in tune with secularization's juridical meaning. As secularization initially signified the transfer of a specific property from the ecclesiastical to the political sphere, it implies that the content that has been transferred remains identical—whether it is a material or, later on, an intellectual content. Furthermore, secularization's pessimistic account of modernity as an inauthentic derivation of Christian thought could also be derived from secularization's metaphorical history. Indeed, the juridical concept of secularization designated an expropriation of territories that belonged to the church originally.

As one of the strongest opponents of the theorem of secularization, Blumenberg elaborated extensively on alternative understandings of the interaction between theology and modernity. Unlike Löwith, Blumenberg did not discover hidden religious traces in secular phenomena but showed how premodern, theological dynamics made modernity possible, preparing its path, so to speak, without however animating it from within. In a meticulous historical analysis of late-medieval and early-modern intellectual history, Blumenberg argued that the theological idea of divine omnipotence implied such a radical humiliation of the human aspirations to reach absolute truth or transcendent redemption that it paradoxically triggered the rise of human self-assertion. In his view, modern human beings were only able to assert their own finite lives on earth after every transcendent aspiration had become in vain. In this regard, Blumenberg did not consider the relation between theology and modernity as an illegitimate transposition of theological contents from one historical paradigm to another. Instead, his analysis focuses on a complex historical dialectic between theological problems that demand nontheological resolutions.

> What mainly occurred in the process that is interpreted as secularization, at least (so far) in all but a few recognizable and specific instances, should be described not as the *transposition* of theological contents into secularized alienation from

their origin but rather as the *re-occupation* of answer positions that had become vacant and whose corresponding questions could not be eliminated.[14]

As a substitute for the notion of secularization, reoccupation (*Umbesetzung*) is as much a genealogical category as secularization itself is. Just like Löwith, Blumenberg disputes the absolute justification and self-foundation of modern rationality by unmasking its contingent historical origins in premodern theology. Unlike the former, however, Blumenberg's genealogical insight into the theological dynamic from which modernity arose implies an affirmation of the modern paradigm, albeit a modest one. Blumenberg does not develop a secularization theory in the traditional sense but his project can be characterized as a genealogy of the secular, insofar as he also uncovers the theological roots of secular modernity.

The same holds true for a range of other figures discussed in this book, who neither made use of the concept of secularization nor strictly belonged to the classic German secularization debate, but who did reflect on the multifaceted, genealogical relations between theology and modernity. In other words, the genealogical project of tracing the origins of modern and secular phenomena cannot only be recognized in secularization theorists such as Löwith and Schmitt or in its fiercest opponents like Blumenberg, but also in the work of German thinkers like Walter Benjamin, Ernst Cassirer, Martin Heidegger, Hannah Arendt, and Jan Assmann. Although it is tempting to associate these thinkers with Schmitt's now popular notion of political theology, this book presents a reading of their work from a perspective that is neither exclusively political nor Schmittian. Indeed, Benjamin's, Assmann's, Arendt's, as well as Jacob Taubes's thinking is presented here in opposition to Schmitt's reflections on political theology and secularization. Attenuating the inevitable political connotation of secularization and political theology in the Schmittian sense, the essays in this book explore their meaning from a much broader and decidedly interdisciplinary perspective.

In sum, this book takes into account a wide range of interactions between theology and modernity—cultural, literary, and philosophical interactions, as well as political lines of influence; continuity as well as discontinuity; legitimacy as well as illegitimacy; disenchantments (Weber), reoccupations (Blumenberg) or theologizations (Assmann), as well as theological genealogies (Agamben), secularizations (Löwith), or political theologies (Schmitt). In spelling out different possible relations between theology and modernity, these concepts can ultimately be understood as presenting different *genealogies of the secular*. In all their variety and heterogeneity, they genealogically trace the historical origins of secular modernity to premodern theology and religion. Referring to the genealogical strategies implied in these concepts avoids some of the pitfalls of secularization and allows for a broader focus. While secularization primarily characterized the relation between theology and secularism as one of immanentization, inauthentic derivation, and continuation, this book encompasses a greater variety of possible interactions between theological and modern contents.

### RELIGION AND GENEALOGY

Evidently, genealogical thinking has a long-standing tradition in continental thought. The genealogical strategy that underlies the German debates on secularization is both in tune and at odds with the way continental philosophy has usually conceived genealogy.

The concept of genealogy itself has a genealogy that goes back to Nietzsche's great project, *On the Genealogy of Morals* (1887). For, in this foundational text already, genealogy presents itself as the project to *historicize* the present and to lay bare overlooked connections with the past. In thus uncovering the origins of the present, genealogical research focuses on the "conceptual transformations," a given idea or belief undergoes in the process of becoming a hidden force and a forgotten dynamic.[15] Nietzsche's main question being "[H]ow was such forgetting *possible?*," he retraces the very contingencies and discontinuities behind concepts that are all too often understood as self-evident.[16] In the later analysis of Michel Foucault, as well, the genealogical project is therefore understood first and foremost as a process of unmasking. Genealogy, that is, proves that the most highly charged and universally cherished concepts that underlie religion and morality, such as human liberty or reason, are neither fundamental to man's nature nor separable from a historical evolution that is colored by chance and conflict. Genealogy, in the words of Foucault, "will never neglect as inaccessible the vicissitudes of history. On the contrary, it will cultivate the details and accidents that accompany every beginning; it will be scrupulously attentive to their petty malice; it will await their emergence, once unmasked, as the face of the other."[17] The German debates on secularization picked up on this thread and scanned through the impurities of history to uncover, within the heart of supposedly modern and secular phenomena and concepts, traces of the premodern.

Nonetheless, the German discourse on religion and modernity that this book focuses on also subverted some of the terms of Nietzsche's seminal work on genealogy. While for Nietzsche religion, and Christian morality in particular, were forces of forgetfulness, here religion itself reveals what is being forgotten and at times even repressed. When religious affinities and theological categories are seen to be at work in the very attempt to create a distance from the premodern past, the genealogical strategies that will be looked at in this book bring out that religions are not, as Nietzsche put it hyperbolically, "at their most fundamental, systems of cruelty."[18] The authors that are studied here in detail have argued that the dynamic of secularization and modernization, including Nietzsche's own rejection of religion, thrives on energies and fields of understanding that are deeply religious. While Nietzsche sought to undermine religion, morality, and theology by unmasking their secular genealogy, the thinkers discussed here did the exact opposite. They sought to nuance the absolutist claims of secularism and modernity by unmasking their origins in religious contexts of meaning.

From these perspectives, the genealogical project of unmasking and uncovering ought not be considered a process of historical purification since it, on the contrary, opens up toward an essential and ineradicable heterogeneity that pertains to all things historical. Genealogy of course suggests lineage, continuation, and inheritance, but for Nietzsche and Foucault genealogy aims to uncover the historical contingency of the origins of ideas, values, and institutions. The act of revealing a forgotten influence of theological concepts within modernization does not merely result from any hope to expel, once and for all, these premodern or anachronistic layers of history. In other words, the genealogical projects discussed in this book revolve around the argument, put forward by some of the most important thinkers of the twentieth century, that identifying human progress with mere rationalization results in an undue reduction. These thinkers contend that it is not just fallacious but even downright suspect to isolate the concepts by way of which modern humanity understands its own position from premodern and theological concepts. In this sense, genealogy typically delegitimizes certain ideas and undermines their immediate and uncritical acceptance. However, pointing to the contingency of these ideas can also make us realize why we attach importance to them. Genealogy undermines the absolute justification of values and ideas but explains at the same time why they can have legitimacy for us. This type of genealogy avoids secularization's pessimistic narrative of false inheritance by gaining insights into the complexities and contingencies of historical development. Ultimately, this strategy could even entail a defense of "the legitimacy of the modern age," as the title of Hans Blumenberg's seminal book suggested.

REFLECTIONS ON THE SECULAR IN TWENTIETH-CENTURY GERMAN THOUGHT (SYNOPSIS)

Part I of the book elaborates on specific methodological and philosophical issues that were already hinted at in the introduction. The two chapters of this section critically reflect on the conceptual scope of secularization and assess its genealogical implications.

The volume opens with Kirk Wetters's "Genealogy Trouble: Secularization and the Leveling of Theory." This essay is programmatic for the rest of the book, as it presents an in-depth critique of the genealogical strategies implied in the concept of secularization. First, Wetters presents a methodological analysis of the role of genealogical arguments in writing intellectual history, distinguishing between "weak," "traditional," and "critical," forms of genealogy. Wetters then analyzes the Löwith-Blumenberg debate in terms of these distinctions. More concretely, he nuances the traditional reception of the debate by showing how Löwith's and Blumenberg's positions do not differ as significantly as is often argued. The historical pictures Blumenberg and Löwith draw are even surprisingly similar. What ultimately motivates Blumenberg's criticism, Wetters shows, is not Löwith's argumentation as such but its specific "weak" genealogical rhetoric. Accordingly, Blumenberg adopts Löwith's historical picture to a large extent but develops it into a "stronger" genealogy. Also taking Max Weber's and Giorgio Agamben's theological genealogies into account, Wetters is combining a historical perspective on secularization theory with a methodological reflection on the practice of genealogical thinking.

In the second chapter, " 'The God of Myth Is Not Dead'—Modernity and Its Cryptotheologies: A Jewish Perspective," Agata Bielik-Robson goes beyond the alternative between an acceptance or a rejection of Löwith's theory of secularization as immanentization. Based on Jewish-messianic ideas borrowed from Gershom Scholem, Ernst Bloch, Jacob Taubes, up to Jacques Derrida and the philosophy of Hans Blumenberg, Jean-Luc Nancy, and Gilles Deleuze, she develops a nuanced philosophical alternative to the concept of secularization through her notion of *cryptotheology*. Affirming the demise of traditional theologies and the belief in the divine absolute, this cryptotheology does not simply give up on the modern translation of the religious content, but applies it to the world. Bielik-Robson is interested in the shift of the messianic interest from the spiritual-otherworldly to the material-innerworldly and the recovery of a *factum brutum* pertaining to the world.

Part II focuses on major German philosophers whose work has rarely been associated with secularization—the chapters respectively discuss Walter Benjamin, Ernst Cassirer and Martin Heidegger, Immanuel Kant, and Hannah Arendt. These chapters show how some of the most influential philosophers of the twentieth century figured as the protagonists of the debate on religion, modernity, and secularism, and how their thinking prefigured the secularization debates proper between Schmitt, Löwith and Blumenberg that took place in postwar Germany.

Sigrid Weigel's chapter "The 'Distance to Revelation' and the Difference between Divine and Wordly Order: Walter Benjamin's Critique of Secularization as Historical Development" renders a substantial analysis of Benjamin's philosophy from the perspective of an interest in the issue of secularization. Contrary to the secularization theorists who describe secularization as a historical evolution, thereby considering the relation between religious and worldly concepts genealogically as one of transferal (Schmitt) or transformation (Blumenberg), Benjamin defines the realm of the secular as always already separated from the sacred. Still, while he thus understands history as being marked by its remoteness from the realm of divine revelation, Weigel argues that Benjamin uses biblical concepts and thought-images as standards that can neither be met nor be avoided. In Benjamin's work, such concepts do not bring the theological and the historical together in one equivocal unity but they reflect a double reference to both profane and religious ideas.

In the chapter "Theology and Politics: Ernst Cassirer and Martin Heidegger before, in, and after the Devos Debate," Jeffrey Andrew Barash recasts the famous Davos Debate in 1929 between Cassirer and Heidegger as a discussion about the phenomenon of religion. Presenting both Cassirer and Heidegger as thinkers who are engaged with the relation between myth, religion, and art, Barash understands Cassirer's views as pertaining to the historical and sociological interest on religion, while arguing that Heidegger's criticism of historical schemas to sketch out the development of religion is indebted to authors like Bultmann, Barth, and Gogarten. Still, one of the most interesting oppositions between Cassirer and Heidegger revolves around the former's emphasis on an unconditioned, ethical truth with an intrinsic validity that is independent of any finite mode of existence. It is from this perspective that Cassirer not only criticizes Heidegger's concept of truth as remaining dependent on the singular finitude of *Dasein*, but also approaches the theme of political theology and theological voluntarism.

In his chapter "Is Progress a Category of Consolation? Kant, Blumenberg, and the Politics of the Moderns," Michaël Foessel develops a philosophical rereading of the Löwith-Blumenberg debate through the figure of Immanuel Kant. After presenting an overview of Blumenberg's objections against Löwith's interpretation of modern progress as secularized eschatology, he shows how Blumenberg's alternative reading ultimately sides with Kant's interpretation of progress, which Löwith interestingly did not discuss. Kant's and Blumenberg's conceptions discard progressivism's paradigmatic triumphalism but present progress as a category of consolation. The modern concept of a progress to infinity thus appears as a regulative idea, in the Kantian sense, which gives meaning to historical disappointments rather than as a secularized eschatological concept that wants to overcome history itself.

The scope of the secularization debate in Germany obviously goes beyond the classic Löwith-Blumenberg debate. As an important intellectual current in postwar Germany, the secularization debate comprised a variety of academic topics and involved a whole range of thinkers from diverse disciplinary backgrounds whose writings and ideas have largely remained under the radar. Although Hannah Arendt is certainly a major figure in twentieth-century continental philosophy, her writings have never been associated with the topic of secularization. In his essay "Hannah Arendt, Secularization Theory, and the Politics of Secularism," Samuel Moyn convincingly shows, however, that Arendt's *On Revolution* implies a reflection on the problem of secularization that can be read as a critical rejection of Carl Schmitt's political theology. Mindful of the double meaning of the concept of secularization, discussed earlier in this introduction, Moyn argues that Arendt does not just develop a *theory of secularization* but also defends the *politics of secularism* as a goal of modern politics. The essay ends by examining how Arendt might reply to currently influential challengers of a secular politics.

Part III is devoted entirely to Jacob Taubes's views on secularization, whose central role in the secularization debates has been largely overlooked. While Taubes's writings have recently received more scholarly attention and have become increasingly influential in the current discourse on political theology, they have not yet been properly read as contributions to the German secularization debate. With the possible exception of his *Occidental Eschatology*, Taubes never discussed to topic of secularization systematically.[19] Nonetheless, his role in the German secularization debates could hardly be overestimated, as he arguably contributed to the perception that the different reflections on secularization in postwar German thought can be conceived as a real debate. Taubes's style of thinking was always very practical and essentially dialogical and confrontational: in every monograph he saw potential for debates and criticism, and from every idea a thinker coined he could make up a topic for a conference, workshop, or essay collection. Taubes, moreover, critically engaged in the work of the main participants of the classic secularization debate, and corresponded with these scholars too—not just with Schmitt and Blumenberg, but also with Scholem, Voegelin, Arendt, Löwith, and Marquard. Part of the reason why Taubes's conception of secularization remains unexplored is the fact that some of his writings on the topic are not easily accessible. This is especially true for his essay "On the Symbolic Order of Modern Democracy," which is reprinted in this book and introduced by Martin Treml.

In "Secularization and the Symbols of Democracy: Jacob Taubes's Critique of Carl Schmitt," Martin Treml elaborates on the intellectual encounter between Jacob Taubes and Carl Schmitt. In spite of radically different backgrounds, Taubes and Schmitt share an interest in the relevance of the history of religion for the current (political) predicament. Especially the figure of the *Katechon* and eschatological theology in general seemed relevant for their discussions. Treml then focuses more specifically on Taubes's interpretation of modern democracy, which implies a critical dialogue with Schmitt. He shows how Taubes traces democracy's political symbolism back to radical Christian heresies that rejected the absolute authority of the church.

In "On the Symbolic Order of Modern Democracy," Taubes elaborates on the theological symbolism applied in secular politics. Initially, theology's hierarchical and authoritarian symbolism seems only at work in monarchical political systems. However, Taubes immediately adds that the symbols of democracy can be similarly traced back to theology, albeit to more heretical, revolutionary, and mystical doctrines that counter traditional orthodoxy. Their mystical emphasis on holiness of the congregation embodying the divine announces, according to Taubes, the democratic values of equality and brotherliness. The chapter closes with a reflection on the theological inspiration of dictatorship in the works Kierkegaard, Marx, Donoso, and Proudhon.

The part of the book on Taubes closes with Sigrid Weigel's chapter, "In Paul's Mask: Jacob Taubes Reads Walter Benjamin." The chapter presents an analysis of Taubes's biased appropriation of Walter Benjamin's thought. Although not explicitly addressing Taubes as a secularization theorist, Weigel discusses some of the genealogical lines he traced between premodern theology and certain modern phenomena or intellectuals. First, she elaborates on Taubes's connection between ancient Gnosticism and Surrealism, meticulously dissecting Benjamin's role in his argumentation. She then shows how Taubes interprets Benjamin himself as a modern Gnostic Marcionite, and finally even as a modern exegete of Paul's letters to the Corinthians and Romans.

The final part of the book, IV, puts another German thinker forward whose work has rarely been associated with secularization. Although the work of Egyptologist Jan Assmann is mainly associated with memory studies, his work deserves to be studied in a book on the German discourse on religion and modernity. The case of Assmann takes up a somewhat exceptional position in this book for two reasons—the first one more historical, the second more philosophical. First, Assmann is much younger than the main participants of the German secularization debate, and only started his academic career when its importance in the German intellectual world was already waning. Nonetheless, he knew some of the main debaters personally, and arguably continues their legacy today. Especially in *Herrschaft und Heil*, he elaborated extensively on the topic of secularization and political theology in dialogue with thinkers such as Schmitt and Blumenberg.[20] In contradistinction to his other works, this book has found relatively little attention in the English-speaking world, especially because it has not been translated. *Herrschaft und Heil* brings us to a second reason why Assmann's work differs from the other authors who are studied here. Assmann develops his own critical alternative to the theory of secularization in the form of a political genealogy of theology. In opposing secularization, however, Assmann himself arguably belongs to the long tradition of German secularization theory, albeit as a late voice in the debate. Assmann's thinking indeed testifies to the heterogeneity of genealogical strategies that are applied in the German discourse on religion and modernity.

Assmann's contribution is introduced by Daniel Steinmetz-Jenkins. His chapter "Secularization and Theologization: An Introduction to Jan Assmann's *Monotheism*" presents an overview of the role of secularization and political theology in Assmann's work at large, and clarifies Assmann's relation to the German secularization debate.

In the final chapter, "Monotheism," Jan Assmann summarizes his main arguments from *Herrschaft und Heil*, making them available in English for the first time. The essay presents an alternative to the theory of secularization in the form of a theory of theologization. Reversing Schmitt's secularization thesis, Assmann argues that theology is not first made political in the process of secularization, but that monotheistic theology itself relied from the outset on secular political concepts it borrowed from the ancient civilizations. In this regard, he presents a genealogy of theology rather than a theological genealogy.

SECULARIZATION, POLITICAL THEOLOGY
AND GENEALOGY TODAY

Today, the concept of secularization has lost much of its credibility, especially as an empirical, sociological tool. It only seems to retain its descriptive validity for the marginal case of Western Europe. Contradicting the traditional secularization narrative, the significance of religious authority has not disappeared in our age. On the contrary, the adherents of desecularization or postsecularism pertinently state that our age is rather confronted with an increasing role of religious sensitivities in the public sphere.[21] However, while this empirical conception of secularization has become problematical today, the more expanded and conceptual view of secularization, central to the German debates, has gained popularity in contemporary academic discussions. The genealogical project that underlies the German secularization debates, tracing modernity back to its Christian, Jewish, or monotheistic roots, is echoed in recent studies such as Jean-Luc Nancy's *Deconstruction of Christianity*, Hans Joas's *The Sacredness of the Person*, Giorgio Agamben's *The Kingdom and the Glory* and *The Time that Remains*.[22] Apart from these significant European contributions, the issue has recently gained particular prominence in the American scholarly world with studies such as Charles Taylor's *A Secular Age*, Mark Lilla's *The Stillborn God*, Gil Anidjar's *Blood*, Thomas Pfau's *Minding the Modern*, Brad Gregory's *The Unintended Reformation*, or Michael Gillespie's *The Theological Origins of Modernity*.[23] These books are generally critical of modern culture and resemble, in that respect, the more pessimistic and conservative interpretations of secularization put forward by thinkers such as Karl Löwith. In comparison to Blumenberg's sophisticated defense of modern thought, Löwith's criticism could initially appear as an outdated nostalgia for premodernity. Today, however, such pessimistic, critical positions are often considered to be more intellectually stimulating and philosophically sophisticated than the optimistic defenses of modern values in Blumenberg's sense, which could now appear as naive or even somewhat clichéd.

In spite of the significant structural parallels to the German secularization debates, these recent studies rarely use the concept of secularization itself, with the exception of Taylor and Gregory, and they enter even less into direct discussion with their German predecessors. Nonetheless, they often introduce or legitimize their intellectual projects through a cursory reference to the German secularization debates: Nancy and Taylor programmatically mention Blumenberg at the very beginning and the very end of their books, respectively; Anidjar and Agamben frame their projects in a critical dialogue with Schmitt, Taubes, and Benjamin. Agamben is also the only one to elaborate on the Löwith-Blumenberg debate.

In order to gain a deeper insight into the stakes of the current debates, it is for several reasons worthwhile to study their German predecessors. First, this return to the German origins of the current debates shows that a genealogy of the secular does not necessarily imply critique, deconstruction, or delegitimation. Genealogy can give rise to the cultural pessimism of contemporary scholars as diverse as Gregory, Anidjar, Taylor, and Pfau, but more positive genealogical projects, which nonetheless refuse to succumb to Enlightenment's naive optimism, can be discovered in their German predecessors like Blumenberg and Taubes. Relying on such thinkers can entail a modest and sophisticated legitimation of the modern paradigm along the lines of Victoria Kahn's recent *The Future of Illusion*.[24] Moreover, getting in touch with the common German origins of the current debates on political theology and postsecularism brings unity to a very heterogeneous scene. Indeed, the contemporary authors that are listed here have often failed to see the connection between their works. At the same time, this approach even bridges some of the conceptual differences between European and American approaches of religion's role in secular society. Finally, and most importantly, the return to the German debates reveals the presuppositions as well as the limitations of current discourses. Not unlike Daniel Weidner's essay, *The Rhetoric of Secularization*, which relies on Weber's and Blumenberg's thought, the appeal to such German thinkers helps answer fundamental questions about the concepts of secularization and the theoretical practices of genealogy:[25] What is actually meant when someone claims that modernity is indebted to theology? What does one try to achieve with such a genealogy? And, what are its normative presuppositions and implications? These are indeed some of the central questions that this book tries to answer.

NOTES

1. Giorgio Agamben, *The Kingdom and the Glory: For a Theological Genealogy of Economy and Government*, trans. Lorenzo Chiesa (Stanford, CA: Stanford University Press, 2011), xi.

2. Carl Schmitt, *Political Theology: Four Chapters on the Concept of Sovereignty*, trans. George Schwab (Chicago, IL: University of Chicago Press, 2005).

3. Agamben, *The Kingdom and the Glory*, 1.

4. Schmitt, *Political Theology*, 36.

5. Although Agamben is probably the first to connect the concept of genealogy to the German secularization debates (see especially the first chapter of *The Kingdom and the Glory*, 1–16), there are other thinkers who approached the problem of secularization from the perspective of genealogy: Brad Gregory, *The Unintended Reformation: How a Religious Revolution Secularized Society* (Cambridge, MA: Harvard University Press, 2012), 3; Hans Joas, *The Sacredness of the Person: a New Genealogy of Human Rights* (Georgetown: Georgetown University Press, 2013). The concept also surfaces in some recent secondary literature on secularization and political theology: Manuel Borutta, "Genealogie der Säkularisierungstheorie: Zur Historisierung einer großen Erzählung der Moderne," *Geschichte und Gesellschaft* 36 (2010) 3: 347–76; Daniel Steinmetz-Jenkins, "Michael Oakeshott's Theological Genealogy of Political Modernity," *European Legacy* 19 (2014) 3, 323–34.

6. Charles Taylor, *A Secular Age* (Cambridge, MA: Harvard University Press, 2007), 3.

7. Hans Blumenberg, *The Legitimacy of the Modern Age*, trans. Robert Wallace (Cambridge, MA: MIT Press, 1983), 10.

8. See Max Weber, *The Protestant Ethic and the Spirit of Capitalism*, trans. Talcott Parsons (New York: Dover, 2003).

9. Walter Benjamin, "Capitalism as Religion," in *Selected Writings, Volume 1, 1913–1926*, eds. Marcus Bullock and Michael W. Jennings (Cambridge, MA and London: Harvard University Press, 2004), 288.

10. Ibid., 288.

11. Ibid., 289.

12. Aby Warburg, "Pagan-Antique Prophecy in Words and Images in the Age of Luther," in *The Renewal of Pagan Antiquity: Contributions to the Cultural History of the European Renaissance*, trans. David Britt (Los Angeles, CA: Getty Research Institute for the History of Art and the Humanities, 1999), 645.

13. Karl Löwith, *Meaning in History: The Theological Implications of the Philosophy of History* (Chicago, IL: University of Chicago Press, 1949), 19.

14. Blumenberg, *The Legitimacy*, 65.

15. Friedrich Nietzsche, *On the Genealogy of Morals*, ed. Keith Ansell-Pearson, trans. Carol Diethe (New York: Cambridge University Press, 2007), 13.

16. Ibid., 12.

17. Michel Foucault, "Nietzsche, Geneaology, History," in *Language, Counter-Memory, Practice. Selected Essays and Interviews*, ed. D. F. Bouchard (Ithaca, NY: Cornell University Press, 1977), 144.

18. Friedrich Nietzsche, *On the Genealogy of Morals*, 38.

19. Jacob Taubes, *Occidental Eschatology*, trans. David Ratmoko (Stanford, CA: Stanford University Press, 2009).

20. Jan Assmann, *Herrschaft und Heil. Politische Theologie in Altägypten, Israel und Europa* (Munich, Germany: Fischer Verlag, 2000).

21. See Peter Berger (ed.), *The Desecularization of the World: Resurgent Religion and World Politics* (Grand Rapids, MI: Wm. B. Eerdmans Publishing Co., 1999); Jürgen Habermas, "Religion in the Public Sphere," *European Journal of Philosophy* 14 (2006) 1: 1–25; Jürgen Habermas and Joseph Ratzinger, *The Dialectics of Secularization: On Reason and Religion*, trans. Brian Mc Neil (San Francisco, CA: Ignatius Press, 2006); Rodney Stark, "Secularization, R.I.P." *Sociology of Religion* 60 (1999): 3, 249–73.

22. See Jean-Luc Nancy, *Dis-Enclosure: The Deconstruction of Christianity*, trans. Bettina Bergo, Gabriel Malenfant, and Michael B. Smith (New York: Fordham University Press, 2008); Joas, *The Sacredness of the Person*; Agamben, *The Kingdom and the Glory*; Giorgio Agamben, *The Time that Remains: A Commentary on the Letter to the Romans*, trans. Patricia Dailey (Stanford, CA: Stanford University Press, 2005).

23. Respectively, see Taylor, *A Secular Age*; Mark Lilla, *The Stillborn God: Religion, Politics and the Modern West* (New York: Vintage Books, 2008); Gil Anidjar, *Blood: A Critique of Christianity* (New York: Columbia University Press, 2014); Thomas Pfau, *Minding the Modern: Human Agency, Intellectual Traditions, and Responsible Knowledge* (Notre Dame, IN: University of Notre Dame Press, 2013); Gregory, *The Unintended Reformation*; Michael A. Gillespie, *The Theological Origins of Modernity* (Chicago, IL: University of Chicago Press, 2008). For other recent books that pursue a similar project see: Slavoj Žižek, *The Puppet and the Dwarf: The Perverse Core of Christianity* (Cambridge, MA: MIT Press, 2003); Eric Santner, *The Royal Remains: The People's Two Bodies and the Endgames of Sovereignty* (Chicago, IL: Chicago University Press, 2011).

24. Victoria Kahn, *The Future of Illusion: Political Theology and Early Modern Texts* (Chicago, IL: Chicago University Press, 2014).

25. See Daniel Weidner, "The Rhetoric of Secularization," *New German Critique* 41 (2014): 1, 1–31.

# Part I.
# Genealogy and Secularization
Conceptual Perspectives

# Genealogy Trouble
*Secularization and the Leveling of Theory*

KIRK WETTERS

WEAK GENEALOGICAL REASON

In a 1937 essay by Theodor W. Adorno on Karl Mannheim, "Neue wertfreie Soziologie" ("New Value Neutral Sociology"), Adorno states that his critiques of Mannheim should be read as representative proxy attacks whose implicit targets include post-Weberian sociology and Max Weber himself. Despite Adorno's stated preference for Weber over Mannheim in terms of "level" and "theoretically constructive energy," he nevertheless passes the following verdict: "My words against Mannheim even reach to the head of the school, Max Weber."[1] Regardless of what one may think about the validity of this judgment, its only possible basis is a vast knowledge of the disciplinary landscape in question—and for this reason it would never be above reproach. Claims of this kind, which are common (yet of questionable persuasiveness), base themselves on forms of implicit authority whose sources are not easily verifiable. Such claims may be refutable only by an equally powerful (and equally dubious) counterauthority. For the sake of argument, however, it might nonetheless be worth posing the question: Do Adorno's claims against Mannheim *really* apply to Weber? To answer this narrow and perhaps prejudicially formulated question would require a tedious and perhaps pointless investigation, a process—as a trial, a forensic or inquisitorial hearing—which might also be at odds with the ideal of free scholarly or scientific study.

Such a literal-minded reading of Adorno's sentence as if it were fully verifiable is evidently absurd. What, then, does the sentence say, if its stated claim is not to be taken at face value? Moreover, why engage in a proxy attack in the first place? The claim that the critique of Mannheim has wide applicability and representativity is, first and foremost, a means of simplification and, second, contains implications about contemporary urgency and relevance. Rather than reconstructing the works of an author, Max Weber, who had been dead for seventeen years, in order to test their consistency philologically and subject the resulting synthesis to a unified critique, it is both simpler and more urgent to judge these older works according to the syntheses and simplifications that the passage of time itself enacted on them. In this sense, Mannheim is what remains of Weber as either a cutting edge or (in Adorno's claim) as a dull epigone.

It almost goes without saying that Adorno's claim also can only be valid from a partisan perspective, a viewpoint that sets itself outside of and against the tendencies represented by Mannheim with respect to Weber. Such are the familiar moves of what might be called "weak genealogical reason," which consistently operates with an implicit metaphorics of succession, lineage, continuity, legitimacy and illegitimacy, relations of friendship and enmity, as well as of family and school. The purpose of the present essay is not only to critique such claims—which are as ubiquitous as they are self-evidently weak—but to question the function and persistence of this particular form of nonanalysis. To this end, not far beyond Weber, my focus will be the German secularization-debates of the 1950s and 1960s. Secularization is a term whose very existence depends on a genealogical claim. From this angle, it also becomes clearer that the central methodological issue of the controversy between Karl Löwith and Hans Blumenberg revolves around the status and admissibility of the historically generated simplifications of weak genealogical reason.

WEBERIAN GENEALOGY

Thanks to Foucault and Nietzsche, the concept of genealogy generally enjoys a good reputation.[2] However, many kinds of claims may be labeled as genealogical, and, as I have already emphasized, not all of them can be characterized as strong. Weak genealogical claims frequently become the targets of critical genealogies. Foucault and Nietzsche are the names most easily associated with the latter approach, which highlighted the contingency, improbability, and uncertainty of all historical derivations. This countermethod deprives established present-day forms and institutions of their unquestioned self-evidence, justification, and legitimation. Critical genealogy thus delegitimates genealogical claims whose authority is derived from "traditional legitimacy" based on continuity, paternity, uninterrupted succession, antiquity, and originariness. Such an idea of traditional legitimacy, though in some sense a commonplace, owes its most influential theorization to none other than Max Weber.[3]

The "trouble" with genealogy, as I understand it, attaches to the unclear differences between its weak, traditional, and critical modes. For example, critical genealogy is in effect antigenealogy, while "weak" genealogies can easily become accepted as quasi-identities and thereby traditionalized. The most notorious example in the background of Blumenberg and Löwith is Weber's thesis on the Protestant ethic and the spirit of capitalism, which could be viewed as a strong and critical genealogy, but which may also have given rise to all manner of traditional or weak genealogical claims. This kind trouble can also be seen in the fact that the quasi-methods of weak, traditional, and critical themselves belong to genealogies in all three senses. Thus, for example, with Nietzsche and Foucault in mind, it is not difficult to imagine the relation between their conceptions of genealogy (and between their works as a whole) in terms of weak, traditional, and critical genealogy. Likewise, a concept like secularization gives rise to genealogy trouble at several levels: (1) secularization, understood as a displaced inheritance of Christianity or religiosity within modernity, relies on a hidden and ambiguous genealogical claim; (2) the phenomenon or event of secularization, to the extent that it can be localized, may itself have a genealogical form, a logic or pseudologic of descendance, derivation, and succession (terms that would also need to be differentiated); and (3) theoretical claims about phenomena thought to comprise secularization may also be imagined as genealogically related. "Secularization" thus lies within and between individual authors, such as Marx and Hegel, as well as within and between intellectual traditions such as the philosophy of history and theology, which are in turn tied to larger discourses and more or less perennial questions about progress, eschatology, and providence.

A genealogical hypothesis reflecting all of these levels is Karl Löwith's 1949 *Meaning in History*, in which he argues that modernity is at once derived from and diametrically opposed to Christianity. He attempts to show this by tracing, in the words of the subtitle, "the theological implications of the philosophy of history." Hans Blumenberg's *The Legitimacy of the Modern Age* responded to Löwith's book with a methodological critique and an alternate hypothesis on the relation of theology and modernity.

The Blumenberg-Löwith debate will be the central topic of the present essay. First, however, I must briefly return to the contribution of Max Weber's *Protestant Ethic* to the problems of genealogy and secularization. Blumenberg alludes to Weber's derivation of capitalism in passing at the beginning of *The Legitimacy of the Modern Age*. Weber's thesis is invoked as an example of a commonplace notion within the prevailing understandings of secularization. Weber is not even named, presumably because the correctness of the thesis is not at issue. Instead, it is a question of the effects of such a thesis after it enters the realm of received opinion and becomes an unquestioned self-understanding of modernity: "There is after all a difference between, on the one hand, saying that in a particular state the 'secularization of the countryside' is very advanced, and that this is indicated by the empirical decline of obligations owed by village communities to the church, and, on the other hand, formulating the thesis that the capitalist valuation of success in business is the secularization of 'certainty of salvation' in the context of the Reformation doctrine of predestination."[4] According to Blumenberg, the generalization and general acceptance of the term *secularization* elides specific differences of context, semantics, and argumentation. At the same time, performative dimensions (signaled in the words *saying* and *formulating the thesis*) are highlighted by Blumenberg but taken for granted in the apparent self-evidence of such claims. Thus, for Blumenberg "secularization" is less a concept than a discursive epidemic, a minimally founded yet self-reinforcing hypothesis.

The *Protestant Ethic* is perhaps the most important of all secularization theses, but the term *secularization* does not occupy prominent place in Weber's work. The *Protestant Ethic* offers a concept of secularization, however, and qualifies as a work of critical genealogy insofar as it shows how capitalism, a present social formation that has often been taken for a progressive or dialectical universality, was a collateral effect of a specific religious ethos. Weber does not always pursue this critical genealogy in a uniformly critical way, but his work nevertheless provides an important model for a style of genealogy that might be called "invertive" or "transformational." On this model, Christianity transforms itself into its opposite, secular modernity, just as an ethics of conviction (*Gesinnungethik*) turns into an ethics of responsibility (*Verantwortungsethik*).[5] On the one hand, this may amount to a negative or decline-oriented version of traditional legitimacy (based on criteria of derivation and originariness), but the transformational-invertive aspect may also be understood as a critique of both the origin (Protestant ethic) and its unintended consequence (capitalism).

A final key aspect of Weber's genealogical strategy is the specificity of his sociological method. Genealogies in this model are not produced by the mute continuity of essences, nor are they based on implicit metaphorics of family and paternity. The power of Weber's sociological model of secularization lies in its analysis of the cumulative effects of actions and practices, which are variably correlated to ideas and beliefs. This is also the reason why the key metahistorical term for Weber is not *secularization* but *rationalization* (*Rationalisierung*)—and to a lesser degree *disenchantment* (*Entzauberung*). I cannot elaborate these concepts here, but I would emphasize that they rest on a different—and less contested—basis than secularization. Rationalization theses are legion, including and especially among the critics of modernity, and very few theorists and philosophers, including Blumenberg, can avoid acknowledging that some things changed since antiquity and the middle ages. "Rationalization" is a consensus-term to generally characterize such changes. The idea of rationalization in Weber's sociology of religion revolves around the specificity of "Occidental modernity" and is thus explicitly based on a Eurocentric and "traditional" genealogy in the comparative context of world history and religion.[6] The implications of rationalization are thus, in the final analysis, universalizing and anthropological. Genealogical method in the humanities and social sciences correspondingly gravitates toward a comparatist rereading of European intellectual history. This may be viewed as a shortcoming, but the only alternative would be to declare that "genealogy" and "theory," including critical theory and critical genealogy, are of no use in a postmodern or globalized era. Such an objection—about the dead end of intellectual history—deserves to be taken seriously, but it also seems to encounter a limit insofar contemporary discourses of all kinds and at all levels remain deeply entangled in genealogical claims. Even the claim that genealogy always leads to a dead end in the incommensurability of the present (a variant of the idea of the "end of history") can only be justified by genealogical analysis.

The concept of "secularization" is a prominent case for such problems, and insofar as it contains an established tradition of self-critique,[7] it offers a chance to ask questions that pertain broadly to the legacies of critical-genealogical thought. The main work of the remainder of this essay will therefore not be the categorization or stigmatization of different genealogical arguments—as "weak," "traditional," or "critical"—but rather to show the interdependence of the various modes and approaches. The distinctions weak-strong-critical are, moreover, subject to transvaluation and perspectivization. The weak and the traditional, which can easily make up a single category, may often turn out to be the strongest, whereas the critical genealogy, to the extent that it focuses on contingency and discontinuity, may not be a genealogy at all and thus may be the weakest when it comes to the positing of substantial and verifiable identities.

#### WEBER'S CHILDREN

In the context of the Blumenberg-Löwith debate, genealogy is not only in play in Weber's analyses of modernity, but also, more implicitly, in controversies about Weber's intellectual genealogy and specifically regarding his work's success and succession. I have already showed something of this in the line from Adorno's review of Karl Mannheim, but tracing the large and small ways that Weber's thought contributed to Weimar-era and postwar discourse would be a huge undertaking. Thus, I limit myself to the relatively well-known case of Weber and Carl Schmitt.

Presupposing that complex situations are always at stake whenever one speaks of an intellectual "genealogy" or "legacy," findings at this level can only be based on the diachronic developments and real-time reciprocal interactions of discrete intellects. Genealogical analogies and "derivations" can only be based on analyses that require a high level of historical and philological detail—without being under any illusions about the fundamental tenuousness of the endeavor. Intellectual genealogies are not actual genealogies any more than they are "inheritances" that can be accurately comprehended through metaphors of paternity. Critical genealogy ultimately depends on philology, and philology, far from providing a simple paternity test, is as likely to dissolve lineages as to unambiguously confirm them.[8]

But the metaphors of paternity nevertheless persist, even in seemingly benign ways, such as in the German convention of referring to the "dissertation adviser" as a Doktorvater—or Doktormutter. And perhaps such assumptions are not always wrong.[9] To further illustrate the problem, I turn to a famous weak-genealogical claim made by Jürgen Habermas, who once declared Carl Schmitt a "natural son" of Max Weber.[10] The source for this claim is the fifteenth meeting of the German Soziologentag, which took place in Heidelberg during the period of "positivism debate of German sociology" (Positivismusstreit der deutschen Soziologie).[11] The date was 1964, and the topic was Max Weber und die Soziologie heute (Max Weber and Sociology Today). Habermas was one of several participants who delivered responses to a paper by Talcott Parsons. Parsons—one of Weber's legitimate children and the leading US

Weberian—gave a paper on "Valuation and Objectivity in the Social Sciences" ("Wertgebundenheit und Objektivität in den Sozialwissenschaften"). From the German critical-theoretical perspective of those days (and perhaps in general), Parsons's sympathetic view of Weber must have seemed overly harmonious, even uncritical: "He [Weber] was unequivocally antagonistic toward all positions that he conceived as conservative and as socialist in the intellectual-political situation of his time in Germany. He nevertheless repudiated neither nationalism nor the demand for 'social justice.' With respect to the capitalist alternative his ambivalence seemed to be much stronger. He viewed capitalism, including the bureaucratization of private and state organizations as the genuine destiny of Western society. But he still had grave fears regarding the human consequences."[12]

In contrast with Parsons's tone and overall approach, Habermas attempts a fundamental critique of Weber's sociological method. The arguments are compressed and perhaps exaggerated, but serious and potentially convincing. The concluding genealogical claim about Weber and Schmitt, however, works at a completely different level. For the sake of context, which has often been neglected in other accounts, I cite the whole passage, starting from Habermas's ironic reference to the mainstream US sociology represented by Parsons: "I envy our American colleagues, who stand in political traditions that allow such a generous and in the best sense liberal reception of Max Weber. We in Germany are still in search of alibis, and would follow only too gladly. But Weber's political sociology had a different history on our soil: during the period of the First World War, Weber formulated the image of the Caesarist Führer-democracy on the contemporary basis of national state imperialism. This militant late liberalism had consequences in the Weimar period, which we need not attribute to Weber but to ourselves, when we receive Weber here and now: we cannot get around the fact that Carl Schmitt was a legitimate student of Max Weber. Viewed in terms of the history of its influence, the decisionist element of Weber's sociology did not break the spell of ideology but rather strengthened it."[13]

Looking for alibis is the one thing—and looking for scapegoats is another. Habermas steers a path between these two alternatives, but it is not easy to decide, more than fifty years later, whether it was brave of him to remind Parsons and the other participants of recent history, or whether this was already a predictable doctrine of the Frankfurt School, which sought to highlight the connection between "positivist" empirical sociology and National Socialism. The path over Schmitt was one of these ways, and perhaps not the most convincing of them. Habermas's adjective "legitimate" implies that Schmitt was not just any student, but a student whose thought reveals direct continuity with Weber's. At the same time, the name "Schmitt" and words like *decisionism* can easily function as red herrings. Generously read, this is a provocative overreaching and at the same time an absolutely conventional strategy. At the time, the remarks were undoubtedly greeted with enthusiasm by some listeners and with exasperation by others. Likewise, the claim seems to have generated some traction in the some lines of reception (legal and constitutional theory), whereas for others Habermas's words may have served as a warning against both Schmitt and Weber.

The more loaded and notorious version of claim was, however, added later to the published text as a footnote: "Adopting a friendly suggestion, I now find a different formulation to be more accurate, assuming one preserves it in its ambivalence: Carl Schmitt was a 'natural son' of Max Weber."[14] Assuming that "ambivalent" and "accurate" (*zutreffend*) are not in outright contradiction, the new version is decidedly more complex. The ambivalence depends on the double meaning of *natural*. Schmitt's relation to Weber is "illegitimate" (by law), but this purely legal relation is trumped by the evident "naturalness" (in the sense of truth or authenticity). The two meanings refer to two different aspects of Schmitt's relation to Weber: Schmitt is an illegitimate son insofar as he, unlike Parsons, does not inherit his father's mantle within Weber's primary discipline of sociology, whereas the other meaning of "natural" implies that Schmitt, though not a part of Weber's officially sanctioned academic offspring, nevertheless takes after his "biological" father.

I do not contest the importance of the relation of Weber and Schmitt—to the contrary, I find it decisive—but I object to Habermas's way of using it to discount both figures. Instead, I see a complex connection that offers a chance of better understanding not only Weber and Schmitt but numerous other contexts in which their thought remains active. In this sense the genealogy remains crucial, but it can only be posed as an ongoing investigation and not as a closed case. "Legitimate" lines in this sense are the prematurely closed cases of traditional genealogy, whereas illegitimacy and problems of legitimation open a space of contestation, ambivalence, and critical availability. If the illegitimate lines are broken or neglected, all that remains is an unquestioned succession, which is paradoxically illegitimate precisely insofar as it presents itself as a purely official and authoritative tradition or school. In opposition to such claims, the coherence of critical genealogy depends on its ability to uncover incoherencies. Critical genealogy does not draw unambiguous lines of descent but unfolds the dialogical embeddedness of thoughts. This is not only a question of what is borrowed or rejected from others—but of the points and purposes by which similar conceptions can be put to different uses.

Habermas's metaphor of paternity suggests that Schmitt can stand for Weber, generally and generically, and further that there is a strict difference between "us" and "them," our "isms" and their "ism."[15] These examples again highlight the weakness—and the strength—of weak genealogy, which can be summarized in a one-liner from Goethe's *Wilhelm Meister's Apprenticeship*: "Fatherhood rests only on conviction; I am convinced, therefore I am the father" ("Die Vaterschaft beruht überhaupt nur auf der Überzeugung, ich bin überzeugt und also bin ich Vater").[16] When Goethe wrote this line—and even in the 1960s—there was no way of definitively ascertaining paternity (*Vaterschaft*) or sonhood (*Sohnschaft*). In Goethe's novel, the reader sees how natural children can be legitimized by the recognition of paternity (regardless of who the father actually is). This remains the case with intellectual-historical genealogies, which have no equivalent of DNA—and no symbolic equivalent of paternity. "Strong genealogy"—traditional genealogy—thereby appears not only as a result of "conviction" (*Überzeugung*), but suggests that this conviction can only be produced by a groundless act of decision. Thus, an unintentional irony can be perceived in Habermas's deployment of genealogical decisionism to condemn Weber for begetting Schmitt's decisionism. Habermas's conviction reveals him to be a true heir, precisely in the moment when he tries to decisively extinguish the line and distinguish himself from it.

Karl Löwith also articulated a viewpoint on the Schmitt-Weber case, which is among the most influential. Löwith's reputation as a Schmitt-critic was second to none, beginning with his 1935 essay, "The Occasional Decisionism of C. Schmitt" ("Der okkasionelle Dezisionismus von C. Schmitt").[17] Only a few years later, in 1940, his "Max Weber and his Successors" ("Max Weber und seine Nachfolger") focused primarily on only one successor: Carl Schmitt.[18] Löwith's writings on Weber display a high degree of intellectual and ethical admiration. He thereby implicitly places himself among Weber's "legitimate" successors. Schmitt, on the other hand, is a characterized as renegade, and the family saga emerges as a tragic reflection of the larger tragedy of the Weimar era: "It belongs to the tragic quality [*Tragik*] of German political life that such a perceptive man as Weber was never able to play a role (*zur Tat kommen konnte*) during the foundational crisis of the Bismarck era, whereas a talented careerist (*Streber*) like Schmitt achieved a level of influence which can hardly be overestimated, over the political thought and legislation of the Third Reich."[19]

Regardless of whether one follows Löwith or Habermas, the maxim applies: "Paternity rests entirely on conviction." The further question, however, in anticipation of the secularization debates: how does the cumulative reception of weak genealogical claims like the ones cited produce strong genealogies? If filiation by conviction is the primary model, then the strength of the identification may itself be Schmittian—dictated by friend-enemy allegiances. Without going quite so far, one might imagine that pronouncements like Habermas's are widely circulated rumors, which may solidify into prejudices and risk being mistaken for simple truths. What is the ultimate effect? Perhaps it is purely intra-academic, a factor in canon-formation and in trends in what is perceived to be "worth reading." But one would also have to at least admit the possibility of deeper effects, for example, the possibility of the unmooring of large discursive fields, even whole disciplines, which are deciding in relatively arbitrary ways, not only about what is worth reading, but where the real problems may lie.

Based on these examples, the reliance on "weak genealogy" seems justifiable and inevitable, insofar as it arises in the context of polemics and fixed positions. Weak genealogy becomes necessary in order to stake out a strong outward definition of complex internal differences and divisions. As already suggested, weak genealogy is decisionistically necessary, as soon as it seems necessary to take sides. The function, however, of securing continuity of self through partisanship guarantees neither intellectual strength nor political rightness. To the contrary, weak genealogy is fodder for an academic-political rumor mill that is only indirectly related to the intellectual and political problems themselves. Ultimately what is at stake is the very possibility of clearly perceiving and coherently acting on such problems in an academic-genealogical framework.

UNSUBSTANTIATED RUMORS
ABOUT "SECULARIZATION"

The rumor mill of weak genealogy is, as I have suggested, one of the most general levels at which Blumenberg poses his critique of secularization. It is one thing to develop a hypothesis about (or against) secularization using the methods of critical genealogy, but it is something else to adopt words like *secular* or *secularized* or even *rational* as if they were attributes of the actually existing world, in whole or in part.

It is famously difficult to ascertain precisely the disagreements and motivations that divided Blumenberg and Löwith in the 1960s. As recently as 2007,

Giorgio Agamben observed in *The Kingdom and the Glory* that the real stakes were not secularization at all, but "the philosophy of history and the Christian theology that constituted its premise."[20] Philosophy of history, for Löwith as for Blumenberg, is a problematic modern inheritance of a theological problem. At the end of the introduction of *Meaning in History*, Löwith writes: "the moderns elaborate a philosophy of history by secularizing theological principles and applying them to an ever increasing number of empirical facts."[21] Certainly one may object to the vagueness and generality of such a sentence, which is not an isolated case in Löwith's book. Blumenberg, by contrast, in his critique of prevailing secularization discourses, expresses himself this way: "The only reason why 'secularization' could ever have become so plausible as a mode of explanation of historical processes is that supposedly secularized ideas can in fact mostly be traced back to an identity in the historical process. Of course this identity, according to the thesis advocated here, is not one of contents but one of functions. It is in fact possible for totally heterogeneous contents to take on identical functions in specific positions in the system of man's interpretation of the world and himself. In our history this system has been decisively determined by Christian theology, which specifically and above all moved it in the direction of increasing expansiveness."[22] Blumenberg goes on to say that theology has no difficulty in answering questions about the origins of humans, the purpose of existence, and so on—but that philosophy is much more constrained.

Based on these passages, it remains difficult to locate a single decisive difference and disagreement between Löwith and Blumenberg. Both focus on the theological inheritance in ways that seem potentially compatible. Certainly, there are differences at the level of nuance, semantics, method, and regarding the precise mechanism historical transformations. Given the apparent proximity (if not partial overlap) of the theses on theology and the philosophy of history, it is important to switch levels and reconsider the implicit consequences of the respective theses, as well as both authors' tone and rhetoric. The prevalent understanding in this regard—for example, that of introduction to the English translation[23]—is that Blumenberg is more optimistic, whereas Löwith is a pessimist. This characterization, however, insofar as it relies on something like an existential attitude, is again rather general and risks glossing over specific differences. Also, labels like "optimism" and "pessimism" are too simplistic, considering that neither Löwith nor Blumenberg ascribe to an emphatically progressive view of history; neither do they overtly contradict Weber's rationalization thesis, which is pessimistic in comparison to Marxian conceptions of history. Instead both Löwith and Blumenberg try to renegotiate the terms and implications of such narratives. Blumenberg goes even further by adding an entirely new (yet somehow familiar) story, which implicitly offsets and recontextualizes the assumptions of the Protestant ethic. The legitimacy of the modern age defines itself, according to Blumenberg's central thesis, as a resurgence of "theoretical curiosity" against "theological absolutism."

Implicit tonal contrasts and divergent narrative consequences can be further illustrated by comparing the conclusion of *Meaning in History* to the first chapter of the third part of *Legitimacy of the Modern Age*, titled "The Disruptability of the Theoretical Impulse" ("Die Störanfälligkeit des theoretischen Antriebs").[24] Starting with Löwith, I would emphasize: (1) His purported pessimism can be confirmed in the declaration that "man's historical experience is one of steady failure."[25] (2) He justifies this pessimism by invoking an ahistorical, positive humanism: "It is not the historical world but rather human nature which persists through all historical changes."[26] (3) He relies on a Weberian "invertive" dialectic, according to which the intents and goals of historical action inevitably reverse themselves: "we have a historical consciousness which is as Christian by derivation as it is non-Christian by consequence."[27] (4) He constantly elaborates and expounds this derivation: "communities of modern times are neither religiously pagan nor Christian; they are decidedly secular, i.e., secularized, and only so far, by derivation, are they still Christian. The old churches of modern cities are no longer the outstanding centers of the communal life but strange islands immersed in the business centers. In our modern world everything is more or less Christian and, at the same time, un-Christian [...]. The modern world is as Christian as it is un-Christian because it is the outcome of an age-long process of secularization. [...]. [O]ur modern world is worldly and irreligious and yet dependent on the Christian creed from which it is emancipated."[28] These lines show how Löwith makes the transition from scholarly genealogy to cultural-critical diagnosis.

I will return to points 3 and 4, but first the comparison-points in Blumenberg: (1) He remains a student of Weber (and Freud) in his emphasis of the milder pessimism of *Unbehagen* and dwindling options: "Between the uneasiness [*Unbehagen*] about science's autonomous industry [*Selbstbetrieb*] and the constraints resulting from its indispensability lies an uncertain latitude of available actions [*ein vager Spielraum des Disponiblen*], which it would be misleading to project upon the totality [*das Ganze*]."[29] (2) The warning against overgeneralization at the end of a sweeping diagnosis betrays discomfort with any attempt to answer questions about the present and future.

Philosophy's competency to speak about the historical destiny of humans is in doubt. Rather than assuming a constant human nature,[30] Blumenberg proposes theoretical curiosity itself as a quasi-anthropological placeholder. In a sentence with many hesitations and qualifications, the indefinite article implies that this supposed constant is only a relative one (one among others): "The 'theoretical attitude' may be *a constant* in European history since the awakening of the Ionians' interest in nature; but this attitude could take on the explicitness of insistence on the will and the right to intellectual curiosity only after it had been confronted with opposition and had to compete with other norms of attitude and fulfillment in life."[31] (3) As in Löwith's Weberian dialectic, modernity here emerges as a reversal of Christianity—but not as an automatic inversion inherent to Christianity's own development. Whereas the broadest version of Löwith's narrative revolves around a historical substitution of belief in Providence by belief in progress, Blumenberg claims that Christianity inadvertently triggered modernity by negating its predominant "attitude" and thereby promoting the idea of a "right and will to intellectual curiosity." Thus, in a way that is different from but not opposed to Löwith, modernity is Christianity's Frankenstein's monster. Blumenberg's conception, like that of Weber's Protestant ethic, motivates historical transformation not by a blind or intrinsic dialectical process of inversion but by the cumulative interplay of beliefs and actions in specific historical contexts. (4) Blumenberg ends his chapter with a modification of Weber's iron cage, proposing a historically "increasing consolidation of the processual structure" (*eine[...] zunehmende Verdichtung [der] Prozeßstruktur*) of theoretical curiosity.[32] Blumenberg suggests that theoretical curiosity was the motor that gave rise to the institutionalized processes of science. At present, however, organized science itself threatens the autonomy of theoretical curiosity: "the lack of room for individual motivation, for authentic initiative, is involved in our uneasiness [*Unbehagen*] with regard to science."[33] From this point on, the concluding tone of the chapter is not optimism—nor pessimism nor resignation—but a declaration that the legitimacy of the modern age represents a corrective against the possibility of a dangerous overreaction. This "corrective" is not a theodicy, nor a justification of the present-day world (in whole or in part), nor a guarantee of future successes and progresses: "To understand the process of the legitimation of theoretical curiosity as a basic feature of the history of the beginning of the modern age certainly does not mean to make curiosity into the destiny [*Fatum*] of history, or one of its absolute values. The legitimacy of the modern age is not the legitimation of its specific constituent elements under all possible circumstances."[34]

These comparisons show that there are concrete differences between Löwith's and Blumenberg's diagnoses of modernity. But they are insufficient to explain why this disagreement seems, on the one hand, to have been one of Blumenberg's major motivations to write and rewrite his *Legitimacy of the Modern Age* and, on the other hand, why this controversy about modernity, which was at once esoteric and multifaceted, turned into a debate about secularization. In short, the concrete intellectual narratives, including their tone and implications, which are quite well established, still do not exhaust the case. Starting from Blumenberg's side, I would surmise that he is less opposed to Löwith's actual theses than to the way in which they seem to promote their own uncritical reception. Blumenberg is above all suspicious of whatever it was that made Löwith's book "influential," which may not rise to the level of scholarly truth-seeking, or it may be the result of a mood—for example of pessimism—than of the of a self-critical genealogy.

In this context, Löwith's linguistic-conceptual weaknesses and shaky methodology can become a main focus. Indeed, Blumenberg makes no effort to hide his view that Löwith's book is a symptom of the crossover of the secularization discourse from scholarly "theory" to widespread popular presupposition: "Among the propositions that in the second generation can already be described simply [*schlicht und knapp*] as 'well-known' ['*bekannt*'] is the thesis that modern historical consciousness is derived from the secularization of the Christian idea of salvation history and, more particularly, of providence and eschatological finitude." According to Blumenberg, this thesis "had an enduring dogmatic effect [*nachhaltig dogmatisierend gewirkt*]."[35] What is at issue is thus not Löwith's thesis itself but its transformation from a genealogical critique of dogmatically presupposed idea of progress into a dogmatic presupposition in its own right. Blumenberg's critique of Löwith makes him responsible for the effects of his own discourse and at the same time demotes this discourse to the effect of a larger discursive trend.

It is not difficult to understand how an author might be upset by a critique of this kind. Later in the same chapter, Blumenberg rubs salt in the wound by offering detailed critiques of Löwith's imprecise language: "There are entirely harmless formulations of the secularization theorem, of a type that can hardly be contradicted. One of these plausible turns of phrase is 'unthinkable without." Blumenberg goes on to agree that "the modern age may be unthinkable without Christianity," but argues that the language of "unthinkable without" masks complex claims and geneses in rhetorical self-evidence. Blumenberg thus argues that the task of philosophy should not be to expound philosophemes and theoremes as the solid results of a traditional genealogy, but should apply itself to the "critique of foreground appearance [*Kritik an der Vordergründigkeit*]—or better: of the apparent background presence—of secularization."³⁶

Blumenberg's use of metaphorology as a form of philosophical *Sprachkritik* could be explored at much greater length. This aspect is, moreover, a significant part of the appeal and influence of his work—especially for those who view themselves as critics more than as philosophers. At the same time, it is unpleasant to be the object of such a critique, especially from someone who (from Löwith's perspective) might have been an ally. Löwith would have also felt—correctly felt—that Blumenberg was making an example of him. Assuming this is the case, it is not easy to draw the line between an outright (and unfair) aggressiveness on Blumenberg's part and the ways in which Löwith's book actually is substantively representative of the problem of the spread of the secularization discourse. To cast some light on this question, I would recall the original context of *Meaning in History* (later published in German as *Weltgeschichte und Heilsgeschehen*). Written during Löwith's stay at the Hartford Theological Seminary, his book has the character of a primer. Rather than a specialized philosophical critique of the philosophy of history, *Meaning in History* is written in clear and accessible English, which still holds up as a good general introduction to the specialty discipline of "philosophy of history" (*Geschichtsphilosophie*).

It is impossible to establish with certainty the level of conversation Löwith encountered in the US, but one might suppose that a similar dynamic motivated *Meaning and History* as Adorno-Horkheimer's much more canonical *Dialectic of Enlightenment*—though with strikingly different results. One has the impression that Löwith wanted to disabuse his American readers of their unquestioned *faith* in progress by showing how this faith was absolutely opposed to the traditional tenets of Christian religiosity. This line of argumentation is clearly reflective of European-American differences, which undoubtedly contributed to Löwith's tendency to oversimplification, overstatement, rhetorical excess and condescension to his reader. Precisely these lapses become the main issue for Blumenberg, because they reveal the ways in which philosophy still wants to be able to provide answers—or at least guidance—to big questions about history as destiny. Löwith, from Blumenberg's perspective, contradicts his own critique insofar as he clings to the shared legacy of theology and the philosophy of history. The English title, *Meaning in History*, could hardly be more explicit in this regard—though it probably should have been called *No Meaning in History*.

Löwith seems to have been aware of his book's shortcomings long before Blumenberg called attention to them. The 1953 German edition begins with a preface (*Vorwort*) invoking the US context to excuse "a certain looseness of the presentation" ("*eine gewisse Lockerheit der Darstellung*"). Löwith characterizes the specific constraints of the American publication and the English language: "Many things are emphasized and handled extensively, which for the German reader probably could have been said more succinctly and less forcefully. The author hopes that this lack of brevity and rigor may be offset by ease of comprehension. He himself found it beneficial that he had to make himself at home in a language that does not lend itself to conceptual subtleties and verbal profundity, but which is in its own way precise and rich."[37]

This is a perfectly reasonable disclaimer, and, as already mentioned, the introductory character of the book could be ranked among its virtues. Thus, it is not difficult to sympathize with Löwith against Blumenberg. For Blumenberg, however, Löwith's lapses reveal the difficulty and confusion that results when philosophy attempts to address contemporary problems and answer questions of general import. This was precisely the mistake of the philosophy of history, which tried to answer the inherited questions of theology, and ended up producing loose and ubiquitous talk of "secularization." This kind of philosophy, philosophy in the public sphere, amplifies itself by way of the genealogical hearsay effect, producing armies of pseudo-authoritative claims—and claims based on these claims, ad infinitum—producing what is these days called an "echo chamber."

Löwith's book's implicit address to a nonspecialized audience is what makes it genuinely exemplary—and a perfect target. Blumenberg turns Löwith's critique of the philosophy of history back on Löwith, arguing that this "critique" is only one more philosophy of history (albeit an antiphilosophy of history). For Blumenberg, the tenor of the critique of the philosophy of history must be different than that of the philosophy of history itself. Löwith may give a negative answer to question of meaning in history, but the very attempt to present such an answer to a general audience is the more acute and virulent legacy of the philosophy of history. This is the crucial point where Löwith falls down, and at the same time it reflects the change of level that Blumenberg hoped to bring about in philosophical-theoretical discourse.

Blumenberg's intervention as such met with little success. Insofar as his work wanted to shut down an echo chamber, it is hard to imagine a different outcome. Now, fifty years later, with a greater appreciation of the dynamics of echo chambers, perhaps it is easier to see the futility. It would thus also be important to ask: Is there actually a problem with Löwith's popularization of the secularization thesis? Is this the real problem, or is it only a symptom of other problems? What if he is doing a public and prophetic service by unmasking historical progress as the "last religion" of a spiritually hollow modernity?[38] These are real possibilities, but these are also precisely the level where serious ambiguities arise, which were a key reason for Blumenberg's position: "The mere observation that the modern world in which we live has in mind very little—and less and less, at that—apart from itself would not justify bringing this 'secularization' into a relation specifically with Christianity, which in such a case would only accidentally and arbitrarily happen to occupy the position of 'unwordliness' in the past that is contrasted with the present. The proposition that the modern world is to be understood as a result of the secularization of Christianity is certainly not meant to convey so little. But what must it say, if it is meant to say more?"[39] The unresolvable implications of the secularization thesis allow it to feed both sides of conflicting tendencies. The most general version of the secularization thesis—that modernity is derived from Christianity—allows Christianity to opportunistically take credit for modernity and to denounce and disavow it. This may be unavoidable in the wider public sphere, but, according to Blumenberg, there is no reason for academic discourses to follow suit (while pretending to lead).

Philosophy should be resisting such configurations, not adding to them. Under the terms of the secularization hypothesis, Christianity can at once take pride in "Christian modernity" and abhor its godless secularism. Ironically, both Blumenberg and Löwith are opposed to such self-serving sociocultural appropriations of the idea of secularization. But for Blumenberg, Löwith lends support to precisely such positions insofar as he maintains and generalizes (without analyzing and critiquing) the Weberian model of the invertive-transformative genealogy. The result is a rather muddy sense of the "derivations" and mechanisms that tie modernity to its Christian past. As soon as these details get lost, the sheer fact of secularization turns into a weak, traditional and ambivalent genealogy. Such a lax reading of genealogical "derivation" is especially evident in the appendix to *Meaning in History*, "Modern Transfigurations of Joachimism," where Löwith declares that "such a derivation usually distorts and perverts the original intention of the historical source. [. . .]. This discrepancy between remote results and the meaning of the initial intentions shows the scheme of derivation by secularization cannot be equated with a homogenous causal determination. [. . .]. In history 'responsibility' has always two sides: the responsibility of those who teach and intend something and the responsibility of those who act and respond."[40] Such vague methodological claims, which undergird the passage, remain in an overtly Weberian register. The case of the Protestant Ethic shines through as an implicit analog of Löwith's interpretation of Joachimism, and Weber's theory of ethics and action—"conscience" versus "responsibility"—is also palpable. Löwith relies on the remnants of Weber's sociological motivation of genealogical transformation, but without explaining why such paradigms "always" (or "usually") apply "in history"? Why do they amount to a "law"?[41] By rereading Weber's theoretical matrices as a quasi-existential rule, Löwith transforms Weber's critical genealogy into a stable metahistorical claim—a fixed point in an uncritical genealogy—against which Blumenberg vociferously reacted.

AGAMBEN'S THE KINGDOM AND THE GLORY

Space does not allow me to treat Agamben's recent *The Kingdom and the Glory* extensively. But there are aspects of this work that merit more than a footnote. First and foremost, I would emphasize Agamben's contextualization of this work within the German secularization debates of the 1960s,[42] and his subtitle—*For a Theological Genealogy of Economy and Government*—specifically identifies his method as genealogical. If one follows these hints, two strands emerge: (1) It is possible to see how Agamben measures his own discourse against the standard set by Blumenberg, Löwith, and Schmitt. The results are compelling: he clarifies points that were fuzzy in his precursors and establishes a practice of genealogy that can at least partly withstand Blumenberg's mode of critique. (2) It is also possible to imagine that Agamben's approach to genealogy was honed through the criticism directed at his *Homo Sacer* project—for example, by Jacques Derrida.[43] The result is a surprisingly long book (by Agamben's standards), which is at the same time leaner and more philological than many of his earlier ones. The tone is oriented toward what Blumenberg would call the "burden of proof," and sweeping philosophical-theoretical claims and overwrought invocations of looming geopolitical crisis are relatively infrequent.

One specific "proof" Agamben seeks to deliver revolves around Schmitt's famous claim in the first sentence of chapter 3 of *Political Theology*: "All pregnant concepts of the modern theory of the state are secularized theological concepts."[44] Agamben attempts neither to prove nor refute this claim in an unqualified way, but focuses more narrowly on the genealogy of the concepts of economy and government (organization, hierarchy, and bureaucracy), power and glory. Compared to Löwith, Blumenberg, or Schmitt, Agamben's more detailed treatment of theology as a specific and uniquely influential discourse can hardly be evaluated by nontheologians—who presumably comprise the majority of Agamben's readership. At the same time, he questions the ability of theology as a discipline to fully plumb the wider genealogical implications of its own textual corpus. I find such a claim plausible, though problematic insofar as it is unclear what it might mean to declare an emphatic "theological turn" in the theoretically informed humanities and social sciences. At the same time, there are indications that such a turn is occurring, for example, in recent scholarship on Walter Benjamin.[45]

One key innovation of Agamben's work with respect to Blumenberg is to understand the term *secularization* neither as a concept nor a metaphor, but as a "signature." This complicates matters, since it forces one to decide what one thinks about Agamben's theory of signatures, which is a cornerstone of his genealogical-archeological method.[46] Even at a nontechnical level, however, the qualifications alone, which Agamben attributes to *the signature* of secularization, strike me as useful in that they maintain secularization as a term without necessarily buying into all of its extended implications. According to Agamben: "Signatures move and displace concepts and signs from one field to another (in this case, from sacred to profane, and vice versa) without redefining them semantically. Many pseudoconcepts belonging to the philosophical tradition are, in this sense, signatures that [. . .] carry out a vital and determinate strategic function, giving a lasting orientation to the interpretation of signs."[47] This definition is somewhat difficult to follow in the case of secularization, because "movement" and "displacement" are a part of the definition of secularization as well as of its semantic function. In *The Signature of All Things*, Agamben conceives the reading of signatures as the core of "the risky operation [. . .] at issue in the tradition of the historical memory of the West."[48] Thus signature operations are part of a more general function, not limited to Agambinian analysis. They might, for example, stand in the place of what Szondi called "hermeneutics" and "philology"—without necessarily being the identical with these terms in all particulars. Without signatures, Agamben states, "there is no passage from semiology to hermeneutics [. . .]. Signs do not speak unless signatures make them speak."[49] What is the advantage of this approach? Perhaps too bluntly, I would say that it shifts the expectations about the idea of secularization, which is no longer a "descriptive concept" of social-scientific terminology but belongs to humanistic—that is: genealogical and archeological—inquiry. Signatures as markers of displacement may also be understood as the building blocks of the history of disciplines and interdisciplinarity: "[A]rcheology is a science of signatures, and we need to be able to follow the signatures that displace the concepts and orient their interpretation *toward different fields*."[50] Within a discipline, there are concepts, between disciplines, there can only be signatures.

Agamben's intervention, though different than Blumenberg's, is in line with Blumenberg's intent with respect to both the "positive" and "philosophical" concepts of secularization. It may also be observed that Agamben relies on an approach that he himself calls "metaphorological."[51] Specifically, he is interested in the "background metaphorics" of the concept of *oikonomia* from its Greek sources through its development as a technical term of theology, up to the current meaning of "economy."[52] *Oikonomia* is at once "a technical notion that designates the Trinitarian articulation of divine life" and "the breach through which Gnostic elements [...] penetrated the orthodox doctrine."[53] The metaphorological reading of patristic theology also contributes to Agamben's ability to perceive interpretive registers overlooked by the theological tradition itself. The genealogical point, perhaps, is that even if Agamben disagrees with Blumenberg on many particulars (which is the case), and even if Blumenberg is not a prominent member of Agamben's well cultivated family tree (which he is not), this does not mean that Agamben takes nothing from Blumenberg (including negative relations in the form of "disagreements").

Agamben also energetically pursues the question of the provenance of the idea of providence and the relation of providence to eschatology, which were stones of contention between Blumenberg and Löwith. For Blumenberg, eschatology was the decisive feature of the early Christian moment, whereas providence was a later compensation, not uniquely Christian and thus not a possible basis for Löwith's narrative of the secularization of providence as progress. Not "Secularization of Eschatology" but "Secularization by Eschatology," as the title of Blumenberg's fourth chapter succinctly puts it. On the first page of this chapter, Blumenberg writes: "A sufficient reason why the idea of providence could not be secularized in a late phase of the history of Christianity is that it had already participated, at the beginning of history, in the one fundamental secularization [*Verweltlichung*] of Christianity that was accomplished by rolling back eschatology and recovering a respite for history."[54] Despite the elegance of Blumenberg's argument, Agamben tends to side with Löwith insofar as he locates the specificity of the Christian idea of providence in the development of *oikonomia* as a technical term of Christian theology. Without speaking to the accuracy of the claim, I would point out that Agamben goes to some length to answer Blumenberg's challenge to establish the provenance of a uniquely Christian idea of providence.[55] Thus, in his emphatic vein, Agamben is able conclude with an italicized sentence: *"Providence is the name of the 'oikonomia,' insofar as the latter presents itself as the government of the world."*[56] This claim provides the basis for Agamben's wider hypothesis, in dialogue with Schmitt's *Political Theology*[57] and Foucault's governmentality, that the very idea of government—of the pairing of "economy and society"—is genealogically related to the theological concept of *oikonomia*, which at once integrates and dichotomizes the general and the particular, the ordered and the random, the foreseen and the spontaneous, and the direct and the mediated. Following the extended implications of this genealogy, Agamben argues that modern governmental power is generated "economically" in a way that stays true to the theological paradigm: "Through the distinction between legislative or sovereign power and executive or governmental power, the modern State acquires the double structure of the governmental machine. At each turn, it wears the regal clothes of providence, which legislates in a transcendent and universal way, but lets the creatures it looks after be free, and the sinister and ministerial clothes of fate, which carries out in detail the providential dictates and confines the reluctant individuals within the implacable connection between the immanent causes and between the effects that their very nature has contributed to determining. The providential-economic paradigm is, in this sense, the paradigm of democratic power, just as the theological-political is the paradigm of absolutism."[58]

Importantly for the degree of differentiation that Agamben is able to develop, the genealogy of glory does not simply replicate that of economy. Glory it is not derived from a specifically Christian heritage, but can be located in an array of sacred and secular sources and exists in a state of constant oscillation between the two: "doxologies and acclamations [...] constitute a threshold of indifference between politics and theology. Just as liturgical doxologies produce and strengthen God's glory, so the profane acclamations are not an ornament of political power but found and justify it."[59] Glory is thus a fundamentally nonsecular (and unsecularizable) category, which Agamben wants to critically destabilize by calling attention to the ways in which glory intrinsically depends on the operation of glorification: "if glory is the very substance of God and the true sense of his economy, then it depends upon glorification in an essential manner and, therefore, has good reason to demand it through reproaches and injunctions."[60] Agamben's genealogy of "the sphere of glory" ends up splitting between (1) the theology of the posteschatological condition, in which glory "occupies the place of postjudicial inoperativity" and the "eternal *amen*" of the hymn stands as "the radical deactivation of signifying language";[6] and (2) its displacement—partial masking and quasi-secularization—in modern democracies "to another area, that of public opinion." This second branch of the genealogy itself has two branches, a constitutional-acclamatory and a communicative-Habermasian variant. "They are nothing but two sides of the same glorious apparatus in its two forms: the immediate and subjective glory of the acclaiming people and the mediatic and objective glory of social communication."[62]

The most important question of genealogy, however, is at the same time the most troubling and unanswerable: in what ways, if any, do such genealogies contribute to a better understanding of the political or intellectual situation of the present and its established forms? For one thing, as I have shown, genealogies can easily lend themselves to the production of alibis and scapegoats. Another answer, which is not quite explicitly stated in Agamben's book, is that the circuitry of political identification might be destabilized to the extent that the rewiring of genealogies suggests that the supposed identities in question are no longer self-identical. What had been understood as "concepts," "identities" and "creeds" are genealogically shown to be the masks of meanings and intents that are fundamentally different from (if not opposed to) the understandings that had been previously presupposed. Though such a claim is largely implicit, in the very last words of the second appendix Agamben approaches it: "Modernity, removing God from the world, has not only failed to leave theology behind, but in some ways has done nothing other than lead the project of the providential *oikonomia* to completion."[63] And what happens after the completion?

Agamben's other answers to the question of the function of genealogy are no easier to decipher, but one of the stated intended results of "an archaeological operation like the one that we have attempted here [. . .], by moving upstream to a time before the separation that took place and that turned the two poles into rival but inseparable brothers," is to "undo the entire economic-theological apparatus and render it inoperative."[64] In that genealogy operates by splitting and division, it makes sense that one can follow the flow backward, not to an origin, but to a point prior to an entrenched and institutionalized dimorphisms. But is the bifurcation itself thereby reversed? How does the operativity of genealogy produce inoperativity? What if genealogy in this sense were only one more operation at the level of the signature, of the shifts and displacements ascribed to the meaning of the developments in question? In the latter case, the results are still not nothing—they are, strictly speaking, "significant"—but they are still far from the shutting down of the entire apparatus, far from the "hymnification" of the political that Agamben envisions.

As I would see it, Weber's paradigm of "invertive" irreversibility—which is less than a completely strict irreversibility—makes more sense than visions of redemption. Just as genealogy can show world-historical geneses happening by way of singular epigeneses,[65] so also further developments must remain possible. It seems less certain, however, whether such courses may be sought out and pursued, planned, or thwarted. Even in the case of global warming—which would seem to be the paradigm of a predictable outcome—the chances of human intention and intervention to produce a historical turning point are very much in question. This train of thought goes against the strongly prevailing preference for agency, solutions, and strategies. But what if, like it or not, such largely rhetorical expectations were actually fueling the problems? This is part of Blumenberg's thesis in his chapter on "the disruptability of the theoretical drive." In the same chapter, he poses the question: who knows how much leeway and unused potential may still exist within the shell of defunct agency?

Genealogy is important, but to look to it for "solutions" would be a misplaced expectation. Moreover, thanks to the incessant splitting and polarization internal to the genealogical pattern, Agamben's analytic practice is intensely productive of ambiguities. He thus exposes himself to Blumenberg's critique of secularization as a motor for producing ambiguity. Modernity as a legacy of Christianity remains constitutively open to transvaluation and polarization: good and bad, positive and negative, heaven and hell, sacred and profane, poetic and bureaucratic language. This is not to say that these terms may not be flipsides of one and the same paradigm, as Agamben suggests, but they also play into Blumenberg's sense that the proliferating paradigms of secularization themselves can only be uttered and heard in the echo chamber of public opinion. For Blumenberg, this space of speaking to the general audience allows the ambiguities to be exploited in ways that cause everything to say whatever everyone wants it to say. For Agamben as well, public opinion is only the negative space of glory. Thus, my suggestion would be to accept Agamben's genealogical analysis but to reject certain of the implications that he draws from it. Specifically, this means putting him into dialogue with Weber by viewing the thesis on economy and glory as an extension of the "iron cage" and a contribution to Weber's inquiry into the processes of rationalization and disenchantment that gave rise to the specificity of Western modernity. In proposing such a recontextualization, I would add that the Agamben does not make it difficult to read him this way. The genesis of polyphonic music, for example, mentioned by Weber as an instance of rationalization, can be easily imagined through Agamben's lens of Trinitarian *oikonomia*. And a sentence like the following could hardly sound more Weberian: "Political economy is constituted, in other words, as a social rationalization of providential economy."[66]

NOTES

1. "Was gegen Mannheim gesagt ist, trifft noch Max Weber, das Schulhaupt." "Neue wertfreie Soziologie" (1937), in *Gesammelte Schriften*, vol. 20.1: *Vermischte Schriften* I, ed. Rolf Tiedemann (Frankfurt am Main, Germany: Suhrkamp, 1986), 44.

2. It would be important to consider Foucault and Nietzsche in detail, but this exceeds the scope of the present study. Giorgio Agamben, whose genealogical method I address in the final section, reconsolidates the genealogical tradition stemming from Foucault and Nietzsche in *The Signature of All Things: On Method*, trans. Luca D'Isanto (New York: Zone Books 2009); see especially "Philosophical Archeology," 81–111.

3. See Max Weber, *Wirtschaft und Gesellschaft*, ed. Johannes Winckelmann (Tübingen: Mohr-Siebeck, 1976), 16–20, 122–58; also Max Weber, "Die drei reinen Typen der legitimen Herrschaft," in *Gesammelte Aufsätze zur Wissenschaftslehre*, ed. Johannes Winckelmann (Tübingen, Germany: Mohr-Siebeck, 1988), 475–88. My characterization of traditional legitimacy makes no special effort to cleave to Weber, but neither do I deliberately deviate from his conception.

4. Hans Blumenberg, *Die Legitimität der Neuzeit* (Erneuerte Ausgabe) (Frankfurt am Main: Suhrkamp, 1999), 18; see also 20. Translated by Robert M. Wallace as Hans Blumenberg, *The Legitimacy of the Modern Age* (Cambridge, MA and London: MIT Press 1983), 10.

5. This terminology is developed in Weber's "Politics as Profession." See Max Weber, "Politik als Beruf," in *Gesammelte Politische Schriften*, ed. Johannes Winckelmann (Tübingen: Mohr-Siebeck 1988), 551–52. See also "Soziologische Grundbegriffe," in *Wirtschaft und Gesellschaft*, 11–17. Regarding invertive structure of historical transformations, Weber is purported to have suggested a such a general formula of his work's implicit philosophy of history: "Weber was profoundly moved ... by the fact that on its earthly course an idea always and everywhere operates in opposition to its original meaning and thereby destroys itself." Cited from the editors' introduction to Max Weber, *The Protestant Ethic and the "Spirit"*

*of Capitalism and Other Writings*, eds. Peter Baehre and Gordon C. Wells (New York: Penguin 2002), xii.

6. On rationalization, see especially Max Weber, "Vorbemerkung" and "Zwischenbetrachtung," in *Geammelte Aufsätze zur Religionssoziologie* I (Tübingen, Germany: Mohr-Siebeck, 1988), 1–16, 536–73. See also Karl Löwith, "Max Weber und Karl Marx," in *Sämtliche Schriften 5: Hegel und die Aufhebung der Philosophie im 19. Jahrhundert—Max Weber* (Stuttgart, Germany: J. B. Metzlersche Verlagsbuchhandlung 1988), 346–60.

7. See Daniel Weidner, "Säkularisierung," in *Blumenberg lesen*, eds. Robert Buch and Daniel Weidner (Frankfurt am Main, Germany: Suhrkamp, 2014), 258–59.

8. See Daniel Heller-Roazen, "Tradition's Destruction: On the Library of Alexandria," in *October* 100 (2002) 2, 133–53. "There could be no philology were tradition not broken, no field of textual interpretation, criticism, and study were the transmission of texts not already obscure, altered, and interrupted: the immediacy and transparency of understanding would forbid the constitution of a discipline of the study of the language of the past. Philology nourishes itself on the erosion of history" (151). When it comes to the relation of philology to the philosophy and theory of the twentieth century, one can observe a strong methodological parting of the ways, which might be characterized as a preference for the "ideas" versus a preference for (historical) "contextualization." If the problem of genealogy as I approach it seems to be more oriented toward the latter, I would still understand it as working in the interest of the former. The Blumenberg-Löwith debate stands as evidence (not an isolated case) that ideas alone quickly become abstract and general, unless one is able to see the direction in which they are pointing. To put this in Blumenberg's terms, it is a question of the status of "constants" (whether proper names, ideas, terms or topoi) in humanistic research. Such constants and identities are never "real"—but they are the necessary precondition of genealogy, philology, and archeology. See also Christian Benne, "Philologie und Skepsis," in *Was ist eine philologische Frage? Beiträge zur Erkundung einer theoretischen Einstellung*, ed. Jürgen Paul Schwindt (Frankfurt am Main, Germany: Suhrkamp 2009), 192–210.

9. Readers may judge for themselves the extent to which my methodology overlaps with that of Richard Wolin, *Heidegger's Children: Hannah Arendt, Karl Löwith, Hans Jonas and Herbert Marcuse* (Princeton, NJ and Oxford: Princeton University Press, 2001), especially the introduction, "Philosophy and Family Romance," 5–20. Obviously each case is different, and Heidegger is evidently a special case. For a contrasting and more intellectually adventurous style of intellec-

tual-biographical "cohort research," see Nicolaus Sombart, *Die deutschen Männer und ihre Feinde: Carl Schmitt—ein deutsches Schicksal zwischen Männerbund und Matriarchatsmythos* (Munich, Germany and Vienna, Austria: Carl Hanser 1991), 17. Wolin's recourse to fatalistic patriarchal-patrilineal imagery ("Greek tragedy," "the sins of the fathers," "anxiety of influence") tends toward a rather deterministic model of genealogy (which may have its grain of truth in the case of Heidegger and his Jewish students), whereas Sombart locates Schmitt at the epicenter of a widespread syndrome, which culminated in the generation of the Weber brothers, and collapsed in that of Schmitt, Heidegger, and Hitler. Both Sombart and Wolin imply that liberalism and democracy are crucial to break the patriarchal spell. This is a crucial insight, but its political pragmatics have not necessarily aged well. The recourse to liberalism and democracy is evidently more difficult in 2018 than it was in 2001 and 1991.

10. Habermas's claim about the Weber-Schmitt genealogy has been the focus of much scholarly attention. See especially John P. McCormick, *Carl Schmitt's Critique of Liberalism: Against Politics as Technology* (Cambridge, UK: Cambridge University Press 1997), 31–82. McCormick speaks of Weber's second-generation "theoretical progeny" in the Frankfurt School. My focus is not primarily the substance of Habermas's claim, which has in the meantime been extensively analyzed, but its rhetorical dimensions. On the accuracy of Habermas's claim (or the lack thereof) see David Dyzenhaus, "The Legitimacy of Legality," *University of Toronto Law Journal*, 46 (1996): 1, 129–80, esp. p. 148, 136, 150; also David Dyzenhaus, *Legality and Legitimacy: Carl Schmitt, Hans Kelsen and Hermann Heller in Weimar* (Oxford, UK: Clarendon Press 1997), 235–39. The Weber-Schmitt case was the subject of two books in the 1990s, both of which reject Habermas's claim and criticize the prejudicial, partisan, and reputation-oriented tendencies of such claims. See G. L. Ulmen, *Politischer Mehrwert: Eine Studie über Max Weber und Carl Schmitt* (Weinheim, Germany: VHC Verlagsgesellschaft 1991), 18–19; and Matthias Eberl, *Die Legitimät der Moderne: Kulturkritik und Herrschaftskonzeption bei Max Weber und bei Karl Schmitt* (Marburg, Germany: Tectum Verlag 1994), esp. 1–6, 100–1. See also Nicolaus Sombart, "Max Weber und Otto Gross: Zum Verhältnis von Wissenschaft, Politik und Eros im Wilhelminischen Zeitalter," in *Nachdenken über Deutschland: Vom Historismus zur Psychoanalyse* (Munich, Germany: Piper Verlag 1987), 22–51. Sombart agrees with Habermas, but for different reasons: "Fascinated by power just like Weber, but much more radical in his thinking, he [Schmitt] has been called an 'illegitimate pupil' [*einen illegitimen Schüler*] of Weber" (47, my translation).

11. Primary documents of the debate are collected in *Der Positivismusstreit der deutschen Soziologie*, ed. Theodor W. Adorno et al. (Neuwied and Berlin, Germany: Luchterhand, 1969).

12. Talcott Parsons, "Wertgebundenheit und Objektivität in den Sozialwissenschaften," in *Max Weber und die Soziologie heute*, ed. Otto Stammer (Tübingen, Germany: Mohr-Siebeck 1965), 61.

13. Jürgen Habermas, "Diskussion über 'Wertfreiheit und Objektivität," in *Max Weber und die Soziologie heute*, 74–81: 81.

14. Ibid., 81.

15. See also Habermas's later and more complex critique of Weber: Jürgen Habermas, "Max Weber's Theorie der Rationalisierung," in *Theorie des Kommunikativen Handelns* (Band 1): *Handlungsrationalität und gesellschaftliche Rationalisierung* (Frankfurt am Main, Germany: Suhrkamp, 1995), 225–366. Dyzenhaus finds that Habermas's later work shares numerous presuppositions with Weber (*Legality and Legitimacy*, 236–37). Thus, Habermas himself might be viewed as a "natural son" of Weber who went on to legitimize himself.

16. Johann Wolfgang von Goethe, *Wilhelm Meisters Lehrjahre* (Münchner Ausgabe), ed. Hans-Jürgen Schings (Munich, Germany: Carl Hanser Verlag), 560. Johann Wolfgang von Goethe, *Wilhelm Meister's Apprenticeship*, ed. and trans. Eric A. Blackall in cooperation with Victor Lange (Princeton, NJ: Princeton University Press, 1989), 342.

17. Karl Löwith, "Der okkasionelle Dezisionismus von C. Schmitt," in *Sämtliche Schriften* 8: *Heidegger—Denker in dürftiger Zeit: Zur Stellung der Philosophie im 20. Jahrhundert* (Stuttgart, Germany: J. B. Metzlersche Verlagsbuchhandung, 1984), 32–71.

18. When Löwith republished the piece in a shortened version in 1964 in the *Frankurter Allgemeine Zeitung*, he gave it the more accurate title of "Max Weber und Carl Schmitt."

19. Löwith, *Sämtliche Schriften* 5, 418.

20. Giorgio Agamben, *The Kingdom and the Glory*, trans. Lorenzo Chiesa (Stanford, CA: Stanford University Press, 2011), 5.

21. Karl Löwith, *Meaning in History: The Theological Implications of the Philosophy of History* (Chicago, IL and London: University of Chicago Press), 19. Unless otherwise noted, citations refer to the English edition.

22. Blumenberg, *Legitimität*, 74; *Legitimacy*, 64 (translation modified).

23. Robert M. Wallace, "Translator's Introduction," in *The Legitimacy of the Modern Age*, trans. Robert M. Wallace (Cambridge, MA and London: MIT Press 1983), xi–xxxi:xvi. See also: Robert M. Wallace, "Progress, Secularization

and Modernity: The Löwith-Blumenberg Debate," *New German Critique* 22 (1981) 1, 63–79.

24. Strangely, the English translation omits to translate this title. The first chapter of the third part is simply called "introduction." Blumenberg, *Legitimacy*, 229.

25. Löwith, *Meaning in History*, 191.

26. Ibid., 200.

27. Ibid., 197.

28. Ibid., 200–1.

29. Blumenberg, *Legitimität*, 264; *Legitimacy*, 230 (translation modified).

30. On Blumenberg's "negative anthropology," see Hannes Bajohr, "The Unity of the World: Arendt and Blumenberg on the Anthropology of Metaphor," *Germanic Review* 90 (2015), 42–59.

31. Blumenberg, *Legitimität*, 267; *Legitimacy*, 232–23 (my emphasis).

32. Ibid., 264; 230 (translation modified).

33. Ibid., 273; 239 (translation modified).

34. Ibid., 275–276; 240 (translation modified).

35. Ibid., 35; 27 (translation modified).

36. Ibid., 39; 30 (translation modified).

37. Karl Löwith, *Sämtliche Schriften 2: Weltgeschichte und Heilsgeschehen: Zur Kritik der Geschichtsphilosophie* (Stuttgart, Germany: J. B. Metzlerische Verlagsbuchhandlung, 1983), 9.

38. Ibid., 192.

39. Blumenberg, *Legitimität*, 34; *Legitimacy*, 25.

40. Löwith, *Meaning in History*, 212.

41. Ibid., 212.

42. See Eva Geulen, *Giorgio Agamben: zur Einführung* (Hamburg: Junius Verlag, 2005), 133–40; also Colby Dickinson, *Agamben and Theology* (London and New York: T & T Clark, 2011).

43. See Jacques Derrida, *The Sovereign and the Beast*, trans. Geoffrey Bennington (Chicago, IL: University of Chicago Press, 2009), 305–49. The published edition of Derrida's 2002 seminar, which came out in French in 2008, could not have directly influenced Agamben's *The Kingdom and the Glory* (Italian 2007) or *The Signature of All Things* (Italian 2008). However, Derrida's critiques should be read in the context of an intense reception of *Homo Sacer*. Derrida criticizes Agamben for his sweeping historicisms, his frequently unguarded language and weak genealogical claims. Derrida seeks to avoid both ahistoricism and simplistic epochal generalizations. This often leads him to take an agnostic position

with respect to terms such as "modernity" and their historical-genealogical premises (rationalization). These critiques are reminiscent of Blumenberg's objections to Löwith and the discourse of "secularization." Even more than Blumenberg, Derrida pursues critical genealogy to a point where the very possibility of genealogy is deactivated. Derrida also evinces great skepticism about the rhetorical point of genealogy as practiced by Agamben (and implicitly also by Foucault): "why all of this effort to pretend to wake politics up to something that is supposedly [...] 'the decisive event of modernity?'" (330). Agamben, in keeping with his earlier critiques of deconstruction, defends his understanding of genealogy in *The Signature of All Things*. Here Derrida's approach represents a dead end and abandonment of genealogy (78–79). Agamben also rejects the criticism which claims that he disingenuously establishes his own originality at the expense of his precursors: "I have [...] preferred to take the risk of attributing to the texts of others what began its elaboration [*Entwicklung*] with them, rather than run the reverse risk of appropriating research paths that do not belong to me. [...]. Every method in the human sciences [...] should entail archeological vigilance. [...]. [I]t must retrace its own trajectory back to the point where something remains obscure and unthematized" (8).

44. "Alle prägnanten Begriffe der modernen Staatslehre sind säkularisierte theologiche Begriffe." Carl Schmitt, *Politische Theologie: Vier Kapitel zur Lehre von der Souveränität* (Berlin, Germany: Duncker & Humblot, 1922), 44; *Political Theology: Four Chapters on the Concept of Sovereignty*, trans. George Schwab (Chicago, IL and London: University of Chicago Press, 1985), 36.

45. See, for example, in addition to the present volume, very recent high-profile collections such as *Messianic Thought Outside Theology*, eds. Anna Glazova and Paul North (New York: Fordham University Press, 2014); *Walter Benjamin and Theology*, eds. Colby Dickinson and Stéphane Symons (New York: Fordham University Press, 2016).

46. See Agamben's "Theory of Signatures" in *The Signature of All Things* (33–80); specifically with respect to the secularization debates of the 1960s (74–76); in defense against Derrida (or comparable criticisms) Agamben articulates his allegiance to Nietzsche and Foucault: "Genealogy goes to war against this idea [of the ultimate disclosure of an original identity]. It is not that the genealogist does not look for something like a beginning. However, what he or she finds 'at the historical beginning of things' is never the 'inviolable identity of their origin'" (83). "The operation involved in genealogy consists in conjuring up and eliminating the origin and the subject" (84).

47. Agamben, *The Kingdom and the Glory*, 4.

48. Agamben, *The Signature of All Things*, 57.
49. Ibid., 61.
50. Agamben, *The Kingdom and the Glory*, 112 (my emphasis).
51. Ibid., 25.
52. On "background metaphors" and the development of "technical terms," see Hans Blumenberg, *Paradigmen zu einer Metaphorologie* (Frankfurt am Main, Germany: Suhrkamp, 2013), 91–109, 116–39; *Paradigms for a Metaphorology*, trans. Robert Savage (Ithaca, NY: Cornell University Press 2010), 62–76, 81–98.
53. Agamben, *The Kingdom and the Glory*, 35, 34.
54. Blumenberg, *Legitimität*, 47; *Legitimacy*, 37.
55. Agamben, *The Kingdom and the Glory*, 47–49 and 109–43.
56. Ibid.,111.
57. Compare Eva Geulen's discussion (135–37) of the dynamics of secularization and political theology in the first volume of Agamben's *Homo Sacer* series.
58. Agamben, *The Kingdom and the Glory*, 142.
59. Ibid., 229–30.
60. Ibid., 226.
61. Ibid., 239, 237.
62. Ibid., 255.
63. Ibid., 287.
64. Ibid., 285.
65. See Anton Schütz, "Epigenesis, law, and the *medium aevum* as medium," *Divus Thomas* 16 (2013), 3–4, 15–36.
66. Agamben, *The Kingdom and the Glory*, 282.

# "The God of Myth Is Not Dead—"
# Modernity and Its Cryptotheologies
## *A Jewish Perspective*

AGATA BIELIK-ROBSON

The light envelops itself in darkness even before becoming subject. In order to become subject, in effect the sun must go down [*decline*]. Subjectivity always produces itself in a movement of occidentalization [...]. That is the origin of history, the beginning of the going down, the setting of the sun, the passage to occidental subjectivity.
—Jacques Derrida, *Glas*

If, as its name suggests, the Occident is a fall, then the body is the ultimate weight, the extremity of the weight sinking from this fall. The body *is* weight. Laws of gravity involve *bodies* in space. But first and foremost, the body itself weighs: it is sunk into itself, according to a specific law of gravity that has pulled the body so far down that it can't be distinguished from its own weight [...]. An unfailingly *disastrous* body: an eclipse, a cold shower of heavenly bodies. Did we invent the sky for the sole purpose of making bodies fall from it?
—Jean-Luc Nancy, *Corpus*

All those thinkers who ever commented on Karl Löwith's thesis on secularization agree that modernity maintains *a* relation with premodern theology. The term *relation* is broad enough to embrace the whole spectrum of rapports ranging from: continuity-with-modification (as in Charles Taylor's *Secular*

*Age*), through secularizing immanentization (as in Karl Löwith, Carl Schmitt, Jacob Taubes, and Ernst Bloch, despite all the differences between them), up to militant rejection (as, to some extent, in Hans Blumenberg's *Legitimacy of the Modern Age*). The purpose of my essay will be to strengthen this theological connection and transform the concept of "relation" from vague and all-encompassing to more narrow and meaningful. First, I will claim that the *immanentization*, which the above thinkers agree to perceive as the most defining feature of modernity, not only does not announce the demise of the transcendence, but, to the contrary, inaugurates *nova era* in uncovering the latter's new modes of being. Modernity, far from being just the age of the "death of God," emerges as the time of God's most surprising *survival*.[1]

There is thus nothing paradoxical in the Hegelian notion of the "death of God religion" as the paradigmatic "religion of more recent times," in which it is the immanence that replaces transcendence as a new object of religious interest.[2] But I would like to introduce into this diagnosis an important distinction which consists mostly in the modification of its emotional register: while in Hegel, it is "the infinite grief of the finite," in which the world mourns the "death of God," in my interpretation, inspired by the Jewish-messianic contribution to the debate on secularization, it will come forward as a more joyous, affirmative and future-oriented attitude in which the theological content is offered possibility of a further, albeit secret, living-on. And finally, I will connect this new religious sentiment with the modern metaphysics of finitude, which I understand as one continuing variation on the theme of the univocity of being: starting with Duns Scotus's famous thesis, developing through Hegel, discussed by Blumenberg, and finding its latest defenders in Gilles Deleuze and Jean-Luc Nancy. In order for the singular beings of the world to come to the fore as the proper object of new metaphysics, God's previously all-powerful and incommensurable existence has to diminish, set down, and hide from sight. Hence the eponymous term, *cryptotheology*: if modernity is cryptotheological, it is because it evolves round the notion of the Hidden God, *deus absconditus*, sent off down to the Derridean crypt but never completely erased and forgotten. Its "atheism" is never pure and simple; it is rather, as in Gershom Scholem's seemingly oxymoronic expression, a *pious atheism*.[3]

It will thus be my aim to show that the debate inaugurated by Karl Löwith, which divided the discussants into two camps, for and against the thesis on secularization, allows for a third option: a "subtler language" of cryptotheology—one that welcomes the demise of traditional theologies, which focused on the divine Absolute, but does not give up on the modern translation of the religious content, which it applies to the new object of attention, that is, the *World*. From the point of view of Jewish messianism—from Scholem, Bloch, Taubes, up to Derrida—the so called death of God may thus be seen as a predominantly affirmative event, shifting the messianic interest from the spiritual-otherworldly to the material-innerworldly.

In *The Legitimacy of the Modern Age*, Hans Blumenberg calls this uniquely modern phenomenon the "migration of the divine attributes to the world,"[4] but he also immediately dismisses it as a dangerous illusion that goes against the very spirit of *modernitas*. According to him, modernity does not attempt to "reoccupy" the position once held by the transcendence and, because of that, does not strive to replace God with the World. He thus violently rejects all modern cryptotheologies of *deus absconditus* as the continuation of the "Gnostic danger," which had resurfaced in the late-medieval nominalistic "theological absolutism" and once again had thrown mankind in the abysses of disorientation and fear, facing it with an all-powerful and inscrutable God the Sovereign. It is precisely the second *overcoming of Gnosticism* that constitutes modernity's *differentia specifica*: modernity resolved to overcome people's dependence on *deus fallax*, the devious and capricious deity, by fostering the attitude of a rational self-assertion based on the systematic avoidance of all metaphysical speculations.

> The Gnosticism that had not been overcome but only transposed returns in the form of the 'hidden God' and His inconceivable absolute sovereignty. It was with this that the self-assertion of reason had to deal.[5]

Here, however, I will try to demonstrate that, pace Blumenberg, the idea of the hidden God who enables the transfer of the infinite to the finite does not have to be encumbered with the shadow of God's inscrutable dominion and that—in the constant reworking of the religious myth—it may actually get us beyond the paradigm of sovereignty: beyond the Gnostic danger into the broad and open land of the messianic philosophy of *saeculum*.

### Which DEATH, OF Whose GOD?

Is the death of God religion, proclaiming the modern passage from transcendence into immanence, truly a Christian monopoly, as Hegel suggests? Almost all thinkers associated with the death of God theology—Thomas Altizer, Jean-Luc Nancy, Slavoj Žižek—insist on the absolute uniqueness of Christianity as the only religion that harbors atheism structurally within itself and as such paves the way to what we tentatively call the modern process of secularization. Yet a similar—even stronger: precursorial—maneuver of atheologization, in which God loses his traditional absolutist attributes, occurs already in Jewish messianism: beginning with the Lurianic kabbalah and ending with Derrida's attempt to pluralize the concept of the death(s) of God(s) religion(s) in his own contribution to the debate on secularization, "Faith and Knowledge."[6]

To some extent, the Christian and the Jewish modernity go hand in hand. The main feature of the new religious sentiment, shared by both and already well spotted by Hegel, is *restlessness*, *die Unruhe*: God, before imagined as an eternal substance beyond any change, enters the path of a dynamic self-transformation. Before a synonym of restful immutability, God now becomes identical with a process: a movement which aims at solving the tensions and aporias tearing apart the original form of the godhead. This seminal change found a paradigmatic expression in Martin Luther's notion of *Anfechtung Gottes*, meaning struggle *within* God himself—*Gott wider Gott*—but also a struggle *with* God, an assertive attempt of the finite being to finds its place in the new metaphysical arrangement.[7]

Yet the very origin of this new theological vision is to be located in the groundbreaking system of Isaac Luria, the sixteenth-century-Safed kabbalist, who introduced change into the very heart of the divine with the invention of *tsimtsum*: the withdrawal/contraction of God. Luria's theory of *tsimtsum* can indeed be seen as the first occurrence of the typically modern self-occlusion of God who retreats in order to make room for the world and subsequently hides behind the created being. By hiding, withdrawing, absenting himself from direct influence; by giving up on his sovereign and unscathed status of the original Infinite (and in this manner playing out his inner contradiction), God *en-crypts* himself in both meanings of the Derridean phrase: he lays himself down in the tomb/crypt and erases any clear signs of his presence within the worldly immanence in which he leaves only oblique and cryptic traces. If modernity is cryptotheology, then it is also a Jewish modernity, because the modern process of the divine *en-cryption* begins not with Luther's *Gott selbst ist tot* [God himself is dead], but rather with Luria's *tsimtsum*.[8]

The assumption of the Lurianic *tsimtsum* as the model of the relation between transcendence and immanence, God and World, but also theology and secularity, is the common characteristic of all the Jewish thinkers who entered the twentieth-century debate on secularization: Gershom Scholem, Walter Benjamin, Ernst Bloch, Jacob Taubes, Hans Jonas (and Derrida, their latest heir). The defining feature of the *tsimtsum* model is the decidedly affirmative emphasis put on the *passage from the infinite to the finite*. Although in the Lurianic system, the Absolute, the primordial *Ein-Sof* [without limits], undergoes a dramatic limitation, this is *not* a cosmic catastrophe: on the contrary, it is a welcome move of creating a room [*makom*] for the other of the world. It is only the next event—"the breaking of the vessels" [*shevirat ha-kelim*], in which the forms/vessels prepared by God to sustain his emanative light give in under its powerful impact—that marks the moment of metaphysical crisis. Yet, even this crisis, announcing the end of all Platonic static forms and eternal universals, can be seen as simply paving the way to a new understanding of being as univocally finite. God had made himself finite and, after the last dispersion of the eternal forms-vessels, exiled himself into the material universe. He is thus setting as a Platonic sun and enters the night of the world in the form of scattered sparks and oblique traces. In Gershom Scholem's description,

> Creation out of nothing, from the void, could be nothing other than creation of the void, that is, of the possibility of thinking of anything that was not God. Without such an act of self-limitation, after all, there would be only God—and obviously nothing else. A being that is not God could only become possible and originate by virtue of such a contraction, such a paradoxical retreat of God into himself. By positing a negative factor in Himself, *God liberates creation*.[9]

This image of a liberated creation will also resurface in Hegel, who concludes his *Phenomenology* with the last lines of Schiller's poem—"Only from the chalice of this realm of spirits foams forth for Him his own infinitude"[10]—which indicates that from now on the infinite can only be interpreted as the community of finite spirits that re-create the divine *Gestalt*, yet without restoring the Absolute to its original ontological infinity. Modern ontotheology, therefore, is all about finite being and *univocatio entis* simply means the absolute rule of finitude. This, for Jean-Luc Nancy, is the ultimate sense or "dis-enclosure" of Christianity as the religion of the death of God: sealing the metaphysical passage from the infinite to finite being, where even—or most of all—God cannot enjoy the infinite existence, but undergoes the paradigmatic exposure, thus becoming an ontological model for all other beings. For Derrida, on the other hand, this passage, although related to the death of God as the Sovereign and Infinite, does not have to be necessarily thought in the Christian way: without automatically connoting negativity of Passion, sacrifice and self-offering, deep down it merely announces that, in modernity, God a/theologizes himself, because he is no longer thought in terms of the unscathed ["*indemne*"]—the sovereign, infinite, eternal, unchanging, invulnerable, safe and sound, whole and holy—but is given over to the continuous trial of the finite immanent reality.[11]

Derrida's deeply affirmative reading of the *tsimtsum* model, where affirmation precedes any negation,[12] is the crowning of a long development within the secret Lurianic line of thinkers who—to use Blumenberg's phrase—had been working on the Lurianic myth in such a way as to adopt it to the modern temper and take it out of the pessimistic Gnostic idiom of Isaac Luria himself. Luria did not leave us anything in writing, but we know that he tended to overemphasize the cataclysmic moment of the breaking of the vessels at the expense of the positivity of *tsimtsum*. We also know that some of his pupils (Israel Sarug most of all) saw God's maneuver of going into hiding as a gesture of anger and wrath (thus confirming Blumenberg's worry about the continuation of the Gnostic danger in *any* later theology of *deus absconditus*). Yet, the *modern* work on the Lurianic inspiration took a precisely reverse turn and by affirming the hazard of creation produced a peculiar cryptotheological line of the self-asserted World—a thread already visible in Scholem, Bloch, Taubes, and Jonas, but becoming fully explicit only in Derrida.[13]

Scholem's classical account of the Lurianic *tsimtsum* is still ambivalent and hesitant, because he tries to be faithful to the historical original doctrine, but Hans Jonas's philosophical paraphrase of the Lurianic myth, deriving from his essay "The Concept of God after Auschwitz," is already free of both Gnostic lament, deploring the cosmic catastrophe of creation, and Gnostic danger, exposing creation to the hidden malignant power. What Jonas offers is a Lurianic myth reworked according to the requirements of the modern temper, which asserts finite existence and thus rejects immortality, ahistorical vision of the cosmos, and divine providence. He interprets *tsimtsum* as the self-limitation of the divine, which deliberately gives itself over to chance, the risk of becoming. God, emptied and contracted, becomes an event of the past-perfect history; always already there in the distant moment of creative decision, but no longer retrievable in the present state of creation. But as a trace of transcendence (or, in Jonas's own terms, as "transcendence awakened in the immanence"), God remains a sense/orientation in the world that makes us prefer something rather than nothing, that is, choose the very *project of becoming* as a nonarbitrary and not fully contingent process, in which the mythic story continues toward its fulfillment (this is why Jonas immediately insists on *not* conflating the Lurianic narrative with pantheism in which the World, fully identical with God, is already complete).

In the beginning, for unknowable reasons, the ground of being, or the Divine, chose to give itself over to chance and risk an endless variety of becoming. And wholly so: entering into the adventure of space and time, the deity held back nothing of itself: no uncommitted or unimpaired part remained to direct, correct, and ultimately guarantee the devious working-out of its destiny in creation. On this unconditional immanence the modern temper insists. It is its courage or despair, in any case its bitter honesty, to take our being-in-the-world seriously: to view the world as left to itself, its laws as brooking no interference, and the rigor of our belonging to it as not softened by extramundane providence. The same our myth postulates for God's being in the world. Not, however, in the sense of pantheistic immanence: if world and God are simply the same, the world at each moment and in each stage represents his fullness, and God can neither lose nor gain. Rather, in order that the world might be, and be for itself, God renounced his being, divesting himself of his deity—to receive it back from the odyssey of time weighted with the chance harvest of unforeseeable temporal experience: transfigured or possibly even disfigured by it. In such self-forfeiture of divine integrity for the sake of unprejudiced becoming, no other knowledge can be admitted than that of *possibilities*, which cosmic being offers in its own terms: to these, God committed his cause in effacing himself from the world.[14]

The question—*which* death of *whose* God: Nietzschean? Hegelian? Lurianic?—constitutes the principal problem of modern cryptotheology, bearing on the multiple shapes of modernity itself. With the Nietzschean death of God, the liberated mankind must finally take superhuman courage to get rid not just of God but also of his lingering shadow. With the Blumenbergian modification of Nietzsche, modernity amounts to a struggle waged by the self-assertive human *cogito* against the devious God (*deus fallax*) who cannot be refuted logically but precisely because of that must be killed. With the Hegelian death of God, it is God himself who consents to die, but then his kenotic self-sacrifice encumbers the world with the guilt that must be bought off/redeemed at the end of history. And finally, with the Lurianic death of God, modernity emerges as the time of the World, a pure liberating *gift*, offering only open possibilities, which is to be remembered [*zakhor*], but in a different way than the remorseful "memory of the Passion."[15]

This is precisely the moment when Christian and Jewish modernity begin to part their ways. Despite some superficial affinities, the Lurianic *tsimtsum* is *not* the same as the Christian *kenosis*: it is not God's self-sacrifice that encumbers the world with the sense of a terrible and scandalous loss. Even if it is a death of God as the Sovereign Infinite, it is also God's *survival*; his only mode of living-on in and with the world which he simultaneously made his own creation and let go as a free other-being. The *tsimtsum* God does not die for us: he limits his primordial infiniteness and becomes finite not in order to make creation eternally guilty and obliged (the infinite grief of the finite), but in order to affirm finite being as the right and final way to be. In the modern reworking of the Lurianic myth, therefore, God himself emerges as the most powerful spokesman for the principle of *univocatio entis*—which also makes spurious all the Nietzschean attempts to kill him, because he no longer poses a Gnostic danger to the reality of the finite world.[16]

But modern univocity does not have a single fate: it bifurcates, by giving way to two very distinct metaphysics of finitude—the difference well reflected in the two epigraphs coming, accordingly, from Derrida and Nancy. The first, taken from Derrida's commentary on Hegel (in which he himself proves to be a sort of a Jewish Hegelian, reading Hegel through Lurianic lenses), connects the modern Occident with "setting down of the sun." Religion travels from the East to the West, which coincides with a crucial passage: *from Substance to Subject*, where God stops being the all-pervasive light and, by negating himself—setting down—becomes reborn as a restless subjectivity. The second, coming from Nancy's *Corpus*, a long commentary on the central sentence of Christianity—*hoc est enim corpus meum*—connects the modern Occident with the Fall: the force of gravity, or sheer weight that makes bodies fall from the sky and far away from the spiritual center of the universe. Here the modern West is the Blakean land of Ulro, made of dead matter obeying the Newtonian laws. What defines the Occident is the Neoplatonic arch of decline: the passage from the infinite spirit to "finite bodies."

Both these positions derive from the matrix offered by the twentieth-century debate on secularization: while Derrida's though can be seen as the last Blumenbergian attempt of the work on (Lurianic) myth, Nancy's effort consists in bringing the (Christian) myth to an end—two deaths of God and two ways of telling their stories. Usually it is Blumenberg's *Legitimacy* that serves as the canvas for the secularization debate, involving all its important participants—Löwith, Schmitt, Taubes, Jonas, Heidegger, Marquard. However, this time I would rather consult his later *oeuvre*, *Work on Myth*, which tells the same story differently—precisely by *telling the story*, that is, insisting on the necessity of a modern narrative that cannot be fully replaced by the successes of instrumental reason (which is often his position in the previous book, too blindly enamored with science and technology). It is here that Blumenberg introduces the alternative notion of a successful story whose success lies precisely in the fact that it does not strike as immediately as a *lie*, that is, one of those Nietzschean "lies necessary for life" that can be easily disenchanted and dismissed. The success of a story consists in depleting the power of the "absolutism of reality," which reduces anxiety caused by the unfamiliar Real.

> What has become identifiable by means of a name is raised out of its unfamiliarity by means of metaphor and is made accessible, in terms of its significance, by telling stories [...]. It will be as a means of maintaining position in the face of an overpowering reality, through millenniums, that stories, which could not be contradicted by reality, were successful.[17]

And it is also here that Blumenberg introduces the idea of "bringing myth to an end": while the work on myth takes some elements of the mythic story seriously and wants to continue them in their transfers and translations, the act of "ending" evacuates the sense of the myth and merely plays parodistically with its emptied form. This, for me, will be the modern materialist idiom, as represented by Nancy (but certainly not by him only): merely an end-game of the religious myth, that is, not as autonomous, atheistic, and safely posttheological as it would like to appear.

### *Factum brutum*, or Matter on the Rocks

Nancy's bringing myth to an end can also be called a Satanic Inversion: not because it is wrong or demonic, but because it can be best summed up by the famous battle-cry of Miltonian Satan: *Evil, be thou my good!*[8] Satan is the prosopopoeia of modernity in its complex relationship with premodern theology: although Satan's intention was to prove his absolute originality, the moment he decided merely to paraphrase God's moral code, he made himself immediately dependent on his Father, thus confirming his authority. Instead of creating a new metaphysical vision that would prove his true novelty, Satan picks the moment of crisis in the divine narrative—evil as the current result of the past fall and the object of future redemption—and claims it for his own, at the same time rejecting the rest of the story. This *unintended dependence*—at once upholding and rejecting the theological narrative—characterizes aptly the process of the inversion that took place in the modern thought praising itself of its strict and unprecedented materialism: instead of proposing a new metaphysics of finitude, it merely inherited the remnants of the old Neoplatonic scheme, already destroyed by the late-medieval nominalistic crisis, and found abode in the midst of its ruins. And if Blumenberg says that "nominalism is a system meant to make man extremely uneasy about the world," materialism calls this Miltonian hell made of the debris of matter precisely—a *home*.[19]

A good illustration of such dubious inheritance, which simultaneously maintains and rejects the mythic story, is offered by Slavoj Žižek in *Absolute Recoil*, and is important for us because it allegedly retells the Lurianic myth—first *tsimtsum*, then breaking of the vessels—in order to propose its materialist paraphrase.

> How should this myth be modified to produce a 'materialist' version? The solution seems obvious: there was no vessel, and so no original breaking, the universe is just a contingent collection of fragments that we can tinker with to produce new assemblages ... What gets lost in this solution is the immanent antagonism/tension/blockage that underlies and sets in motion the movement of fragmentation.[20]

If the "Lurianic myth" constitutes a kabbalistic modification of Neoplatonism, with the vessels standing for universals and *shevirat ha-kelim* for the dispersion of matter, then the materialist "paraphrase" does away with the whole plot of the story—"no vessel, no original breaking"—and leaves us with the dedramatized final result, yet presented as if it was there from the start as something irreducibly factual, a *factum brutum*: the universe as "*just* a contingent collection of fragments."[21] The mythic narrative is thus simultaneously upheld (the result is right) and destroyed (it is not a result of anything, *just* a primal fact), which not only loses all dialectical tensions that can only form themselves within a *mythos*, a narrative drama, but also invalidates the very language in which this "result" is described.

Such bastardized and deeply aporetic secularizing "paraphrase" of both Luria and Hegel can indeed be called, after Karl Löwith, "illegitimate." Its most characteristic feature is the *absolutization of the moment of crisis*, which—although taken from the "mythic" narrative where it means exactly "crisis"—detaches itself from its former normative "significance" and becomes a *factum brutum*, the primal fact, something that "remains" *after* the destruction of the meaningful narrative. For Blumenberg, this is also the essence of the procedure he calls "bringing myth to an end." He demonstrates it in reference to Franz Kafka's parody/paraphrase of the myth of Prometheus, which ends with the depiction of the posthuman and posthistorical landscape. After all the *persona* of the drama—Prometheus, the eagle, the gods—had forgotten what it was all about and had become "weary" of repeating it ...

> There remains the inexplicable mass of rock. The legend tries to explain the inexplicable. As it comes out of the substratum of truth it has in turn to end in the inexplicable.[22]

Kafka's intention coincides here with T. S. Eliot: *in myth's beginning, is myth's end*. What made us invent stories to break the seal of the inexplicable—the obtuse and terrifying "absolutism of reality"—is also what eventually claims them back and forces us to face the "naked truth," the stony *factum brutum*. Blumenberg comments,

> What remains, here too, is the stone, because it is ground [*Grund*, earth] and therefore needs no ground [*Grund*, reason]: Not needing explanation is the ground of its incontestability. The metaphor of an original stratum underlying all events, which itself no longer requires justification [. . .] extends from Goethe's 'granite' to Kafka's 'inexplicable mass of rock' [. . .]. Kafka makes the 'action' disappear in nature, in its simply unmoved, indestructible, unhistorical form as the mass of rock.[23]

The materialist "paraphrase," therefore, would consist in the *inversion* of the very movement of the mythic story: while the latter is apotropaic, that is, turns away from the "simply unmoved, indestructible, unhistorical," the former goes back to find itself as close as possible to the Real. For Nancy, also an advocate of the materialist "paraphrase," such inversion is the only thing left after the ultimate expiration of the Greco-Judeo-Christian metaphysical story. In *The Sense of the World*, Nancy asks,

> Does not the deconstruction of both tragedy and Christianity—of their combination, which dialectically culminates in the unhappiness of sense as and *end* in all senses—does this deconstruction not have to take the form of another turn, return, detour, or turning-back of this dialectical knot?[24]

Yet, according to the Kafkian logic as reconstructed by Blumenberg, this "turning-back" is already inscribed in the Christian revelation itself: its end is already implied in its very beginning, when it proclaims the "death of God." This, for Nancy, is precisely the perpetual Christian tragedy, the absolutized moment of crisis. The "good news," seemingly announcing the advent of "the sense taken to its point of excess," in fact declares the exhaustion of all revealability.

> In that sense it is certainly surpassing, the *Aufhebung*, the Jewish departure outside Judaism, for the idea of Christian revelation is that, in the end, *nothing is revealed*, nothing but the end of revelation itself [. . .]. Sense is then completed, or, to say the same thing differently, used up. It is *complete sense in which there is no longer any sense*. That is what ends up being called 'the death of God,' in a phrase that is not accidentally of Christian provenance (it comes from Luther),

for it states the very destiny of Christianity. In other words, closer to Nietzsche, Christianity is accomplished in nihilism and as nihilism, which means that nihilism is none other than the final incandescence of sense, that it is sense taken to its point of excess.[25]

Christianity is thus the last religion, *dying*—as Freud would have said—the death of her own, not by external but only by internal causes, ending the whole story of revealability (*Offenbarkeit*) with the "revelation of nothing": the "nothing" as the ultimate premise of "no more gods," "no more sense," and "no more stories," that insinuates itself in the place of the dead God.

At the same time, however, Nancy insists that this is *not* a negative proposition and that the nihilistic horror of negativity thus revealed can be inverted into the positive of *affirmation*: into the "glory" of creation finally set free, because *abandoned* only to itself. Yet, as such, this "affirmation" does not depart from the deconstructed story, beyond its end toward a new beginning. It merely feeds off it, as if in a prolonged Beckettian "end-game" that "brings myth to an end," but still remains, parasitically, within its decomposing body. It is not a destructive secularization of the mythic narrative, as Löwith would like to see it, but rather its *exhaustion*. In the end, therefore, "there is nothing more to say," as Nancy so often concludes his musings. The "Christian myth" ends in absolute receding, which only shows an empty place, as if in a parody of *tsimtsum*. In *Corpus*, which by no accident is Nancy's meditation on Descartes (paralleling Blumenberg's reflections on *cogito*), it is not the self-asserted human subject, but only the dead extended bodies that are the only thing *left* after the final expiration of the myth.

> Thus, indeed, he's the one who's exposing himself *dead* like *the world of bodies* [. . .]. In other words: no God, not even gods, just *places*. Places: divine through an opening whereby the whole 'divine' collapses and withdraws, leaving the world of our bodies bare. Places of bareness, of destitution, place of *limon terrae*.[26]

But what is gained with this deconstructive operation? The material world is all in ruin—it's just groundless earth, dust and ashes, rocks and stones—but at least it is *free*. After all, it is better to reign in hell of "brutal facts" than serve in heaven of "meaningful ideas." The very obverse of autonomy is thus alienation pushed to its extreme, beyond any possibility of recall (the Hegelian *Er-innerung*). Being can be truly liberated, only when "abandoned" as a waste product; or, in Schelling's idiom, precursorial to this line of modern cryptotheology, being can find freedom only at the furthest fringes of its *Ab-fall*, where this "fall-away" means also garbage, scraps, and waste.²⁷ If there is an element of modern self-assertion here, it boils down to the Beckettian bleak vision of a sovereign dominion over the "pile of crap," or to Benjamin's portrait of a baroque tyrant presiding over of the material universe in ruins, the prince of the "permanent catastrophe." And even Blumenberg himself can be seen as falling for this vision which he interprets as the positive grounding of modern instrumental reason and its *Herrschaftsrationalität*: the rule over the worthless material waste—the easier, the more barren the matter appears.

Indeed, this logic of bringing the myth of Christianity to 'the end of revelation itself' until all is left is *factum brutum*, is structurally analogous to the one described by Blumenberg as governing the passage to the posttheological modernity in *The Legitimacy of the Modern Age*. The "New World" emerges out of the disenchanted remnants of the nominalistic theology, itself already a remnant/ruin/end of the Neoplatonic metaphysics—an atomistic disarray of material beings, out of joint and deprived of any structure and hierarchy—and becomes accepted precisely *as such*. Says Blumenberg,

> The radical materializing of nature is confirmed as the systematic correlate of theological absolutism. Deprived by God's hiddenness of metaphysical guarantees for the world, man constructs for himself a counterworld of elementary rationality and manipulability.²⁸

This "counterworld," however, does not even deserve to be called a "World": it is merely a chaotic correlate of the nominalistic theology that grants God absolute omnipotence and, accordingly, perceives matter as infinitely malleable and compliant to the unbound divine power—with this difference only that now matter becomes subservient to human mind and hand.²⁹ What then immediately follows is the *inversion* which, as in the case of Descartes, "transforms the late medieval *crisis* of certainty into an *experiment* with certainty," and as such "rests upon the presupposition of the crisis, in that it constructively intensifies them."³⁰ And just like *cogito* maintains its absolute validity only in the worst possible metaphysical scenario as the *only* moment of certitude, being the obverse of an equally absolute doubt caused by the "malignant demon"—the modern matter is also a product of the destruction of the once meaningful medieval cosmos, its absolutized moment of crisis. Next comes the stage of *neutralization*, or adaptation to the permanent catastrophe of the material universe in ruins: the skeptical phase that "argues for the *irrelevance* of the physical answers to the shaping of life in the world."³¹ And though Blumenberg himself would be more than happy to stop at this Neo-Epicurean solution, which "frees the phenomenon of nature from its affective reference,"[32] modern philosophy evolves and eventually demands that we show an affect of *affirmation* for the world, even if—or rather precisely because—it seems so indifferent, brutally factual, and itself unaffected by any "human story": a Miltonian "hell without heaven" . . .[33]

## "EARTH WITHOUT HEAVEN": THE STORY CONTINUES . . .

Yet, this tendency, although prevalent, is counteracted by another, truly innovative cryptotheology which—once again paraphrasing John Milton, one of the greatest prophets of modernity—can be called: "World Regained." This line is less emphatically materialistic than *worldly*: its theme is the modern *saeculum*, "worldliness." It does not approach it in terms of secular materialism, but rather in terms of an implicit "religion of the world": *implicit* not because it "illegitimately" avails itself of old metaphysical schemes, but because it proclaims a truly new metaphysics of the finite existence, which champions a figure of an *implicit God*—a God who wants to conceal himself and withdraw in order to make room for modern *saeculum*, the Age of the World. And if the former materialist paraphrase deliberately wishes to lose in translation the whole metaphysical *story*, this one is uniquely concerned with the "transfer of the infinite into the finite," involving a complex, continuous, and often secret work on what Jonas calls the "Lurianic myth."

The World Regained is also the main subject of Blumenberg's *Legitimacy*: modernity is the recovery of the material dimension of the world, which for him means the final and irrevocable demise of theology. In this strictly disjunctive logic, it is either God, serviced by theological absolutism—or the World, coming to the fore only with the dissipation of the former. But we could also say, partly pace Blumenberg, that the modern *Verweltlichung* announces a new, so far unknown, "religion of the world," which simultaneously evokes a more ancient theology of creation: very much present in Judaism but forgotten with the advent of the apocalyptic Christianity, along with its "a-cosmic" distaste for the material reality and longing for the otherworldly transcendence. If we insist on reading Blumenberg cryptotheologically (which is always a serious impeachment of his own position), we could even state a hypothesis that modernity is an *inverted Marcionism*, where it is creation that is once again affirmed *against* redemption.[34] This implicit *cryptotheology of creation*, encrypted in Blumenberg's writings, would not simply adopt the truncated "result" of the nominalist theological absolutism, but go truly against the grain of the "permanent catastrophe" and regain what has been lost for the ages of the dominance of the absolutist paradigm, namely, the World.

Blumenberg rightly criticizes Karl Löwith, who claimed that modernity is a secularization of Christian theology, for not taking into account that Christianity has always been marked by the eschatological *Entweltlichung*, and as such could not become a matrix for the modern interest in worldliness. But such refutation of Löwith does not yet lead to the negation of *all* theology: to the contrary, it may just as well pave the way to an alternative theology of *Verweltlichung*, where it is the World now gaining the whole attention. And although it is not completely in harmony with his intentions, Blumenberg is honest enough to notice the dialectical sequence connecting the modern result of the "World Regained" with the previous "loss of the world":

> Thus the possibility of talk of secularization is conditioned by the process that established 'worldliness' in the first place. There was no 'wordliness' before there was the opposite of 'unwordliness.' It was the world released to itself from the grip of its negation, abandoned to its self-assertion and to the means necessary to that self-assertion, not responsible for man's true salvation but still competing with that salvation with its own offer of stability and reliability. This true 'creation of the world' [*Weltwerdung*] is not a secularization [becoming worldly] in the sense of transformation of something preexisting but rather, as it were, the primary crystallization of a hitherto unknown reality.[35]

Again, it is Milton who best articulates this dialectic: in the ironic conclusion to the *Paradise Lost*, the eponymous loss is met not with "mourning and melancholy," but immediately replaced by the gain of the World, which presents and crystallizes itself before Adam and Eve as indeed a "hitherto unknown reality."

> They, looking back, all the eastern side beheld
> Of Paradise, so late their happy seat,
> Waved over by that flaming brand, the gate
> With dreadful faces thronged and fiery arms:
> Some natural tears they dropped, but wiped them soon;
> The world was all before them, where to choose
> Their place of rest, and Providence their guide,
> They, hand in hand, with wandering steps and slow,
> Through Eden took their solitary way.[36]

*The world was all before them*: this is not a nontheological statement. Rather, if there is a reason to wipe the tears of sorrow and rejoice again, it is because the World offers itself as a place no less divine and no less implicated in the religious plot than Paradise, or perhaps even more so. The peculiar "Jewish" effect of Milton's conclusion derives from the way in which he deliberately conflates the two topoi that Christianity always kept strictly contrasted and that Judaism often interposes: the *Exile* and the *Exodus*. Instead of deploring the fact of humans being exiled from the paradisiac state of existence, Milton affirms it as an exodus from their infantile stage of dependence, thus anticipating Kant's *Ausgang aus der selbstverschuldeten Unmündigkeit* and Marx's, in an even more secular translation, modern *Auszug* out of the "idiocy of village life." This "brave new world"—new, because it never existed before, and brave, because there is an exciting plot linked to its sudden emergence—cannot be thought of as some impoverished result of the one-sided removal of the antithesis: it is not just a "pale shadow," remaining after the death of God, a *nihil* left over after the higher hierarchy of spiritual being had been "cut off." Although, as we have seen, this danger of nihilizing deprivation/impoverishment is indeed incipient in the modern project of *Verweltlichung*, it will be counteracted by the modern cryptotheology that prevents the World Regained from sliding into nothing by keeping it in the mode of self-assertion. The worldly cryptotheology, allowing a full "transfer of the infinite in the finite," is thus the beginning of a *rich immanence*, which does not lose anything in the process of the World-forming translation. It takes over the whole richness of theological meanings and it will be now the role of the World to answer the Tillichian questions of "the ultimate concern"—most of all, the issue of redemption, no longer to be solved by the otherworldly mysticism.[37]

It needs to be stated clearly, however, that in his analysis of the modern *Verweltlichung*, Blumenberg does not share Milton's enthusiasm. He sees the transfer of the infinite into the finite as a dangerous practice that will charge [*belasten*] the World with theological tasks it cannot sustain and will once again awaken the specter of maximalist messianic expectations that he wishes to see gone for good. Blumenberg's ideal vision would be to revert to the small Epicurean *Lebenswelt* in which humans lead a finite existence, merely counting on a kind indifference of gods and fate. But he knows that, in modernity, which has discovered the World, such return is either no longer possible or requires a special effort of the "active forgetting" that aims at wiping out the whole infinite horizon (and which Blumenberg joins, by offering his own version of the Nietzschean "sponge": the 600-page-long refutation of the thesis on secularization). The transfer of infinity on the World, *All-World*, is a *possibility* that Blumenberg does not deny, even though he tirelessly proves that it is doomed to fail.[38] This broad open land of worldwide empty spaces immediately becomes an object of a new *theological curiosity* (as juxtaposed with Blumenberg's "theoretical curiosity"), causing, on the one hand, the Pascalian fear and trembling, but also, on the other, giving rise to the *tremendum fascinans* of the Romantic Sublime. What modern philosophy often deplores as the problem of *Weltlosigkeit*, the unprecedented and disorienting loss of the *Lebenswelt*, the world-of-life[39]—is thus compensated by the cryptotheology of "worldliness or worldwideness,"[40] no longer conducive to the local sense of being-in-the-world, but, as in Milton, vertiginous and ambivalent: both exciting and terrifying.[41] Perhaps, all *living* religious thought in modernity is silver-lined with this cryptotheology of Worldwideness, dealing with the crucial transfer of the infinite into the finite: Nancy's and Derrida's, though often opposite, included.[42]

The messianic passion for the "religion of the world" is the main theme of Jacob Taubes's *Occidental Eschatology*, yet another Hegelian/Lurianic contribution to the debate on secularization—and it is precisely this passion that makes Taubes decidedly different from Löwith, pace the latter's claim that this book simply plagiarized his ideas.[43] Taubes fully endorses the *passage from transcendence to immanence*, in which God becomes incarnate in the process of mundane history: the "earth without heaven."[44] This transition, however, does not occur according to the logic of secularization. If secularization, the way Löwith understands it, is a failed translating procedure in which more is lost than preserved, the passage Taubes has in mind, on the other hand, constitutes the Benjaminian type of translation, which merely enhances the truth hidden in the original.[45] The emphasis, therefore, is not on the *loss* and its melancholy commemoration, but on the *gain*: it is not so much the loss of the transcendence, as the translation that finally allows for elucidation of the meaning of the transcendence for the immanent being. For, claims Taubes, this significance can become clear only if the transcendence becomes *operative* within the immanence, that is, instead of hovering over it in an unmoved perfection, begins to signify something for the immanent being and thus becomes able to transform it from within. Taubes, therefore, far more convincingly than Löwith, explains how the divine, once torn away from the static mystery and turned into the dialectical process, can finally produce a "meaning in history."[46]

For Taubes, the Copernican Turn—"earth without heaven"—far from announcing the era of secularization, inaugurates modernity as the epoch in which the main tenets of Jewish messianism can finally find their perfect conditions for realization. If "history only reveals its essence as eschatology,"[47] then also the reverse is true: religious faith, culminating in eschatological belief, can only fulfill itself in the worldly historical dimension. Modern demise of metaphysics ("earth without heaven") or, more subtly, modern *temporalization of metaphysics* (where *saeculum* means, very much like the Hebrew *olam*, simultaneously the time and the world, or the "time-of-the-world"); modern appreciation of a dynamic change which transforms being without looking up to eternal archetypes; and modern rupturous "all that is solid, melts into air"—all these moments point to a revolutionary break with the Greco-Christian cosmos of the Neoplatonic harmony, yet without just leaving it in ruins. The new dialectical method, which continues to move forward, has to steer between the two essentially static views: the Scylla of premodern theological absolutism, concentrated solely on the transcendent God; and the Charybdis of modern materialism, which accepts the posttheological world the way it is, as a *factum brutum*, that is, the disenchanted end-result of the former. Aware of both these dangers simultaneously, Taubes states firmly: "In a Copernican universe a theology that takes its symbols and presuppositions seriously can only proceed by the method of dialectic."[48] Dialectic, therefore, is not a domain of secular philosophy only; it is rather a new method of doing theology within the worldly immanence—a cryptotheology.[49]

To capture this very transformation—the new dialectical focus on "earth without heaven"—Ernst Bloch, Taubes's most direct precursor in assimilating the elements of Jewish messianism into modern philosophy, coined the term: *mystical nominalism*. Appearing only in passing in *The Spirit of Utopia*, this enigmatic concept signifies the rich and ecstatic reverse—a true *silver-lining*—of modern nominalism.[50] Yet, for Bloch, the World regained after the destruction of the universals—the World made of infinitely mysterious singular beings—is not just a destitute remnant of old metaphysics, the end of its theological story. The factuality hailed by Bloch is not barren and brute; the halo surrounding it—the light of the "setting sun," or the Derridean specter of the God who retreated into hiding—transforms the nominalistic spectacle of ruins into a joyful vision of the World as the self-celebration of the ontological multitude that only begins to emancipate itself from the Neoplatonic hierarchy, but also from God's sovereignty. Yet, the emancipation of the World does not proceed here by the way of "abandonment," which ends the entire story; it is still a not yet realized promise that allows the story to continue. And although Bloch's God is "hidden" in the immanent "traces" scattered all over the world, this "hiddenness" has nothing to do with the "Gnostic danger" of his inscrutable sovereignty. It does not hide a mystery of power; it hides a mystery of promise.[51]

YES, YES, BUT NOT YET: THE SPECTER

Could it thus be that the Jewish messianic way of retelling the "Lurianic myth" overcomes Gnosticism in a manner more efficient than modern materialism cutting all stories short? Opposing Derrida to Nancy along the Blumenbergian axis of continuing/ending the myth, is not necessarily in harmony with their intentions, the latter's especially. On the surface of things, rather, it should be Nancy who contributed creatively to "the modern history of our finitude," with his insistence on the nonprivative and fully affirmative "finite thinking"—and not Derrida who always warned us against the immanentist closure and totalitarian effects of the modern ontology in which "something got missing."[52] And yet, it is precisely Derrida who arrives at a richer metaphysics of finitude that, simultaneously, allows the "transfer of the infinite into finite" and does away with the "Gnostic danger" (which, for Blumenberg, is always intrinsically linked with the very idea of the Infinite).

The key to the Derridean advantage is the *suspended affirmation* that leaves room for that "something missing," which Adorno, in dialogue with Bloch, calls the "spirit of utopia": *Yes, Yes,* but not yet, not right now, not cutting the story short, still maintaining the suspense.[53] The difference between Nancy and Derrida can thus also be seen as the difference between Christian and Jewish messianism in their latest modern re-elaborations: while the former is bound to affirm the finite being *hic et nunc,* without delay, by following the *consummatum est* and *hoc est enim corpus meum* of incarnation; the latter can still wait, reserving the space of *not yet* for a future, always only coming, fulfillment. Nancy's model of the transfer as the instantaneous immanentization—"to make without respite *that which is designated as the 'beyond' of the world pass back into the world*"[54]—meets thus a counterproposition in Derrida's *reserve*: exactly a respite, patience, and suspense, allowing the story to continue, that defers the moment of affirmative reduction to the *hic et nunc.*

This reserve, in case of Derrida, would be, as he defines it in *Ghostly Demarcations,* "a certain *irreducible* religiosity (the one that commands a discourse on the promise and justice)."[55] *Irreducible* means here most of all: resisting the primacy of univocal ontology that threatens to bring down everything to *der Bannkreis des Daseins,* the immediate "circle of being," yet without impeaching the very principle of modern univocity.[56] From the ontological perspective, the ghostly *specter*, which in Derrida's thinking becomes the last manifestation of the Taubesian Spirit, does not exist, because it does not fit the regime of univocity: it is not a finite body which, in Nancy's system, remains the only thing *left* after the ultimate end of all gods, passions, myths, stories, even living flesh.[57] But it nonetheless *survives* "in line with another modality" as

> the experience of the non-present, of the non-living present in the living present (of the spectral), of that which lives on (absolutely past or absolutely to come, beyond all presentation or representability).[58]

It, therefore, survives in the modality of a very special *experience*: the powerful imperative of *zakhor* [remember] forming a Jewish/Derridean counterpart to the Christian/Hegelian "memory of the Passion," which does not make us look back, at the *skandalon* of God's sacrifice and the loss of transcendence, but always forward, within this World, toward always newer versions of the messianic story: "*In the future, remember to remember the future.*"[59] By agreeing to deconstruct the onto-theological version of transcendence as "the unscathed," Derrida nonetheless insists on paraphrasing it in a nonmaterialist manner, which would not lose everything in translation—as the possibility of radical otherness *within* the immanence: the not yet fulfilled, and as such nonexistent promise of a messianic justice which, as the last task of thinking in the World, remains beyond any deconstruction.[60]

Just like Taubes and Bloch try to find a modern "silver lining" to the nominalistic doctrine which they continue in a positive way, so does Derrida with his "non-Gnostic" reworking of the Lurianic myth, which is based on the image of a "hidden God"—contracted to the form of a specter/halo/setting sun, which surrounds the World with an aura—but without all the Gnostic *horror metaphysicus* that Blumenberg attached to it in a seemingly insoluble knot. The Jewish line of the "work on myth" has avoided this consequence, by elaborating on the motif of *tsimtsum* as a "perfect gift" in which God gives up on his sovereign status and thus liberates creation. So, if the "Gnostic danger" indeed returns in modernity, it is not because of the cryptotheologies of *deus absconditus*, but rather because of those materialist thinkers who insist on the "naked truth" of *factum brutum*. The paradox here is the unintended consequence of the "death of God," who, in the prolonged act of dying—the Blanchotian "*nunc stans* of dying"[61]—projects his inscrutable sovereignty on the Real which, in the lack of any "successful stories," confronts us again with the un-overcome "absolutism of reality." Thus, although Nancy claims triumphantly that there are "no hiding places" for the dead God and that "monotheism is in truth atheism,"[62] the result is far from liberating. For, as Blumenberg warns us in *Work on Myth*,

> The 'naked truth' is not what life can live with; for, let us not forget, this life is the result of a long history of complete congruence between man's environment and 'signification'—congruence that is only shattered in its most recent phase. In this history life itself continually deprives itself of an immediate relation to its abysses ... [63]

Modernity can thus be seen as an age of shattering the texture of "signification," killing all gods and putting a violent end to mythical narratives in the manner announced by Maurice Blanchot, who so often inspires Nancy, in the last words of *The Madness of the Day*: "A story? No. No stories, never again."[64] But it can also continue a cryptotheological work on myth that "knows no Sabbath on which it would confirm, retrospectively, that the god of myth is dead."[65] So, perhaps, pace all the late modern "eschatological melancholy," which put all "grand narratives" into disrepute, the last word could go to Blumenberg himself, who ends *Work on Myth* with an open question: "But what if there were still something to say, after all?"[66]

NOTES

1. My proposition is thus fully consistent with the general project of this book, which aims at the detection of theological genealogies of modernity, with a special emphasis paid to *Nachleben*—afterlife or survival—of religious categories, not their demise and dissolution. As Willem Styfhals and Stéphane Symons say: "Instead of describing the supposed disappearance of religion in the modern age, this second meaning of secularization designates the hidden survival of structural religious contents in modern culture. Uncovering the tacit continuation of religion within the secular, the second meaning of secularization problematizes the first. It conceptualizes not so much the decline but the changed nature and possible continuation of religion in modernity. What is at play is not the *death* of religion but its *afterlife*" (my emphasis). See page 4.

2. See G. W. F. Hegel, *Faith and Knowledge*, trans. Walter Cerf and H. S. Harris, (Albany: State University of New York Press, 1977), 190.

3. Gershom Scholem, "Reflections on Jewish Theology," in *On Jews and Judaism in Crisis. Selected Essays*, ed. Werner Dannhauser (New York: Schocken Books, 1976), 283.

4. Hans Blumenberg, *The Legitimacy of the Modern Age*, trans. Robert M. Wallace (Cambridge, MA: MIT Press, 1985), 79. The very idea of the transfer of the infinite into the finite does not come from Blumenberg himself but from the German Romantics, most of all Novalis, who in his most famous aphorism advocates the romanticization of the world, consisting also in seeing "the finite as infinite." Novalis depicts the movement of the Infinite Subject as passing into finite beings without diminishing its glory: "Das absolute Ich geht vom Unendlichen zum Endlichen . . .": Novalis, *Werke, Tagebücher und Briefe Friedrich von Hardenbergs: Werke in drei Bänden*, eds. Hans-Joachim Mähl, Richard Samuel, Hans Jürgen Balmes (Munich, Germany: Carl Hanser Verlag, 1987), vol. 2, 126.

5. Blumenberg, *Legitimacy*, 135.

6. Jacques Derrida, "Faith and Knowledge. The Two Sources of 'Religion' at the Limits of Reason Alone," in *Acts of Religion*, ed. Gil Anidjar (London: Routledge, 2001).

7. For Hans Blumenberg, Luther's *Anfechtung* is the very beginning of modern self-assertion [*Selbstbehauptung*], that is, the existential attitude paralleling the nominalistic thesis on *univocatio entis*, in which singular creatures begin to claim their share of being against God and his absolutist privilege to be the only and the highest being himself: ". . . [God] left to man only the alternative of his natural and rational self-assertion, the essence of which Luther formulated as the 'program' of antidivine self-deification." *Legitimacy*, 178.

8. To appreciate the astounding career of this seemingly obscure kabbalistic notion see most of all: Christoph Schulte, *Zimzum. Gott und Weltursprung* (Frankfurt am Main, Germany: Suhrkamp, Jüdischer Verlag, 2014), which gives a very exhaustive panorama of thinkers engaged with *tsimtsum*: from Luria himself, via Hegel and Schelling, up to Scholem, Benjamin, Jonas, and Levinas.

9. Scholem, "Reflections on Jewish Theology," 283 (my emphasis).

10. G. W. F. Hegel, *Phenomenology of Spirit*, trans. A. V. Miller (Oxford: Oxford University Press, 1976), 493.

11. Derrida, "Faith and Knowledge," 58.

12. "Negativities may ensue, but even if they completely take over, this *yes* can no longer be erased": Jacques Derrida, "Ulysses Gramophone: Hear Say Yes in Joyce," in *A Derrida Reader. Between the Blinds*, ed. Peggy Kamuf (New York: Harvester Wheatsheaf, 1991), 593.

13. Most probably beginning already with Spinoza. In many respects, Spinoza emerges a precursor of the modern Jewish cryptotheology, especially when seen through the lenses of Leo Strauss's *Spinoza's Critique of Religion*, itself a classical position on the twentieth-century debate on secularization. Leo Strauss grants

Spinoza the invention of the truly modern understanding of the word *progress*: a dynamic, open, nonteleological and hopeful process of the worldly transformation and striving, which never wishes to go back to anything that was "before." Though Strauss does not make this connection explicitly, we can immediately interpret the epochal change he notices in Spinoza as the crucial moment of the work on the Lurianic myth: "His speculation resembles Neo-Platonism; he understands all things as proceeding from, not made or created by, a single being or origin; the One is the sole ground of the Many. Yet he no longer regards this process as a descent or decay but as an ascent or unfolding: *the end is higher than the origin* [...]. Spinoza thus appears to originate the kind of philosophic system which views the fundamental *processus* as a progress: God Himself is not the *ens perfectissimum*. In this most important aspect he prepares German idealism": Leo Strauss, *Spinoza's Critique of Religion* (Chicago, IL: University of Chicago Press, 1997), 16 (my emphasis). Luria's modification on Neoplatonism is crucially modified once more: emanation is no longer a fall of beings into lower material regions of existence, but, to the contrary, a proper expansion of God's power; the created world is thus "greater" than God himself alone. And if Strauss's last statement may not be completely true in case of Schelling, it certainly is in case of Hegel.

14. Hans Jonas, *Mortality and Morality. A Search for the Good after Auschwitz*, trans. Lawrence Vogel (Evanston, IL and Chicago: Northwestern University Press, 1996), 134.

15. Derrida, "Faith and Knowledge," 50.

16. It is by having in mind *tsimtsum* as the perfect nonsacrificial gift, Derrida writes in his commentary on Hegel, whom he tries to read along a secret Lurianic curve. For Hegel, who understands creation in terms of the Christian *kenosis*, it simply must take on the form of self-offering: "The gift can be only a sacrifice, that is the axiom of speculative reason": Jacques Derrida, *Glas*, trans. John P. Leavey and Richard Rand (Lincoln and London: Nebraska University Press, 1986), 242. On the not so "secret" dependence of Derrida on Lurianic kabbalah, see a very competent article of Elliot R. Wolfson, "Assaulting the Border: Kabbalistic Traces in the Margins of Derrida," *Journal of the American Academy of Religion* 70 (2002): 3, 475–514.

17. Hans Blumenberg, *Work on Myth*, trans. Robert M. Wallace (Cambridge, MA: MIT Press, 1985), 6–7.

18. In fact, the whole of Satan's speech in the Book 4 of *Paradise Lost* is relevant here, as we shall yet see: "So farewel Hope, and with Hope farewel Fear, / Farewel Remorse: all Good to me is lost; / Evil be thou my Good."

19. Blumenberg, *Legitimacy*, 151.

20. Slavoj Žižek, *Absolute Recoil: Towards a New Foundation of Dialectical Materialism* (London: Verso, 2014), 143.

21. I derive the idea of the modern *factum brutum* as the product of the crisis of a previously meaningful philosophical system from Jacob Taubes, who, in *Occidental Eschatology*, applies it to the transition from Hegel's idealism to Marx's materialism. Jacob Taubes, *Occidental Eschatology*, trans. David Ratmoko (Stanford, CA: Stanford University Press, 2009), 130. In that sense, by playing on Žižek's allegiance to psychoanalysis, we can call this modern version of materialism *posttraumatic*.

22. Franz Kafka, "Prometheus," trans. Willa and Edwin Muir, in *The Complete Stories*, ed. Nahum N. Glatzer (Schocken Books: New York, 1971), 432.

23. Blumenberg, *Work on Myth*, 635.

24. Jean-Luc Nancy, *The Sense of the World*, trans. Jeffrey S. Librett (Minneapolis: University of Minnesota Press, 1997), 147–48.

25. Jean-Luc Nancy, *Dis-enclosure: The Deconstruction of Christianity*, trans. Bettina Bergo (New York: Fordham University Press, 2008), 147.

26. Jean-Luc Nancy, *Corpus*, trans. Richard Rand (New York: Fordham University Press, 2008), 63.

27. See F. W. J. Schelling, *Philosophy and Religion*, trans. Klaus Ottmann (Thompson, CT: Spring Publications, 2009). On the precursorial role of Schelling's theosophy in shaping the idiom of modern materialism, see most of all Jürgen Habermas, "Dialectical Idealism in Transition to Materialism: Schelling's Idea of a Contraction of God and Its Consequences for the Philosophy of History," trans. Nick Midgley and Judith Norman, in *The New Schelling*, eds. Judith Norman and Alistair Welchman (New York: Continuum, 2004).

28. Blumenberg, *Legitimacy*, 173.

29. Which, in Blumenberg's idiom, means that the only way to overcome the Gnostic danger posed by the *deus fallax/genius malignus*, the devious God-Demon of nominalistic theology and the Cartesian "metaphysical fable," is to become one: "If Descartes' wicked demon could not be refuted, then the only thing left to do was to become this demon oneself—through the 'will to power." *Work on Myth*, 608.

30. Blumenberg, *Legitimacy*, 187.

31. Ibid., 181.

32. Ibid., 181.

33. If Blumenberg had ever commented directly on Deleuze's and Nancy's imperative to affirm being as it is, he would have most probably dismissed it as an "unlivable" proposition, although also perversely desirable: a kind of a death wish

to end all myths sustaining life and face the naked Real with all its killing truth. In *Work on Myth*, where he sees something similar in Ernst Jünger, he calls it the "epitome of new desires" and immediately adds that such *gelassen* attitude is possible only thanks to the "achievement of distance through 'work on myth' itself. It is a necessary condition of everything that became possible on this side of the terror, of the absolutism of reality," *Work on Myth*, 9. Blumenberg thus confirms the "Satanic" rule of the unintended dependence: the material Real, only seemingly immediate, can only be approached via the "end-game" of the mythic story and only as its end result.

34. For Blumenberg, only "the great Marcion" understood that in Christianity there can be no reconciliation between the created World and the salvation, which can be stated as true also on modernity, with this only difference that, unlike Marcion himself, it rather chose creation.

35. Blumenberg, *Legitimacy*, 47.

36. John Milton, *Paradise Lost*, Book XII, 665.

37. In her contribution to this volume, "The 'Distance to Revelation' and the Difference between Divine and Worldly Order: Walter Benjamin's Critique of Secularization as Historical Development," Sigrid Weigel also notices the modern survival of postbiblical categories as salient metaphors capturing the new status of the secular world. While analyzing Benjamin's attitude towards the *saeculum*, that is, to the emergence of the historical time, she emphasizes most of all the relevance of the thought-image of the expulsion from paradise as the figure of separation: "In his entire theory, he defines the historical life of men primarily as an existence that starts simultaneously with a radical caesura that expels men from the state of human being in an a-historical biblical site, be it by the expulsion from Paradise, be it by the separation from the existence as a creature of Genesis. Since the caesura that separates historical life from Creation is the very moment in which the *saeculum* emerges for the first time, Benjamin's concept of history may be read as a theory of the secular in the literal sense of the word: a theory not of secularization but of a theory of the secular. Its main method is working on and with distinctions ... the 'historical man' in his theory acts primarily under the condition of being expelled and separated from the sacred order." See page 89. Because of the radical separation, the postbiblical categories cannot be transferred or translated into the secular order, but they nonetheless provide a point of reference. In my approach, however, the negative metaphor of expulsion has an ambiguous meaning, because it also interferes—already within the "sacred order" itself—with the positive image of exodus, which bestows the passage into the *saeculum* with religious justification.

38. The whole fourth part of *Legitimacy*, dealing with Nicolas of Cusa and Giordano Bruno, is devoted to this refutation which sometimes takes on in Blumenberg a slightly obsessive form: "the infinitisation of the cosmos is not simply the transposition of an essentially divine attribute—not a surreptitious divinization of 'Nature'—but rather a process of *reoccupation* of 'function positions' within a system of self- and world-understanding": Elisabeth Brient, *The Immanence of the Infinite. Hans Blumenberg and the Threshold to Modernity* (Washington, DC: Catholic University of America Press, 2002), 100.

39. Most of all Hannah Arendt in *The Human Condition* (Chicago, IL: University of Chicago Press, 1999).

40. Nancy, *The Sense of the World*, 174.

41. Which Marshall Berman, by calling it a "Maelstrom vision," attributed very rightly to the basic existential setup of modernity; see his *All That Is Solid Melts into Air: The Experience of Modernity* (London: Verso, 2010).

42. But how does Heidegger stand in this context? Is his *Weltlichkeit*, constituting one of the basic *existentialia* characterizing Dasein, a variant of the Blumenbergian *Verweltlichung*? Certainly *not*: whereas the latter is a dialectical outcome of ontotheology, which could not have come to being without the earlier stage of theological absolutism, the former is a deliberate result of an existential analysis that ventures beyond ontotheology into a "new beginning," finding an inspiration in the early Greek thinking of *physis* from where the "last God" will eventually emanate. In *Beiträge* Heidegger says explicitly: "the *being-in-the-world* of Dasein. 'World,' but not the Christian *saeculum* and the denial of God, Atheism! *World* through the essence of truth and of the *Da!*" Martin Heidegger, *Beiträge zur Philosophie (Vom Ereignis)*, vol. 65 of *Gesamtausgabe*, ed. F. W. von Hermann (Frankfurt am Main, Germany: Vittorio Klostermann), 295. The return to Greek *physis* as the new/old matrix of sacredness, advocated by Heidegger, leads to yet another attempt to "overcome Gnosticism," undertaken by Leo Strauss and his recent commentator, Benjamin Lazier, who, in his *God Interrupted*, fuses Straussian teaching with Blumenberg. My reading of Blumenberg differs from Lazier's, even if I share the idea of "overcoming of Gnosticism," which unites the whole group of thinkers—Strauss, Scholem, Jonas, Arendt—who in their youth fell under the spell of the Gnostic negation of worldliness. But, by wanting to prove his point—that despite their initial fascination with Gnosis, most of the important Jewish thinkers of the Weimar era eventually turned away from it—Lazier becomes completely insensitive to the *dialectical* use of Gnosticism that they never completely abandoned. Lazier stakes his claim on Scholem's apparent anti-Gnosticism by arguing that he was disgusted by the transgressions of the

Frankists. Indeed, he may not have been a fan of Jacob Frank, but he never changed his favorable opinion of Sabbatai Sevi, who certainly cannot be listed as an ally of Lazier's favorite hero, Leo Strauss, and his anti-Gnostic quest after "natural law." The subtle Lurianic-Hegelian line that I am pursuing here cuts into the straightforward dualism of nature/immanence versus antinature/transcendence. If it "overcomes Gnosticism," it is not because it reverts to the Greek idea of nature-*physis* as the self-sufficient and self-sustaining immanent system that does not need any transcendent justification, but because it shifts the theological curiosity from the Creator to his creation. Thus, although it blocks the simple "negation of the world," which often forms a Gnostic component of otherworldly mysticism, it does not affirm the world as a natural autotelic immanence. What Lazier, following Strauss, perceives as the *return* to nature, I rather see as a *turn* toward creatureliness (*Kreatürlichkeit*), which constitutes a new category of worldliness, coming to the fore only due to *tsimtsum*, that is, the self-withdrawal of God. In Lazier's own words, uttered in the article which summarizes the content of his book, "Overcoming Gnosticism: Hans Jonas, Hans Blumenberg, and the Legitimacy of the Natural World": "As the political philosopher Leo Strauss put it in a letter to Jonas, gnosticism may well have been the most radical rebellion in Western history against the Greek notion of *physis*" (*Journal of the History of Ideas*, 64 (2003) 4, 620). Yet the "third overcoming" of Gnosticism that I am reconstructing here has nothing to do with the Heideggerian-Straussian recovery of the Greek idea of *physis*. It is not the legitimacy of the *natural* world, but the legitimacy of the *creaturely* world that is at stake. See Benjamin Lazier, *God Interrupted: Heresy and the European Imagination between World Wars* (Princeton, NJ: Princeton University Press, 2012).

43. As is related by Hans Jonas in his memoirs: Hans Jonas, *Memoirs*, ed. Christian Wiese, trans. Krishna Winston (Lebanon, NH: Brandeis University Press, 2008), 168.

44. "In the Copernican view of the world there is an earth but no heaven. The earth mirrors no heaven, and the reality of the world is gained by *Copernican* man, not by having the world emulate a superior archetype, but by revolutionizing the world in terms of an ideal that lies in the future." Taubes, *Occidental Eschatology*, 88.

45. Walter Benjamin, "The Task of the Translator," in *Selected Writings*, vol. 1, eds. Howard Eiland, Michael W. Jennings (Cambridge, MA: Harvard University Press, 1996), 261.

46. See Karl Löwith, *Meaning in History: The Theological Implications of the Philosophy of History* (Chicago, IL: University of Chicago Press, 1949). On the rela-

tion between Löwith and Taubes see Peter Gordon, "Jacob Taubes, Karl Löwith and the Interpretation of Jewish History," in *German-Jewish Thought Between Religion and Politics. Festschrift in Honor of Paul Mendes-Flohr on the Occasion of His Seventieth Birthday*, eds. Christian Wiese and Martina Urban (Berlin, Germany: de Gruyter, 2012), 351. We can only confirm his diagnosis: "Unlike Löwith, Taubes does not consider the religious inheritance of modern philosophy a sign of syncretion or corruption. Eschatology is not a foreign intrusion upon history but its very essence and completion" (ibid., 362). A line of critique of Karl Löwith, similar to Taubes, was found in Blumenberg by Kirk Wetters who, in his contribution to this volume, writes: "Löwith, from Blumenberg's perspective, contradicts his own critique insofar as he cleaves to the shared legacy of theology and the philosophy of history. The English title, *Meaning in History*, could hardly be more explicit in this regard—though it probably should have been called *No Meaning in History*." See page 35.

47. Taubes, *Occidental Eschatology*, 13.

48. Jacob Taubes, *From Cult to Culture. Fragments Towards a Critique of Historical Reason*, ed. Aleida Assmann (Stanford, CA: Stanford University Press, 2009), 171–72.

49. In his essay, "Is Progress a Category of Consolation? Kant, Blumenberg, and the Politics of the Moderns," Michaël Foessel makes a similar point and claims that for Kant (and *a fortiori* for Hegel) religion only begins to make sense in modernity, which is capable of elucidating its prophetic imagery in philosophical concepts that concern earthly immanence. While commenting on Kant's *Idea of a Universal History*, which concludes with a philosophically interpreted "chiliastic vision," Foessel writes: "Far from a secularization, with Kant (though already with the Lessing of *Education of the Human Race*) we are assisting in a correction of course. Religious expressions become symbolic approximations of what human reason, having reached maturity, learns to think through its own means." See page 124. At the same time, however, Foessel does not share our enthusiasm for the modern discovery of the infinite All-World and opts for a more nostalgic attitude that deplores the loss of the Neoplatonic sense of cosmic hierarchy: "Although mathematizable, the moderns paid for the infinity of the universe by the loss of knowledge concerning the cosmic hierarchy, where each man could claim a choice place." See page 125.

50. This enigmatic but also thrilling term promising the other, still unfinished, project of modernity appears in Bloch's *Spirit of Utopia* in the sentence that also issues a warning: "modernity's paths, the irreversible eruption of its mystical nominalism, have to be followed through to the end, or Egypt [...] will again be

enthroned": Ernst Bloch, *The Spirit of Utopia*, trans. Anthony Nassar (Stanford, CA: Stanford University Press, 2000), 27. It is worth noticing that in our context the Blochian Egypt—in Jewish messianism the synonym of irredeemable hopelessness—names precisely the twin brother (Esau) of mystical nominalism, that is, the Ockhamian-Baconian doctrine that provided the impetus to the creation of modern science based solely on disenchantment and instrumental reason. In other words: reduced to its purely secular aspect and deprived of its "spectral" crypto-theology, modernity, instead of realizing the promise of universal liberation, turns into yet another "house of bondage."

51. On the positive modifications of the nominalistic doctrine undertaken by the line of modern Jewish messianic thinkers, see my: *Jewish Cryptotheologies of Late Modernity. Philosophical Marranos* (London: Routledge, 2014), especially the chapter "The Promise of the Name: Jewish Nominalism as the Critique of the Idealist Tradition."

52. Nancy, *The Sense of the World*, 29–33.

53. Though Derrida's messianicity is even more effervescent and spectral than "anything utopian." See: Ernst Bloch, "Something Missing: A Discussion between Ernst Bloch and Theodor W. Adorno on the Contradictions of Utopian Longing," in *Utopian Function of Art and Literature. Selected Essays*, trans. Jack Zipes and Frank Mecklenburg (Cambridge MA: MIT Press, 1988), 16.

54. Nancy, *The Sense of the World*, 183.

55. Jacques Derrida, "Marx & Sons," *Ghostly Demarcations : A Symposium on Jacques Derrida's "Specters of Marx,"* ed. Michael Sprinker (London: Verso, 1999), 234.

56. Having in mind the dangers of ontological reduction, Derrida says: "I think it is the most problematic aspect of Marx, namely, the unrestrained, classical, traditional desire to conjure away any and all spectrality so as to recover the *full, concrete reality* of the process of genesis hidden *behind the spectre's mask*." Ibid., 258 (my emphasis).

57. Nancy, *The Sense of the World*, 149.

58. Derrida, "Marx & Sons," 253–54.

59. Jacques Derrida, *Archive Fever. A Freudian Impression*, trans. Eric Prenowitz (Chicago, IL: Chicago University Press, 1996), 76.

60. This dual possibility of perceiving the modern world as either a hopeless "heap of broken articles," left in ruin after the nominalist crisis, or an incomplete project that still awaits its fulfillment appears also in the already mentioned essay of Michaël Foessel who sees in the latter option the only chance of metaphysical consolation. Following Kant, for whom "an ideal history that has all the markings

of a *novel*," that is, a story in which "all the seeds nature has planted in it can be developed fully and in which the species' vocation here on earth can be fulfilled," see page 121. Foessel quotes Friedrich Schlegel, who "would later establish the link between the incompleteness of time and 'practical command' in his Jena lectures, held precisely on the topic of transcendental philosophy: 'This proposition, that the world is still unfinished, is extremely important in every respect. If we think of the world as complete, then all our doings are nothing. But if we know that the world is unfinished, then no doubt our vocation is to cooperate in completing it." See page 126. Friedrich Schlegel, *Neue philosophische Schriften*, ed. Josef Körner (Frankfurt, Germany: Schulte-Bulmke, 1935), 155–56. Derrida would certainly have agreed: the incomplete modern world is something to work on and not something to accept as an irreparable *factum brutum*.

61. Maurice Blanchot, *The Space of Literature*, trans. Ann Smock (Lincoln & London: Nebraska University Press, 1982), 155.

62. Nancy, *Dis-enclusure*, 35.

63. Blumenberg, *Work on Myth*, 110. Although Nancy, in *The Sense of the World*, says something seemingly similar and even mentions Blumenberg at one point (*The Sense of the World*, 174), while introducing the opposition between "sense" and "truth," his own proposal to "make sense" and thus tell stories about the World against the "nihilistic" regime of truth always inevitably shatters on the rocks of the latter and emerges as nothing but a *lie*.

64. Maurice Blanchot, *The Madness of the Day* (Barrytown, NY: Station Hill Press, 1995).

65. Blumenberg, *Work on Myth*, 633.

66. Ibid., 636.

Part II
# Philosophy and the Secular
An Alternative History of the German Secularization Debate

# The "Distance to Revelation" and the Difference between Divine and Worldly Order
## Walter Benjamin's Critique of Secularization as Historical Development

SIGRID WEIGEL

ON THE VIRTUALITY OF
MERE LANGUAGE (*Reine Sprache*)

In his famous article "The Task of the Translator" (1921), Walter Benjamin concedes that "all translation is only a somewhat provisional way of coming to terms with the foreignness of languages."[1] This insight implies a break with the idea of a perfect and totally appropriate translation and, accordingly, with the search for it. Benjamin's theory of translation is based on a completely different idea. This is evident from a dense passage of the text, one that is often overlooked.[2] Here, Benjamin approaches the task of translation by considering it a matter of proving the *distance* that separates the languages (of mankind) from revelation. This understanding ensues from the Babylonian confusion, that is, the moment in which the multiplication of human languages coincides with the departure of this kind of language from an absolute other kind of communication, namely, from a perception through revelation. In contrast to *revelation*, that is, the idea of an unambiguous perception, Benjamin characterizes the language in its historical state by the separation of two aspects: the "way of meaning" (*die Art des Meinens*) and the "what is meant" (*das Gemeinte*). Due to the proliferation of languages spoken in the historical life of men, the different languages (Benjamin mentions German and French) have developed different "ways of meaning" when they refer to the same thing, whereas their common "what is meant" always remains hidden within the languages. In the historical state of languages, "what is meant" (*das Gemeinte*) is never found independently. One can only think of it as such, that is, independent from the different "ways of meaning," when it "is able to emerge from the harmony of all the various ways of meaning" as sheer language.

What follows from this insight is a concept of "mere language" (*reine Sprache*) that may only be ascribed to a virtual totality (*Allheit*) of all different languages and "their intentions supplementing each other."[3] However, this totality is only imaginable beyond history, since the intention in all existing languages has to be distinguished into "what is meant" and the "way of meaning." Therefore the totality of all intentions is only imaginable at the messianic end of history, at the end of history as such and of any historical state of languages.

> So long it [*das Gemeinte*] remains hidden in the languages. If, however, these languages grow in this way until the messianic end of their history, it is up to the translation that catches fire from the eternal life of works and the perpetually renewed life of languages to put ever anew the holy growth of the languages to the test: as far as what is hidden in them [*ihr Verborgenes*] is removed from revelation, it may become just as present by the *knowledge of this remoteness*.[4]

The idea of mere language (*reine Sprache*) belongs to the register of often misread and misunderstood concepts in Benjamin's thought.[5] His mere language is neither something mystical nor theological; instead, it is a term that circumscribes a part of languages that can only be virtually thought of as separated from languages as they exist in written and spoken form: namely that "what is meant" in all languages, in the *Allheit* of languages. Here "all communication [*Mitteilung*], all sense, and all intention finally encounter a stratum in which they are destined to be extinguished."[6] Since the totality of language cannot be reached in reality or history, the state of mere language is virtuality—or in a different perspective: latency toward the hope for redemption. This idea resembles the insight Benjamin would develop two decades later in his theses *On the Concept of History* (1940): "Admittedly, only a redeemed mankind receives its complete past. Which is to say: only to the redeemed mankind has its past become citable in each of its moments."[7] In contrast, the historical subject involved in a certain historical constellation always cites—that is, revives—certain images, scenarios, and moments of the past, on which his own situation casts a light.

In the article on translation, Benjamin therefore places existing languages in a site that is defined by its distance and distinction from qualitatively radical different realms. On the one hand, the foreignness of human languages is separated from revelation; on the other hand, the historical growth and change of these languages is limited by the messianic end of history—and as we well know, the messianic end does not refer to an end in the dimension of time but to the termination of any historical state of existence. This central passage from "The Task of the Translator" is characteristic for the specific way in which Walter Benjamin conceptualizes history as a literal space of time beyond chronology, development, or continuity. In his entire theory, he defines the historical life of man primarily as an existence that starts simultaneously with a radical caesura that expels people from the state of human being in an ahistorical biblical site, be it by the expulsion from Paradise or be it by the separation from the existence as a creature of Genesis. Since the caesura that separates historical life from Creation is the very moment in which the *saeculum* emerges for the first time, Benjamin's concept of history may be read as a theory of the secular in the literal sense of the word: *a theory not of secularization but of a theory of the secular*. Its main method is working on and with distinctions.

In his historico-theoretical rereading of biblical narratives, Benjamin reads the scenario of the expulsion from Paradise as primal scenes for the beginning of an historical existence of humans and a human-made world; and this world's first distinction functions as the main matrix for all his reflections. It stands for the simultaneous emergence of history, human language, human judgment, and other symbolic systems. "History comes into being at once with meaning in human language,"[8] as he puts it in the short essay "On the Role of Language in the Mourning Play and Tragedy" (1916). History is conceptualized in his reflections as the scene of human life and language between Genesis and the Last Judgment, between revelation and redemption. It is conceptualized not as a development in time but as a realm radically distinct from the Divine order: the space in which people act from which the idea of time emerges.

However, this does not mean that biblical ideas play no role in human history; precisely the opposite is the case. In the state of being separated from revelation, human concepts and actions remain dependent on the world and ideas of the biblical language. In this way *law* is distinct from *justice*, but at the same time divine justice functions as the guideline and orientation of law within a human-made order—one that can never be achieved within history. Benjamin's emphasis on the simultaneous relation *and* difference between biblical ideas and worldly concepts is more visible in the German language than in English. This can be seen, for example, in the interplay between *Recht* and *Gerechtigkeit* (law and justice), *Anklage* and *Klage* (accusation and lament), *Lösung* and *Erlösung* (solution and redemption), *Aufgabe* and *Auftrag* (task and mandate), *Aussöhnung* and *Versöhnung* (conciliation and atonement), and the like.

## TRANSFORMATION AND TRANSFERAL: BLUMENBERG AND SCHMITT

When discussing a critique of secular reason, Benjamin's approach to history is of paramount interest because it does not criticize any particular theory or idea of secularization. Rather, it calls into question the fundamental preconditions of the concept. For nearly all predominant concepts of secularization tend to position secularization in the dimension of historical development, whereby the latter is conceived as a progression in time. This is above all the case for the ubiquitous rhetoric of secularization as *Verweltlichung* (becoming worldly) or de-Christianization and, hence, as a steady decline of the power of theological interpretation and the loss of religious certainty. But it is also true for that conception of secularization which defines it as a strict separation of church and state and deploys this separation as a primary indicator of modernization or democratization. The respective positions of Hans Blumenberg and Carl Schmitt in their theoretical controversy over secularization are ultimately based on the notion of an historical development, even if neither author operates with concepts of disappearance or loss, but with such figures as reoccupation or transformation (Blumenberg) and transferal (Schmitt).

Carl Schmitt explicitly refers to *transferal* in one of the often cited arguments of his *Political Theology* (1934), thus situating the transfer of theological concepts into concepts of modern theories of the state within the course of their historical development. He writes,

> All significant concepts of the modern theory of the state are secularized theological concepts not only because of their historical development—in which they were *transferred* from theology to the theory of the state, whereby, for example, the omnipotent God became the omnipotent lawgiver—but also because of their systematic structure, the recognition of which is necessary for a sociological consideration of these concepts. The state of exception in jurisprudence has an *analogous* meaning to the miracle in theology.[9]

A double limitation arises out of this argument concerning the phenomena of secularization. Methodologically, Schmitt's thinking becomes tied to the figures of *analogy* and *transferal* between theology and the law, while thematically it becomes tied to the scholarly field of state theory. This constellation of a conceptual transfer not only adheres to a relatively mechanistic notion of secularization; it also has a problematic theoretical consequence. Namely, *after* a transfer of theological concepts into other registers has taken place, there is no further need to take religious aspects within the latter into consideration, nor is there the need to question the afterlife of religion within a secular world. If the legitimacy of sovereignty in the modern age has been entirely subsumed into the law of the state, then—paradoxically—religion is excluded from this kind of political theology: the latter has totally replaced the former. Schmitt's figure of transferal forecloses the possibility of conceiving relationships between politics and theology any other way than in the figure of transference.

This consequence is explicitly addressed in the epilogue of Schmitt's *Political Theology II* (1970) with the revealing subtitle *The Legend of the Expendability of Any Political Theology*. In this text he comments on the significance of the turn to the modern era (*Neuzeit*) for his Political Theology: "On the 'era's threshold' of this turn"—herewith he refers to Blumenberg's term *Epochenschwelle*— "sounded the *Silete Theologi!* of Albercius Gentilis, who was a contemporary and fellow countryman of Giordano Bruno from Nola with whom he shared a fate even though he was himself happier."[10] Indeed, Schmitt's concept of the political remains de facto subjected to the commandment *Silete Theologi!* And thus the question of whether and how the traces of religious violence continue to operate within the "secularized theological concepts" of the political remains obscured. This means that Schmitt has to be seen as a representative, rather than an analyst, of secularization. Moreover, he is an agent of the type of secularization that traces the genealogy of modernity from a preceding Christian tradition that ends in the sublation of Christian concepts in secular terms. The result, however, is in effect a (more or less) unacknowledged theological charging of these terms. In this respect, political theology in Schmitt's sense ultimately amounts to a theologization of the political.[11]

By contrast, in his book *The Legitimacy of the Modern Age* (1966) Hans Blumenberg undertakes a critique of the secularization paradigm as a "final theologumenon." Yet even when he questions the logic of the threshold to the epoch (*Epochenschwelle*) of the modern world and critically analyzes its grounding in secularization or *Verweltlichung*, the concept of secularization he uses remains bound to the logic of historical development. In his critique of the paradigms of secularization, Blumenberg describes the latter as an *Umbesetzung*, a "reoccupation of answer positions that had become vacant and whose corresponding questions could not be eliminated."[12] It is when he argues that in such reoccupations a "continuing acceptance of the religious sphere in which language originates"[13] can be discerned that he judges such practice of secularization as the "final theologumenon"[14] and criticizes the rhetoric of secularization in general as being a secularization-theology. Not only the term *final theologumenon* indicates a situating of the reoccupation discussed by Blumenberg on an axis of historical progress; both the discussion of the "presumed migration of attributes" (chapter VII) and his analysis of the structure of reoccupations repeatedly refer to new occupations, so that even the reoccupation theorem of secularization moves within the pattern of a replacement of the old with the new. The limits of a critique that concentrates on the rhetoric of secularization, and discovers in it above all a succession or inheritance, can be scrutinized in Blumenberg's critique of secularization as a "category of historical illegality." In this manner, within the corresponding first part of *The Legitimacy of the Modern Age*, the modern world inherits theology. The logic of historical development thereby proves to be one of the fundamental dilemmas of a critique of secular reason. It seems nearly impossible in epistemological terms to get rid of the idea of development when addressing the idea of secularization. All the more challenging is the way in which Benjamin reconceptualizes the question of secularization by grounding it in the radical qualitative difference of the secular vis-à-vis religious ideas.

REFERENCE TO BIBLICAL TERMS:
BENJAMIN'S LANGUAGE THEORY

Walter Benjamin's approach to the historical state of life and language provides a quite unique way of analyzing the tension-filled relation between the registers of religious ideas and mundane concepts. His approach to the afterlife of religious meanings in worldly concepts is neither theological nor secular. Rather, his thinking can, in my view, be most accurately described as *postbiblical* because it is based in the awareness of the relevance of biblical ideas as a crucial reference point of philosophical, social, and ethical concepts developed in European history. His theoretical reflections arose from an acknowledgment of the uncircumventable relevance of biblical language, the Divine order, and the idea of salvation, without himself being tied to it by confession. One of the leitmotifs of his writings is the conviction that the terms of the Divine order have singular meanings that cannot be transferred into concepts of the profane order, of human action or social communication. Alternatively, the historical man in his theory acts primarily under the condition of being expelled and separated from the sacred order. His values, actions, and institutions are distinct from the ideas handed down by biblical language, but they are simultaneously dependent on the latter.

Benjamin's references to biblical narratives or terms have often been misread as theological interpretations. This initially occurred in the context of his famous theory of language in a text from 1916. Therein he presents an epistemological reading of the Genesis that provides the ground for his whole epistemology. Benjamin's utilization of biblical scenes as primal scenes in his texts is not a matter of a discourse of theology or faith, but of an epistemological reference to paradigmatic scenes of handed-down narratives of origins. It is in this sense that he used the Genesis narrative to reconsider the question of the origin of language, and not the question of the beginning or emergence of human language as in Herder's sense. Rather, he names as the starting point of his reflections in *On Language as Such and on the Language of Man* (1916) the academic dispute, in his time nearly unresolvable, between the mystical and the modern theory of language, the latter of which was described by Benjamin as the "bourgeois understanding of language."[15] The difference between the two theories was the following: on the one hand, there was the notion of an onomatopoetic similarity between word and its designated referent, which goes back to the pre-Socratic idea of words as names (*onomata*); on the other hand, there was the thesis of the conventionality or the arbitrariness of words in the modern theory of language conceived as a theory of signs. Instead of aligning himself to one side or another within this controversy, Benjamin transforms the opposition into a *historical dialectic*. In this way, he provides an approach to analyze the interplay *and* the tensions between moments of linguistic magic (similarity, mimesis, or the noncommunicable) and conventionality (the symbolic or semiotic) in language. Benjamin writes: "Language is namely in every case not merely communication of the communicable but also a symbol of the non-communicable."[16] In a later variation, in the *Doctrine of the Similar* (1933), which forgoes any reference to the primal biblical scene and instead relies on anthropological proof, it is formulated in the following way:

> This, if you will, magical side of language, as well as of script, does not however run alongside the other, the semiotic, without any relation to it. Everything

mimetic of language is rather a founded intention that can only appear at all in connection with something alien as its basis [*Fundus*], namely the semiotic, communicating element of language.17

The emergence of this relationship is in the early essay, *On Language*, cast as a primal scene. Benjamin constructs this scene as a caesura that is contained in the biblical narrative of creation. This caesura separates the language that followed the expulsion from Paradise or language as it has developed in human history from the Paradisiacal or Adamitic language in which the human being is called on by God to give names to nature and things. In this caesura the end of the condition of Paradise coincides with the beginning of historical existence—or, in other words, of human conditions. Benjamin stresses this when he writes, "History comes into being at once with meaning in human language."18 In Benjamin's reading of the biblical narrative as an historical primal scene, the Fall of the first human couple becomes the "Fall of the spirit of language" (*Sündenfall des Sprachgeistes*) through which not only knowledge of good and evil—and hence judgment—is attained. At the same time, language also becomes a means by which human beings speak *about* nature and things. In naming, however, the word comes apart as name and designation. In this respect, this text does not develop a theology of language. Rather, it devises a theory of language in which the views of opposed theories of language refer to different elements or aspects of language. Their antagonism is itself the result of a historical dialectic.

## THRESHOLD-KNOWLEDGE: THE SPAN BETWEEN CREATION AND LAST JUDGMENT

Instead of referring to an epochal threshold to the modern age, which plays a central role as the saddle period of *Verweltlichung* in the grand narratives of secularization, Benjamin considers different configurations of the *threshold* (*Schwelle*) itself: the threshold as border and turning point of distinct meanings. However, this is less a matter of cultic practices that traditionally were used to separate the sacral from the profane, as described by the history of religion and the anthropology of ritual, where the differentiation of sacred and profane spaces happens simultaneously with the modification of the state of the persons who move within them or perform cultic practices. In contrast to this, Benjamin characterizes the main figures of his texts by staging their language, their representations and gestures in the very topography of history significant for his thought. They act with a distance toward the world of creation but with a view toward it, or, in other words, in "the span between Creation and Last Judgment [*Weltgericht*],"[19] as it is phrased in the essay "Karl Kraus" (1931).

In this article Benjamin presents Kraus as a *persona* operating in a complex and complicated intermediate space between the world of Genesis and the present, thus neglecting the historical state of the latter. By neglecting history, which would fill this intermediate space in the form of a time span, Benjamin's Kraus finds himself in a position on "the threshold of the Last Judgment."[20] Benjamin compares this perspective to the visual (aesthetic) perspective of foreshortening found in Baroque altar painting. Where Creation and Last Judgment are brought together in a relation of immediacy (that is, with no intervening historical time), their orders collide directly in a conflictual constellation, namely, as a conflict of principles. In order to emphasize the distinction between the different reference points of his protagonist, Benjamin positions Kraus on a threshold from which he turns either to the world of Creation or toward the *Weltgericht* on the other side. In arguing against Adolf Loos's statement that Kraus "stands on the threshold of a new age" Benjamin writes,

> Kraus is no historic genius. He does not stand on the threshold of a new age. If he ever turns his back on *Creation*, if he breaks off lamenting [*Klagen*], it is only in order to accuse [*anzuklagen*] at the Last Judgement [*Weltgericht*].[21]

In this condensed thought-image Benjamin presents a dialectical constellation of irreconcilable expressions, namely, lament and accusation, and depicts a position in which he either turns to the one or the other, thus alternating between these different expressions. *Klage*, the language of creatures, and *Anklage*, the language of guilt and law, are primarily distinct in that they are directed at different authorities: the latter to the court, the former to the Maker. They are not only incompatible but contradictory.

One of the consequences of the lack of consciousness for the historic state of his present is the way in which Kraus's critique of language and of the existing law refers to the idea of justice (*Gerechtigkeit*). In this context, Benjamin characterizes his protagonist as a zealot who places the legal system itself under accusation, attacking the law not for individual judgments (i.e., misjudgments) but "in its substance." For he accuses the *law* of its betrayal of *justice*—and Benjamin adds: "More exactly, betrayal of the word by the concept, which derives its existence from the word."[22] This abbreviation holds the key. The claim is: just as the *concept* derives from the *word*, so is the *law* derived from *justice*. Thus, Kraus charges both derivations (law and concept) with high treason vis-à-vis the idea to which they owe their existence. His accusation thus relates to the betrayal of concepts such as justice and the word in whose name the complaint is simultaneously filed. In other words, complaint of this kind, conducted within history or within the order of the profane, even though appealing to notions of Divine order, produces a paradox. In it, the victims of the betrayal (justice and the word) and the authorities to whom the appeal is made are identical. It is only on the basis of this constellation that the full sense of the *salto mortale* becomes clear, which Benjamin discerns in Kraus's rhetoric of accusation. The latter is characterized by Benjamin as a *Sprachprozeßordnung*, which is an artificial term meaning something like a judicial procedure toward language: "To worship the image of divine justice as language—even in the German language—this is the genuinely Jewish salto mortale by which he tries to break the spell of the demon."[23]

This passage presents Benjamin's engagement with the idea of *justice* in a condensed form: his repeated reflection on the fact that justice is an idea that precedes positive law and originates in a biblical context. Insofar as the legal order (as an historical order) takes the idea of divine justice as its point of orientation, while positive law (as human law or the law made by human beings) simultaneously marks the distance from the sphere of divine justice, the law is characterized by a structural equivocality. Indeed, Benjamin speaks in the Kraus article of "constructive ambiguities of law." This formulation expresses the insight that an unavoidable equivocal meaning is inscribed into the constructive function of the law within history, because justice (with a small *j*, that is, the institution of law) carries within itself a reference to the idea of Justice (with capital letter) in a prejudicial, biblical sense. The consequence is that the emphatic reference to Justice in this latter sense has a destructive impact against the law if it is appealed to in the critique of present concrete jurisdictions. As Benjamin states in the last passage of "Karl Kraus," "Destructive is therefore that Justice which calls a halt to the constructive ambiguities of law."[24]

Unfortunately, the English translation fails to convey several of such interplays of ideas and concepts that reflect the tension between the religious and the profane registers, or it fails to convey those counterstriving constellations that are typical for Benjamin's reflections on the impact of biblical concepts in political theory. For example, this is the case with the aforementioned scenario of Kraus on the threshold between Creation and Last Judgment. First, the translation of *Selected Writings* appears as "if he breaks off *in* lamentation" for the original formulation "bricht er ab mit Klagen" that means he stops lamenting. Second, the word *anklagen* is completely lacking in the rendition of the English Benjamin, because it is translated as "to file a complaint."[25] This passage is just one example of the way in which Benjamin's specific mode of writing and thinking gets lost in translation. It is not only that his thinking-in-images gets lost because his thought-images are either translated as concepts or as metaphors, although they often deal with the literal meaning of words taking the word by its name. In addition, his emphasis on the interplay between ideas from the biblical or religious register and political or ethical language is obscured in translation.[26]

## BENJAMIN'S CRITIQUE OF PEOPLE CLAIMING A "DIVINE MANDATE"

For example, this interplay forms the main argument of Benjamin's reading of Goethe's novel *Elective Affinities*. In this text he develops an alternative model to that of the George School and Gundolf. By elevating Goethe in particular, and the writer in general, Gundolf ascribed divine attributes to poetic works themselves, and thereby turned art into a pseudo- or quasi-religion. Although, as Benjamin establishes, the separation of art and philosophy in antiquity coincides with the decline of myth (and its indifference to the category of truth), he observes a tendency toward remythologization in the program of poetry as a quasi-religion. He counteracts this tendency by drawing a strict line of demarcation between the discourse of art and a speech vis-à-vis God. Precisely because of this, his essay touches on a modern phenomenon, namely the reestablishing of art *as* cult or *as* mystery, which takes place not least in the aesthetic of the sublime: art as a substitution for religion in a seemingly postsecularized age.

At the beginning of the second part of the essay, in which he grapples with problems of biography, namely, in the context of his commentary on Gundolf's book on Goethe, Benjamin develops his critique of the hubris of claiming a *divine mandate*.[27] His critique concerns the commingling of art and religion—above all in Gundolf's understanding of the author as a mythic hero, a "demigod," a "hybrid of hero and creator," and as a "superhuman type of savior" whose work represents humanity in the starry sky. Departing from this critique, a strict line of distinction runs through Benjamin's article. It distinguishes the terms of discourse on art from concepts belonging to another, divine system of meaning. Although his critical reflections on myth (which represent a kind of leitmotif, especially in the first section) have found much attention in scholarship on Benjamin, this work on language, in which reflections on the terms play a fundamental and structuring role, has been largely ignored. In what follows I will explain some of these terms:

Task (*Aufgabe*) versus Exaction (*Forderung*)

For Benjamin, "the poetic work in the true sense" can emerge only where the word frees itself from the spells of the task.[28] His critique of the confusion of literary works of art and divine mission or mandate targets the image of the poet in the George circle.

> This school assigns to the poet, like the hero, his work as a *task*; hence, his *mandate* is considered *divine*. From God, however, man receives not *tasks* but only exactions [*Forderungen*], and therefore before God no privileged value can be ascribed to the poetic life. Moreover, the notion of the *task* is also inappropriate from the standpoint of the poet.[29]

This radical rejection of any "task" in the field of art and poetry seeks to prevent the legitimization of the poetic work on the basis of an authority alien to it, whatever its nature and description. Only with language's liberation from a determination of tasks can the "true work of art" spring forth. With the suggestion that only exactions and not tasks would come from God, the secular reason of poetic theory or aesthetics is also criticized, as it makes divine authority into a type of employer and thereby levels the inevitable difference between God and humans without which the divine terms forfeit their meaning.

Creation (*Geschöpf*) versus Shaped Form (*Gebilde*)

In the same context Benjamin criticizes the contemporary "heroizing attitude of the poet" as being a perpetuation of the hubris already connected to the old concept of the genius. This is evident in his reflections on the discourse of the production of art that refers to the metaphor of Creation: "And indeed the artist is less the primal ground or *creator* than the origin or *form giver* [*Bildner*], and certainly his work is not at any price his creation but rather his *shaped form* [*Gebilde*]."[30] This difference between *Gebilde*, that is to say something produced, and *Geschöpf* does not, however, resolve itself in the simple differentiation between culture and nature. This is apparent in the following passage, in which Benjamin discusses art's specific kind of life and brings the concept of redemption into play: "To be sure, the shaped form, too, and not only the creation, has life. But the crucial difference between the two is this: only the life of the creation, never that of a shaped form (*des Gebildeten*), partakes, unreservedly, of the intention of redemption."[31] Here, Benjamin returns to his idea that art possesses a certain kind of life that he had elaborated more intensively in "The Task of the Translator," where he discusses translation as part of the "afterlife" (*Nachleben*) of works. When he now ascribes redemption exclusively to the life of the creation this implies the exclusion of the artwork from the sphere of the messianic. Only life that stays in the line of (God's) Creation may be endowed with the intention of redemption and the capacity to express it. The worldly idea corresponding to redemption in literature, art, and the human-made world is hope. However, Benjamin does not talk of the hope of protagonists or other artificial figures, but the hope the author expresses for them; hope can be expressed only in the author's or artist's attitude toward his own figures. This kind of hope applies the happiness and nonmessianic redemption of his characters. He, for example, claims that Goethe, in Ottilie's name, truly tried to "rescue someone perishing, to redeem a loved one in her."[32]

## Choice (*Wahl*) versus Decision (*Entscheidung*)

The line of demarcation between the two registers also plays a significant role in the discussion of the concepts of love and marriage. Here, Benjamin qualifies the way Gundolf appraises marriage a mystery and sacrament as being an act of mysticism itself. In contrast to this, Benjamin discusses "marriage" in terms analogous to those he developed in the *Critique of Violence*. There Benjamin explains that concepts such as "life" and "man" are notions that possess a double meaning determined by their relationship to two different spheres, namely, a natural sphere and another sphere surmounting bare naked life that he calls *übernatürlich*, more than natural, a sphere called moral or ethical. The meaning of marriage is thus derived from the interplay between its "natural moment" (sexuality) and "divine component,"[33] namely, fidelity. He names fidelity (*Treue*) the "Divine logos of marriage," referring to the idea of Divine fidelity in the biblical narrative of the covenant of God and his people. He by no means talks of a divine aspect or moment of marriage, but of the idea of fidelity (*Treue*) as a divine *logos*, that is to say, a term derived from a biblical world. In this interpretation Benjamin ascribes a transcendent moment to the decision to marry in order to establish a lifelong covenant of matrimony. Being aware that "the dark conclusion of love, whose daemon is Eros," implies a natural incompleteness of love, insofar as Eros is "the true ransoming of the deepest imperfection which belongs to the nature of man himself."[34] Marriage, in contrast, is an expression of the will for continuance in love (i.e., for its supranatural endurance) and for seeking fulfillment and perfection. And it is exactly this aspect that Benjamin sees in the moment of decision, a concept he would like to understand as strictly distinguished from choice (*Wahl*). The decision "annihilates choice in order to establish fidelity: only the decision, not the choice, is inscribed in the book of life. For choice is natural and can even belong to the elements: decision is transcendent."[35]

If this decision is bound to a legal act, then religious ideas emanate from civilian life in the "divine moment" of matrimony, "For what is proper to the truly Divine is logos: the divine does not ground life without truth, nor does it ground the rite without theology."[36] Thus, it is important to him to stress that marriage does not draw its justification from legislation, because then it would be regarded merely as an institution. Rather, for Benjamin marriage is motivated only by being an expression of the decision for continuance in love. Furthermore, when he writes that love seeks this expression (of constant love) "by nature rather in death than in life," he again explains the supernatural (not: unnatural) element of marriage: continuance in life. Thus, Benjamin's readings do not see the presentation of competing laws in Goethe's novel, which is often interpreted as a struggle between natural and marital laws. For him, in contrast, the destructive forces emerge from the deterioration of marriage due to the fact that the characters compare themselves with the natural elements when they refer to the paradigm of "elective affinities" that is a kind of relationship of chemical elements. What becomes recognizable in the novel through the ignorance of marriage's meaning that transcends the natural life "are surely the mythic powers of law."[37] The characters of Goethe's novel exemplify how misjudgment of the "divine moment" in marriage leads to a return of the mythic. The inability to decide, the relapse into a sacrificial myth, and the evocation of "fate," which characterize the actions of the two couples—all of this Benjamin explains on the basis of their "chimerical striving for freedom,"[38] that is, with their secular reason. As educated, enlightened people, superior to the order of nature, they believe they have outgrown the need for the ritual, as is most evident in the scene in which the gravestones are rearranged.

> One cannot imagine a more conclusive detachment from tradition than that from the graves of the ancestors, which, in the sense not only of myth but of religion, provide the ground under the feet of the living. Where does their freedom lead those who act thus? Far from opening up new insights for them, it blinds them to the reality that inhabits what they fear.[39]

DOUBLE REFERENCE: BENJAMIN'S
WORK ON DIFFERENCE

To conclude, among the dominant theories of secularization, the most prominent version assumes that secularization is to be understood as a phenomenon of transferal or translation in the line of historical development. This places the rhetoric of secularization at the center of attention. Benjamin appears distinctly within this horizon, because he rather operates in a historical scenario in which the secular is reconceptualized as a world in distance from Creation or revelation—that is, always in terms of being *different to Creation*, but in full awareness of one's own present language originating from biblical language, of its derivation from a beginning that must be thought of as always already irretrievably lost. The terms of this language cannot be simply transferred into secular concepts—justice into law or ethics, for example. Instead, they function as a standard that can neither be avoided nor met. Yet in this space, one defined by its remoteness from revelation, language acquires its double sense only via a detour through the clear distinction between concepts that are derived from a Divine or biblical order and those of a worldly order. These orders' referentiality and specific ways of alluding, each according to its kind, to biblical language, divine justice, and the idea of Creation can be discussed only on the basis of a clear distinction. A *reflexive and critical theory of the secular* acting in the knowledge of this constellation of history does *not* express itself in transferals and translations, the results of which present themselves as the products of complete secularization while in fact being marked by the precarious ambiguity of their Janus-like form. In contrast to these, Benjamin sets forth thought-images and figures that do not seek to reconcile Creation and history or bring them onto the same level, but reflect the double reference to both profane and religious ideas: *double reference* instead of *equivocality*. Benjamin's theory provides an alternative to secular reason in that it develops a reading and deciphering of the permanent traces of secularization. His attention to the interplay and tensions between the register of words originating from biblical ideas and the register of words denoting mundane concepts for human-made products and institutions can be described as a work on difference and a work of difference: secularization not understood as an historical process but the production of the secular as a permanent, repeated separation or divergence from religious ideas and an orientation on them at the same time.

NOTES

The article is based on my book *Walter Benjamin: Die Kreatur, das Heilige, die Bilder* (Frankfurt-am-Main, Germany: Fischer, 2008). The English translation of this book is *Walter Benjamin: Images, the Creaturely, the Holy*, trans. Chadwick Smith (Stanford, CA: Stanford University Press, 2013).

1. Walter Benjamin, *Selected Writings, Volume 1*, eds. Marcus Bullock and Michael W. Jennings (Cambridge, MA: Harvard University Press, 2003), 257.

2. Not a few of the misreadings of Benjamin's theory result from the fact that they overlook central statements that imply groundbreaking differences to the conventional understanding of the subject. For a preeminent example see the analysis of Benjamin's most overlooked reference to the commandments in *Critique of Violence* in the third chapter of Weigel, *Walter Benjamin*.

3. Benjamin, *Selected Writings, Volume 1*, 257.

4. Ibid., 257 (translation modified, emphasis mine).

5. A widespread misunderstanding of Benjamin's theory of translation stems from the fact that "reine Sprache" is translated as "pure language," although Benjamin here talks of "reine Sprache" in the sense of "language and nothing else," that is, of mere or sheer language. For more on the issue of language in Benjamin's philosophy, see Eli Friedlander, *Walter Benjamin. A Philosophical Portrait* (Cambridge, MA: Harvard University Press, 2012), 9–36.

6. Benjamin, *Selected Writings, Volume 1*, 261.

7. Benjamin, *Selected Writings, Volume 4*, eds. Howard Eiland and Michael W. Jennings (Cambridge, MA: Harvard University Press, 2006), 390 (translation modified).

8. Benjamin, *Gesammelte Schriften. Band II*, eds. Rolf Tiedemann and Hermann Schweppenhäuser (Frankfurt-am-Main, Germany: Suhrkamp, 1977ff.), 139. The English translation fails the meaning of the sentence "Geschichte wird zugleich mit Bedeutung in der Menschensprache" by giving it as "History becomes equal to signification in human language" (Benjamin, *Selected Writings, Volume 1*, 60).

9. Carl Schmitt, *Political Theology. Four Chapters on the Concept of Sovereignty* (1934), trans. Georg Schwab (Cambridge, MA: MIT Press, 1985), 46 (my emphasis).

10. Schmitt, *Politische Theologie II: Die Legende von der Erledigung jeder Politischen Theologie* (Berlin, Germany: Duncker & Humblot, 1970), 86. Albercius Gentilis (1552–1608) was an Italian jurist who taught at University of Oxford. He specialized in civil law and international law.

11. For a more extended critical engagement with Schmitt's political theology see the second chapter of Weigel, *Walter Benjamin*.

12. Hans Blumenberg, *The Legitimacy of the Modern Age* (1966), trans. Robert M. Wallace (Cambridge, MA: MIT Press, 1985), 65.

13. Ibid., 104.

14. Ibid., 119.

15. Benjamin, *Gesammelte Schriften. Band II*, 144. For more on these issues, see Winfried Menninghaus, *Walter Benjamins Theorie der Sprachmagie* (Frankfurt-am-Main, Germany: Suhrkamp, 1995).

16. Ibid., 156.

17. Benjamin, *Selected Writings, Volume 2*, eds. Michael W. Jennings, Howard Eiland and Gary Smith (Cambridge, MA, Harvard University Press, 2005), 697 (translation modified).

18. Benjamin, *Gesammelte Schriften. Band II*, 139.

19. Benjamin, *Selected Writings, Volume 2*, 437.

20. Ibid., 443.

21. Benjamin, *Gesammelte Schriften. Band II*, 349; *Selected Writings. Volume 2*, 443 (translation modified, emphasis mine).

22. Benjamin, *Selected Writings, Volume 2*, 444.

23. Ibid., 444 (translation modified).

24. Ibid., 456 (translation modified).

25. Benjamin, *Selected Writing, Volume 2*, 443.

26. For more examples and a more extended analysis of Benjamin's double reference to biblical and profane language lost in translation see the seventh chapter of Weigel, *Walter Benjamin*.

27. Benjamin, *Selected Writings, Volume 1*, 323.

28. Ibid., 323.

29. Ibid., 323 (emphasis mine).

30. Ibid., 323 (translation modified, emphasis mine).

31. Ibid., 324 (translation modified).

32. Ibid., 354 (translation modified).

33. Ibid., 326.

34. Ibid., 345.

35. Ibid., 346.

36. Ibid., 326.

37. Ibid., 301.

38. Ibid., 332.

39. Ibid., 302 (translation modified).

# Theology and Politics
## Ernst Cassirer and Martin Heidegger before, in, and after the Davos Debate

JEFFREY ANDREW BARASH

In December 1923, nearly six years before the debate that brought them face to face in Davos, Switzerland, in 1929, Ernst Cassirer invited the young Martin Heidegger, who at the time was *extraordinarius* professor at the University of Marburg, to give a talk before the Kant Society (*Kant-Gesellschaft*) in Hamburg where Cassirer taught. During his stay in Hamburg, which lasted several days, Heidegger spoke on the theme, "The Task and the Ways of Phenomenological Research" ("Aufgabe und Wege der phänomenologischen Forschung"). In a still unpublished letter that Heidegger wrote to his wife Elfride, dated December 19, 1923, which was not included in the published collection of their correspondence, he wrote that he was a guest in the home of the psychologist William Stern, professor at the University of Hamburg and father of Günther Stern (Günther Anders), the future husband of Hannah Arendt. "My talk went well," Heidegger wrote,

> [before] a large audience [...]. The city is wonderful [...]. Cassirer and other professors who attended my lecture would like to invite me for a talk next year at the Warburg library [...]. The Sterns are extremely nice und would like me to prolong my stay until Friday morning. They haven't left me for a moment.[1]

Several years later, Heidegger referred to this first encounter with Cassirer in Hamburg in a footnote found in section 12 of *Sein und Zeit*, titled, "Existential

Analytics and the Interpretation of Primitive *Dasein*" (*Die existenziale Analytik und die Interpretation des primitiven Daseins*). In this reference Heidegger notes a certain agreement, an "*Übereinstimmung*," he reached with Cassirer during the discussion following the talk concerning the need to elaborate an "existential analytic."[2]

In spite of this statement of their accord in Hamburg, it would be difficult to imagine two more divergent personalities and philosophical orientations. Later in Davos, it is above all this discordance that came to light. The different points of their disagreement have recently become a topic of detailed analysis and my purpose here will not be to reexamine the different interpretations of this debate that I have considered elsewhere.[3] In the brief space of this chapter, my aim, rather, will be to revisit the Davos debate in order to place it in a somewhat unusual perspective.

The angle of approach I will adopt was suggested to me by a critical appraisal of Heidegger's philosophy that Cassirer presented in Davos on the evening before the first debate in a preliminary talk, the "Heidegger-lecture" ("*Heidegger-Vorlesung*"). This lecture remained unpublished until it appeared in 2014, among the previously unpublished writings included in the recent Hamburg edition of Cassirer's collected works.[4] In this lecture, Cassirer identified what he took to be the deep sources of Heidegger's philosophy of existence, arising from presuppositions of an essentially *theological* order. Oddly enough, however, Cassirer never returned to this theme, neither in his debate with Heidegger at Davos, nor in later writings. In my present effort, I will scrutinize Cassirer's reference to theological presuppositions that animated Heidegger's orientation. According to my argument, an examination of Cassirer's and Heidegger's divergent attitudes toward theology permits us to set their respective philosophical positions in a novel light. And, as I will attempt to illustrate in the concluding sections of this chapter, analysis of their respective attitudes toward theology at the same time reveals an important source of the political philosophy that Cassirer elaborated in the decades following the debate in Davos.

CASSIRER AND HEIDEGGER: THE INITIAL SETTING

We do not know today if the theme of theology arose in the discussions that took place between Cassirer and Heidegger in 1923, during Heidegger's brief sojourn in Hamburg. Perhaps Cassirer was able to discern the importance of this topic for Heidegger's philosophical orientation in this period preceding the publication of *Sein und Zeit*. Heidegger had taken a certain distance from the Catholic tradition in which he had been brought up and with which he had been closely affiliated during the period of his studies at the University of Freiburg im Breisgau. Following his marriage in 1917 with a Protestant woman, Elfride Petri, and his intensive study of the writings of Martin Luther, themes related to Protestant theology began to have a profound impact on his thought, as witnessed by the courses he taught as a young *Privatdozent* at Freiburg during the years following World War I that are collected in volume 60 of his *Complete Works* (*Gesamtausgabe*) under the title *Philosophy of Religious Life* (*Philosophie des religiösen Lebens*). In regard to Luther and Christian religiosity, Heidegger wrote the following lines to his wife in a letter he sent her in September 1919:

> Since my reading of Luther's commentary on the *Epistle to the Romans*, many things that were previously troubling and opaque have become clear, and are a source of liberation for me. I understand the Middle Ages and the development of Christian religiosity in a fully different light. And this has opened completely new perspectives in regard to the philosophy of religion.[5]

Heidegger maintained his strong interest in theology, above all in the writings of Martin Luther, during the period of his teaching at the University of Marburg after 1923. During his four years at Marburg, Heidegger collaborated with the Protestant theologian Rudolf Bultmann. In 1927, the year in which *Sein und Zeit* appeared, he wrote to Bultmann that "Augustine, Luther, Kierkegaard are philosophically essential for the formation of a radical comprehension of *Dasein*."[6] And, in the introduction to *Sein und Zeit*, Heidegger asserted that theologians, in light of a renewal of interest in Luther's writings, had begun to formulate more original questions.[7] Moreover, the reflections proposed throughout this work on Paul, Augustine, Luther, and Kierkegaard illustrate their profound significance for his philosophical analyses.

If we bear in mind this role of theology for the elaboration of Heidegger's ontological standpoint, it is curious that this theme was never directly mentioned in his commentary on Cassirer's philosophy. In his book *Mythical Thought*, the second volume of the *Philosophy of Symbolic Forms*, which appeared in 1925, Cassirer dealt in detail with Christian theological themes in the more general context of analysis of the distinction between myth and religion. Following the publication of this work, Heidegger wrote a review in which he examined Cassirer's theory of myth, without, however, paying any attention to Cassirer's conception of the phenomenon of religion and, more specifically, of the Christian religion. Not only in this review, but also in subsequent remarks on Cassirer's philosophy, whether in his contemporary Freiburg courses, in *Sein und Zeit* or later at Davos, Heidegger never mentioned this theme. It is as if the topic of religion, considered from their respective viewpoints, were too present, too close, perhaps too troubling, to be evoked in a direct confrontation.

Be this as it may, the criticism Heidegger elaborated on of the epistemological foundations of Cassirer's theory of myth clearly challenged his manner of historical reflection on myth, and did so in a way that touches at least indirectly on his conception of religion. It is therefore to Heidegger's oblique critique of Cassirer's conception of religion that I will now turn, in order to set in relief the countercritique Cassirer developed at Davos and during the years that followed.

The manner of historical reflection that Cassirer adopted in his interpretation of myth and of its relation to religion owed a good deal to the inspiration of his mentor Hermann Cohen. For Cohen, as for Cassirer, Jewish monotheism, above all as represented by the prophets, as well as Christian monotheism, each contributed to a general movement elaborated over the course of history: Judaism and Christianity, through faith in a unique transcendent God, surmounted the rudimentary forms of mythical thought that had identified its deities with occult forces deployed by things in the immanent world. The great contribution of the Jewish prophets, which was reaffirmed in another sense by early Christianity and reinforced by the Protestant Reformation, lay in a firm rejection of an alleged magical potency deployed by idols and other worldly objects. Over the course of their historical development, the great monotheistic religions reinterpreted the sense of religious faith in directing it toward divine transcendence beyond the tangible things of this world. In situating the specific contribution of Christianity, which the Protestant Reformation raised to its fullest expression, Cohen recognized in Luther's work a continuation of the movement inaugurated by the Hebrew prophets. In Cohen's words in his work *Ethics of Pure Will* (*Ethik des reinen Willens*, 1904),

> As the Prophets struggled against sacrifice, so Luther opposed faith to works, above all works in the sense of the Church [...]. The works of the Church are like ancient sacrifice, transformed into mystery.[8]

In Cohen's eyes, this contribution of Jewish and Christian monotheism was reinforced by the rationalism of the ancient Greek heritage, above all through the Platonic and neo-Platonic legacy which, from the Hellenistic period onward, had a decisive impact on the two religions.[9] Ancient Greek rationalism and Judeo-Christian monotheism each progressively set in motion the historical movement that led to the subduing of the most rudimentary forms of myth, and subsequently to the overcoming of the remnants of mythical-magical belief still at work in Christianity. In this manner, each also brought an essential contribution to the *ethical* development of humanity. Indeed, over the course of human history, the progressive challenge directed against the assumption that human destiny is ruled by occult forces opened the way to the idea of individual liberty as the source of moral responsibility.

While Ernst Cassirer reaffirmed the broad outlines of Cohen's interpretation of human history, his philosophy of symbolic forms modified it in an essential way. According to Cassirer's original perspective, myth and religion, science and art, like the words and signs through which they are articulated, are so many symbolic forms in terms of which humans make sense of reality. It is through the historical elaboration of symbolic forms for Cassirer that human awareness of the spiritual character of religious symbols emerged, enabling humanity over the course of history to overcome the mythico-magical belief in their occult power. At the same time, the spiritualization of symbols reinforced the redirection of religious faith toward transcendence.

Even more firmly than Cohen, Cassirer underlined the significance of Plato and of the Platonic heritage which, to his mind, represented a decisive turning-point that led to the overcoming of the mythical-magical world image, since Plato accorded a preeminent role to the autonomous power of reason in its capacity to reveal sovereign goodness that is not conditioned by the things of the sensuous world, but reigns from a realm of pure transcendence beyond their purview. In this sense, according to Plato's celebrated words in *The Republic*, the Good is "beyond being or essence" (*epekeina tês ousias*).[10] On this basis, Cassirer rejoined Cohen's interpretation in reaffirming the contribution of both Jewish and Christian doctrines of divine transcendence to the liberation of the human spirit, and in emphasizing the role of Martin Luther in his struggle against what he took to be the vestiges of idolatry in the rites of the Catholic Church. Cassirer wrote in this regard,

> The entire history of dogma, in its evolution from the most primitive forms until Luther and Zwingli, shows us in an immediate way the perpetual combat that opposes the primordial historical sense of symbols, their meaning as "sacraments" and "mysteries," and their derivative, purely "spiritual" sense. There, too, the "ideal" wrests itself only very slowly from the sphere of material things, from effective reality.[11]

Like the Platonic heritage, the monotheistic religions reinforced this conviction concerning the spiritual significance of symbols and, in this manner, for Cassirer as for Cohen, religion, in leading toward the gradual liberation from the hold of beliefs in magical forces, contributed to the development of the conviction of human ethical responsibility.

While Cassirer was in agreement with Hermann Cohen's conception of the ethical role of the monotheistic religions, he nonetheless evaluated the historical significance of religion in a way that essentially differed from the ideas of his former mentor. This difference appears in its clearest form in relation to Cohen's late work, *Religion of Reason from the Sources of Judaism* (*Religion der Vernunft aus den Quellen des Judentums*). In this book Cohen stressed, more strongly than ever before, the uniqueness of Judaism as a religious faith and the specific role of Jewish messianism for the orientation of human history, which he distinguished in this context from Christian eschatology. Whereas Christian eschatology maintains a sharp distinction between the transcendent realm and the sociopolitical world, Jewish messianism aims to realize a universal ideal in the world itself and conceives this task as the ultimate goal of its faith.[12] Cassirer's symbolic interpretation of religion, however, led him in a different direction. Indeed, as we glean from the final part of *Mythical Thought*, Cassirer interpreted the history of the monotheistic religions in terms of what he saw as their tendency to come ever closer to the domain of aesthetics. Even if religion can never fully divest itself of its mythical foundations, the more it is able to free itself from the trammels of mythical belief in magical forces and to conceive of itself in spiritual and symbolic terms, the closer it approaches the domain of art. Whereas religion, in its historical development, is continually condemned to face the problem raised by the ultimate *reality* of its objects, this problem disappears, and religious consciousness is "calmed" (*beruhigt*) and "placated" (*beschwichtigt*), as soon as it beholds itself in the perspective of art. As Cassirer wrote on the final page of the *Mythical Thought*,

> Myth always sees in the image a fragment of substantial reality, a part of the world of things endowed with forces that are equal or superior to those of the world. The religious conception strives forward from this initial magical aim to an ever purer spiritualization. And yet, even here it finds that it is continually led to a point where the question of its meaning and truth is converted into that of the reality of its objects, a point at which, in a hard and sudden way, the problem of "existence" arises. Only with aesthetic consciousness is this problem truly left behind.[13]

## PHILOSOPHY AND RELIGION IN HEIDEGGER

During the early period of his teaching at the University of Freiburg im Breisgau, between 1919 and 1921, several years before the publication of Ernst Cassirer's *Mythical Thought,* Heidegger elaborated a sharp critique of the method of investigation in philosophy and in the human sciences that sought to understand the phenomenon of religion in terms of its historical manifestations. This, indeed, was the kind of historical investigation that inspired Cassirer's research. Like the advocates of neo-orthodox theology, notably Karl Barth, Rudolf Bultmann, or Friedrich Gogarten, Heidegger challenged the liberal theology that had predominated before World War I; the orientation of theologians like Adolf von Harnack or Ernst Troeltsch, who, from a Protestant perspective, had underlined the historical role of Protestantism and its importance for the emergence of modern culture. This method had clear affinities with that adopted by Hermann Cohen in the period of publication of his work *Ethics of Pure Will.* Indeed, even if during these years prior to World War I Hermann Cohen and Ernst Troeltsch engaged in an intense debate concerning the role of Judaism in the history of religions, both of them, like Ernst Cassirer at a later point, agreed that the meaning of religion is to be sought in the domain of its *historical* development. And, in his early lectures on the phenomenology of religion, Heidegger railed against this method. In his eyes, the search for objective continuities linking together the different epochs of history, capable of revealing historical meaning beyond the transformations of history, was nothing more than a modern expression of the Platonic quest for transcendence beyond the flux of living experience.[14]

Animated by this conviction, Heidegger placed in relief a very different aspect of Luther's teaching than that which had been advanced by Hermann Cohen or Ernst Cassirer. From his standpoint, Heidegger stressed, not Luther's reproof of mythico-magical vestiges in the Catholic faith and possible affinities between this aspect of Luther's doctrine and the Platonic quest for supersensuous truth but, on the contrary, a wholly different viewpoint: Luther's radical *critique* of modes of conceptualization bequeathed by the ancient Greek metaphysical tradition, above all by the Platonic heritage. In its traditional role as the metaphysical model for the self-interpretation of Christian spirituality, Greek philosophy, for Heidegger, had deformed (*verunstaltet*) Christian existence, and the only way to retrieve a pristine Christian religiosity was by liberating it from the spell of Greek conceptual presuppositions.¹⁵ Here the uniqueness of religious experience for human existence had to be made palpable independently of the conceptual paradigms to which it had traditionally been assimilated, in accord with which modern adaptations of Platonic assumptions identified it with one among many incarnations of a superior truth, the expressions of a transhistorical continuity beyond its historical manifestations. In taking as his model what he described as the authentic "factical life-experience" ("*faktische Lebenserfahrung*") of the primitive Christian community, Heidegger sought to underscore the unique existential significance of a religiosity that was in no way commensurable with schema of historical development or extraneous categories of analysis. Foremost among these was the Platonic and neo-Platonic valorization of *aesthetic* qualities, designating them, like religious phenomena, as touchstones of a superior, transcendent truth manifested in the immanent realm.¹⁶ In interpreting Luther's Heidelberg *Disputatio* of 1518 in his early Freiburg course lectures, Heidegger emphasized that the Reformer's rejection of ancient Greek metaphysical concepts equated them with mere forms of idolatry that *aesthetically* glorify what are seen to be the wonders of the created world.¹⁷ From Heidegger's standpoint, authentic religious experience, far from an ongoing incarnation of a transhistorical idea of truth comparable to the perdurable luster of aesthetic phenomena in the immanent realm, could serve as a source of philosophical insight into the illegitimacy of such expressions of the Greek metaphysical tradition. All such forms of Greek metaphysics, as he exclaimed in this and other contexts, must be resolutely deconstructed—"*abgebaut*," submitted to phenomenological *Destruktion*.¹⁸ In Heidegger's eyes, the inspiration above all of Paul, Luther, and Kierkegaard serves to guide the attempt to retrieve the original sense of religious experience. They, above all, give insight into the significance of human finitude as it is faced with the necessity of choosing a mode of existence in the light of future death. Here Heidegger's understanding of Luther and Kierkegaard presents a striking anticipation of his interpretation of the finitude of human existence elaborated in *Sein und Zeit*. In a lecture presented in 1924 in the seminar of Rudolf Bultmann in Marburg on "The Problem of Sin in Luther," Heidegger paraphrased Kierkegaard as follows:

> The principle of Protestantism embraces a particular presupposition: [that of] the anguished man who sits in the face of death in a state of fear and trembling before a harsh trial.¹⁹

PHILOSOPHY AND THEOLOGY:
AESTHETIC PRECONCEPTIONS

In view of Heidegger's philosophical and theological orientation, it comes as no surprise that he sharply contested Cassirer's theory of symbolic forms and, with it, his conception of myth. Whereas Cassirer in *Mythical Thought*, as we have seen, interpreted myth, religion, and aesthetics as so many symbolic forms, Heidegger, well before Davos, identified a chasm separating primordial Christian religiosity from any other form of experience. Whereas Cassirer presupposed the historical articulation of symbolic forms leading to an ongoing spiritualization of the mythical components of religion and suggested that the problem posed by their ultimate reality might be attenuated through appreciation of their quality as aesthetic symbols, Heidegger sharply questioned the assimilation of religious and aesthetic experience to the same conceptual schema of explanation in an ongoing process of historical development. In a course lecture presented in 1925, the year of publication of Cassirer's *Mythical Thought* and of his review of this work, Heidegger signaled what was to his eyes the inappropriateness of Cassirer's methodology where it indifferently subjects aesthetic, mythical, or religious phenomena to the same "formal models" (*formale Leitfäden*): "what proves to be a suitable approach in aesthetics," as he wrote, "may impede elucidation and interpretation of other phenomena." On this basis, Heidegger qualified as "inadequate" Cassirer's general conception of symbolic forms.[20]

In his review of *Mythical Thought*, Heidegger's critique of Cassirer centered above all on the developmental schema in terms of which Cassirer interpreted the historical articulation of the symbolic forms. If Heidegger did not specifically allude here to Cassirer's interpretation of Christianity, he radically rejected Cassirer's idea of a fundamental historical *progression* of modernity beyond the mythical world-image. Indeed, at the fundamental level, all human existence—whether mythico-magical or modern—is marked by the same finitude. And finite existence necessarily comprehends itself in light of the facticity of a being thrown into the world, preoccupied by unavoidable everyday concerns in the world, and faced with the inevitability of future death. No historical progression can overcome this universal existential situation.

In view of the role that Cassirer attributed in *Mythical Thought* to the development of a capacity for aesthetic appreciation of mythical and religious symbols as the mark of historical progression beyond the more rudimentary forms of belief, Heidegger's sarcastic reproof of the universal schema elaborated by what he called "aesthetes" at the Davos debate, in a comment made in its aftermath, takes on a curious significance. A few months following his encounter with Cassirer at Davos, in a letter addressed to Karl Löwith on September 3, 1929, Heidegger lauded younger members of the audience, who showed signs of "resolution of a singular, effective Dasein," and he contrasted their attitude with what he characterized as the

> [...] Olympic and pretentious world-encompassing objectivity, which, for aesthetes of the institution, becomes an obscure and ephemeral form of enjoyment.[21]

In view of the aestheticized interpretation of the general schema of historical development of symbolic forms that Cassirer proposed in *Mythical Thought*, was he not, in the context of Davos, the most likely target of this critique?

## CASSIRER'S "HEIDEGGER-VORLESUNG" AND THE THEOLOGICAL BACKGROUND TO THE DAVOS DEBATE

Following his initial reading of Heidegger's *Sein und Zeit*, Ernst Cassirer began to elaborate an analysis of this work and, as early as 1928, he wrote a critical commentary on it in the text *'Geist' und 'Leben'* (*Spirit and Life*), which he never completed and which, in its preliminary form, was posthumously published. In this text Cassirer began to reflect on the theological sources of Heidegger's philosophy,[22] and it is this theme that he would treat in greater depth in the *Heidegger-Vorlesung* written some months later and presented in Davos on the eve of his first debate with Heidegger.

What is immediately striking in Cassirer's *Heidegger-Vorlesung* is not only that he examined the theme of the theological sources of *Sein und Zeit* that nowhere was evoked in the debate itself; more remarkable still was the manner in which Cassirer, in function of his critique of Heidegger, modified his appraisal of Luther in comparison to his earlier interpretation of the Reformer in *Mythical Thought*. In his portrayal of Luther in this work Cassirer, we have seen, underlined what he identified as his contribution to a long historical process of desacralization of sensuous things in the world. According to Cassirer, this long process of "spiritualization of the sensuous" ("*Vergeistigung des Sinnlichen*") flowed from the double source of Platonic philosophy and the Judeo-Christian tradition. In the *Heidegger-Vorlesung*, however, Cassirer presented a wholly different side of Luther: the Luther of "fear and trembling" in a guise prefiguring the analytic of *Dasein*. In this lecture, Luther poses the radical problem of human finitude, for he recalls the impending demise that no one can avoid. In the face of death, any quest for stability and security collapses; the search for an ideal order beyond human finitude and the contingencies of this world proves futile. Cassirer develops his analysis in relation to Luther's *Eight Sermons* ("*Acht Sermone*"), professed at Wittenberg in 1523. Luther there proclaimed,

> We all must die and no one can die for another [...]. Each one must seek his own rampart and engage his own struggle against the enemies that are the devil and death. At that moment I will not be with you, nor you with me.[23]

Cassirer labeled Luther's doctrine "religious individualism"—a characteristic, according to him, that also emerged in the Catholic tradition in the writings of Pascal. Religious individualism challenges every "objective form" of religion. Heidegger interprets death in an analogous way: in his eyes, finite existence, when relying only on itself, dissolves all illusory ties, whether physical or social. According to Cassirer's paraphrase of Heidegger, death obliges each individual to turn away from the inauthentic world of anonymous, everyday existence. This critique of the objective forms of religion, in Luther as in Heidegger, places in question the certitudes of the metaphysical tradition. Luther had emphasized the inscrutability of the Divine will and, in light of human fallibility and mortality, he contested the role accorded by the Platonic and Stoic-Christian tradition to the quest for an ideal order of the universe and to the intelligibility of "eternal certitudes" in this order beyond existence in its radical finitude.[24] From a novel twentieth-century perspective, Heidegger presented an analogous challenge to the Platonic and Stoic presupposition concerning the fundamental status of an autonomous cosmic order, beyond the finitude of mortal perspectives. It is here that Cassirer broached the principal theme of his lecture: Heidegger drew from the interpretation of human finitude the conclusion that all truth is relative to the finite beings we are.[25] And Cassirer opposed to this conclusion the Platonic-Stoic idea of an unconditioned ethical truth, the intrinsic validity of which in no way depends on the finite mode of existence of the one who affirms it. This conviction, as Cassirer emphasized, was a source of inspiration for a broad intellectual tradition in the West. It also served to orient Kant's transcendental idealism, independently of the critique he directed against traditional metaphysics. As we recall, on the day following Cassirer's lecture this topic stood at the center of his debate with Heidegger.

THEOLOGY AND POLITICS: CASSIRER'S
LATER CRITIQUE OF HEIDEGGER

During the years after the Davos debate, Cassirer did not pursue the interpretation he proposed in the *Heidegger-Vorlesung* of the theological sources of Heidegger's philosophy of existence. Nonetheless, if we examine for a moment the development of his thinking in the years following Davos, one aspect of his orientation is particularly noteworthy for our present analysis. Indeed, in the framework of his conception of politics which, in the early 1930s became an ever more central topic of his reflection, Cassirer resumed his interpretation of the Lutheran heritage in a manner that bore a striking affinity with the topic of his lecture on Heidegger at Davos. Independently of the question of Heidegger who, in any case, had at that time not yet announced his political position, Cassirer began to turn his attention to theologico-political topics, and he deepened his investigation of the theological sources of the challenge launched by Luther and Calvin against the Platonic-Stoic tradition.

Cassirer's most detailed analyses of theologico-political topics in this period are found in two books published in 1932: in *The Platonic Renaissance in England and the Cambridge School* and in *The Philosophy of Enlightenment*. These were the last works Cassirer published in Germany. Several months after the printing of *The Philosophy of Enlightenment*, Hitler rose to power and Cassirer left Germany for England and then Sweden.

In view of the dire political situation in Germany in the early thirties, Cassirer presented much more in these works than a simple history of modern European thought. Rather, the books' themes and contents represent a plea in favor of the aspect of the European intellectual heritage that was in his eyes particularly important to defend.

In this context, Cassirer placed in a new perspective the antinomy he had developed at Davos between Luther and the Platonic-Stoic tradition. He underscored the contribution of this tradition in examining what he considered to be the precise political implications of the radical attack Luther and Calvin directed against it. The theological doctrine concerning the fallen condition of humanity and the weakness of human reason led the Reformers to adopt positions of political voluntarism. In view of human finitude and the fallibility of human reason, both Luther and Calvin concluded that it was necessary to promote political doctrines in favor of strict obedience to the sovereign will. Calvin and his successors, as Cassirer noted, had called for the creation of a theocracy to provide absolute orientation for the State.

The originality of Cassirer's thought during this period lies in his identification of a curious affinity between the political voluntarism of the Reformers and the radical absolutism that Hobbes advocated later on. Hobbes, in order to contest the legitimacy of theocratic principles in politics, concluded that only absolute sovereign authority could controvert the danger posed by the claims of the theologians and thus maintain the stability of the State. Thus, on the basis of starting points that were diametrically opposed to each other, the Reformers and Hobbes drew the conclusion that only absolute sovereign authority, representing Divine authority in the temporal realm, could prevent the outbreak of civil war and the reign of chaos. Only the sovereign—either the sovereign church or the political sovereign—was authorized to establish legitimate government and to decree what is just and unjust. It is on this basis that Luther and Calvin, on one side, and Hobbes, on the other, contested the ideal of an autonomous political truth endowed with intrinsic validity and intelligible in the light of human reason. In spite of all other differences between them, the sixteenth century Reformers and the theoretician of the absolute State of the seventeenth century shared this common assumption.[26]

In opposition to political voluntarism, Cassirer invoked the argument of Hugo Grotius who, in drawing on Platonic and Stoic sources, affirmed the principle of the intrinsic rational validity of truth that depends neither on the Divine will, nor on human will, since neither God nor humans can transform what is intrinsically good into evil, nor evil into good. As Cassirer stipulated, Kant, on the basis of critical theory, set this conviction as the cornerstone of his ethico-political orientation. Kant, indeed, opposed any conception of politics that would make laws depend on the arbitrary sovereign will, and it was here that Kant's philosophy had inspired the earlier response to relativism he had mobilized at Davos. Even when Cassirer limited his analysis to the history of political thought without making direct reference to his contemporary period, the implications of his arguments in regard to the growing influence of new forms of political voluntarism were evident. Under the label of decisionism or of political theology, this new contemporary form of voluntarism drew on the analogy between Divine omnipotence and absolute sovereign power to legitimate the idea that political decisions cannot be limited by any established norm.[27]

If Cassirer approached the theme of political theology in historical perspective in this period of sharp political radicalization that witnessed the first important victories of the Nazi Party, he nonetheless abandoned all reference to Heidegger, not only during this period, but during his years of emigration to England and Sweden, from 1933 until his departure for the United States in 1941 at the beginning of World War II. It was in the United States, in his final work *The Myth of the State*, posthumously published in 1945, that he resumed his critique of Heidegger. In this context, Cassirer focused on the political implications of Heidegger's philosophical questioning of any rational or traditional order capable of claiming a fundamental status beyond the singular perspective revealed in light of human finitude, and of the call to decision in the face of nothingness and of death. Nonetheless, in *The Myth of the State* it is no longer in relation to *theological* voluntarism that Cassirer developed his analysis. He no longer even suggested that there might be a link between the philosophy of Heidegger and Luther's theology, or political theology in any precise sense of the term. His attitude toward Heidegger changed in close relation to a broader transformation in his theoretical orientation: in the final context of *The Myth of the State*, Cassirer accorded to Heidegger's philosophy a novelty that set it beyond the scope of all earlier forms of both myth and theology, corresponding to what Cassirer took to be the unprecedented status of the modern political myths he chose to serve. Myths of the twentieth century, from this perspective, by virtue of their calculated ideological design, transform the function of spontaneous belief systems of earlier peoples, while mobilizing their archaic force; this modern transformation contrasts sharply with the otherworldly orientation and ethical concern of traditional theology. Hence Heidegger's decision in 1933 to lend his support to the arbitrary power of a dictator who was subjected to no limit beyond his own will cannot be attributed to a traditional theological inspiration, but reveals the inner affinity of his thought with novel twentieth-century forms of political mythology. In a passage of *The Myth of the State* that the American editors of the work chose not to include in the posthumously published edition, Cassirer made a remark that illustrates his position regarding theology with particular clarity. Heidegger's critique of universal standards of truth in the sense of the Platonic tradition, as Cassirer noted, and his tendency to relativize the idea of truth in function of the singular finitude of *Dasein*, brought him onto the ideological territory of the most arbitrary forms of twentieth-century political mythology. The sixteenth-century theology of Luther, however, shared no affinity with the novel forms of myth in the twentieth century, which Heidegger chose to embrace. In reference to Luther, mentioned in company with Kepler, Winckelmann, and Herder, Cassirer laconically stated: "it is impossible to read the National-Socialist ideology into the entire text of German culture."[28]

This ultimate development in Cassirer's thought reveals a theoretical conclusion drawn on the basis of the terrible experience of World War II that informs *The Myth of the State* as a whole: in this final interpretation, traditional theological categories, however radical they may be, can in no way account for the archaic force of the myths of the twentieth century and for their accompanying philosophical ideologies that had recently demonstrated the full range of their devastating potency.

NOTES

1. *"Mein Vortrag ist gut abgelaufen [...] grosser Zuhörerkreis [...]. Die Stadt ist Herrlich [...]. Cassirer und andere Professoren die in meinem Vortrag waren, wollen mich im nächsten Herbst für eine Vorlesung in der Bibliothek Warburg haben [...]. Sterns sind äusserst nett und wollen dass ich noch bis Freitag früh bleibe [...]. [Sie] lassen mich nicht los."* Martin Heidegger to Elfride Heidegger, December 19, 1923, unpublished. I am grateful to Dr. Thomas Meyer for this information. Unless otherwise indicated, all translations are my own. Since the pagination of the German edition of *Sein und Zeit* is indicated in the English translation of this work and in the Heidegger *Gesamtausgabe*, I indicate only the pagination of the original German edition.

2. Martin Heidegger, *Sein und Zeit* (Tübingen, Germany: Niemeyer, 1972), 51.

3. See, in this regard, my review article concerning Peter Eli Gordon's book, *Continental Divide: Heidegger, Cassirer, Davos* (Cambridge, MA: Harvard University Press, 2010), which was published in *History and Theory* 51 (2012) 3, 436–50. Gordon's work is the latest in a number of attempts to comprehend this seminal philosophical event. These works include: *The Symbolic Construction of Reality: The Legacy of Ernst Cassirer*, ed. Jeffrey Andrew Barash (Chicago: University of Chicago Press, 2008); Massimo Ferrari, *Ernst Cassirer, Dalla scuola di Marburgo alla filosofia della cultura* (Florence, Italy: Olschki, 1996); Michael Friedman, *A Parting of the Ways: Carnap, Cassirer, and Heidegger* (Chicago, IL: Open Court, 2000); *Symbolic Forms and Cultural Studies: Ernst Cassirer's Theory of Culture*, eds. Cyrus Hamlin and John Michael Krois (New Haven, CT: Yale University Press, 2004); D. Kaegi and Enno Rudolph, *Cassirer–Heidegger: 70 Jahre Davoser Disputation* (Hamburg, Germany: Meiner, 2002); Thomas Meyer, *Ernst Cassirer* (Hamburg, Germany: Ellert und Richter, 2006); Birgit Recki, *Kultur als Praxis: Eine Einführung in Ernst Cassirers Philosophie der symbolischen Formen* (Berlin, Germany: Akademie, 2004); Edward Skidelsky, *Ernst Cassirer: The Last Philosopher of Culture* (Princeton, NJ: Princeton University Press, 2008).

4. Ernst Cassirer, *Davoser Vorträge. Vorträge über Hermann Cohen. Mit einem Anhang: Briefe Hermann und Martha Cohens an Ernst und Toni Cassirer, 1901–1929, Nachgelassene Manuskripte und Texte*, vol. 17, ed. Jörn Bohr (Hamburg, Germany: Meiner, 2014), 3–76.

5. *"Seit ich Luthers Römerbriefkommentar gelesen, ist mir vieles vordem Quälende und Dunkle hell und Befreiend geworden—ich verstehe das Mittelalter und die Entwicklung der christlichen Religiosität ganz neu; und es haben sich mir ganz neue Perspektiven der religionsphilosophischen Problematik ergeben."* Martin Heidegger to Elfride Heidegger, September 9, 1919, *"Mein liebes Seelchen!" Briefe Martin Heideggers an seine Frau Elfride. 1915–1970* (Munich, Germany: Deutsche Verlags-Anstalt, 2005), 100.

6. *"Augustin, Luther, Kierkegaard sind philosophisch wesentlich für die Ausbildung eines radikalen Daseinsverständnisses."* Martin Heidegger to Rudolf Bultmann, December 31, 1927, Rudolf Bultmann, Martin Heidegger, *Briefwechsel, 1925–1975*, eds. Andreas Grossmann and Christof Landmesser (Frankfurt am Main, Germany: Klostermann, Tübingen: Mohr/Siebeck, 2009), 48.

7. Martin Heidegger, *Sein und Zeit*, 10.

8. *"Wie die Propheten das Opfer bekämpften, so bekämpft Luther mit seinem Glauben die Werke, nämlich die Werke der Kirche [. . .]. Die Werke der Kirche sind das alte Opfer, das sich hier in ein Mysterium verwandelt hat."* Hermann Cohen, "Luther," *Ethik des reinen Willens* (Berlin, Germany: Bruno Cassirer, 1921), 303.

9. Ibid., 516.

10. Plato, *The Republic*, 509b (Cambridge, MA: 1980), 107; Ernst Cassirer, *Das Mythische Denken, Philosophie der symbolischen Formen*, vol. 2 (Darmstadt, Germany: Wissenschaftliche Buchgesellschaft, 1994), 300.

11. *"Die gesamte Entwicklung der Dogmengeschichte, von ihren ersten Anfängen bis zu Luther und Zwingli hin, zeigt uns sodann den ständigen Kampf zwischen dem geschichtlichen Ursinn der 'Symbole,' nach dem sie noch ganz als 'Sakramente' und 'Mysterien' erscheinen und ihrem abgeleiteten, rein 'geistigen' Sinn. Auch hier arbeitet sich das 'Ideelle' nur ganz allmählich aus der Sphäre des Dinglichen, des Real-Wirklichen heraus."* Ernst Cassirer, *Das mythische Denken, Philosophie der symbolischen Formen*, vol. 2, 297.

12. Hermann Cohen, *Religion der Vernunft aus den Quellen des Judentums. Eine jüdische Religionsphilosophie* (Frankfurt am Main, Germany: J. Kauffmann, 1929), 341–68.

13. *"Der Mythos sieht im Bilde immer zugleich ein Stück substanzieller Wirklichkeit, einen Teil der Dingwelt selbst der mit gleichen oder höheren Kräften wie diese ausgestattet ist. Die religiöse Auffassung strebt von dieser ersten magischen Absicht*

*zu immer reinerer Vergeistigung fort. Und doch sieht auch sie sich immer wieder an einen Punkt geführt an dem die Frage nach ihren Sinn- und Wahrheitsgehalt in die Frage nach der Wirklichkeit ihrer Gegenstände umschlägt, an dem sich, hart und schroff, das Problem der 'Existenz' vor ihr aufrichtet. Das ästhetische Bewusstsein erst lässt dieses Problem wahrhaft hinter sich."* Ibid., 311.

14. Martin Heidegger, *Einleitung in die phänomenologie der Religion (1920–21)*, *Philosophie des religiösen Lebens, Gesamtausgabe*, vol. 60 (Frankfurt am Main, Germany: Klostermann, 1995), 39–50; see in this regard chapter 4 of my book, *Marin Heidegger and the Problem of Historical Meaning* (New York: Fordham, 2004), 132–56.

15. Martin Heidegger, *Philosophie der Anschauung und des Ausdrucks* (1920), *Gesamtausgabe*, vol. 59 (Frankfurt am Main, Germany: Klostermann, 1993), 91.

16. According to Heidegger's early Freiburg lectures of 1921, "Augustinus und der Neuplatonismus," even Augustine, who had been a principal source of Luther's theology, fell prey to the enticements of neo-Platonic metaphysics, as may be seen nowhere more distinctly than in his aesthetic viewpoint, which took worldly beauty to be an emanation from an absolute transcendent source. Martin Heidegger, "Augustinus und der Neuplatonismus," *Philosophie des religiösen Lebens, Gesamtausgabe*, vol. 60, 284.

17. Heidegger, "Einleitung in die phänomenologie der Religion," *Philosophie des religiösen Lebens*, Anhang II, 282

18. Martin Heidegger, "Augustinus und der Neuplatonismus," *Philosophie des religiösen Lebens*, Anhang I, 247; Martin Heidegger, "Anzeige der hermeneutischen Situation" (1922), *Phänomenologische Interpretationen zu Aristoteles* (Stuttgart, Germany: Reclam, 2003), 32–35.

19. *"Das Prinzip des Protestantismus hat eine besondere Voraussetzung: ein Mensch der in Todesangst da sitzt in Furcht und Zittern und viel Anfechtung"*; Martin Heidegger, "Das Problem der Sünde bei Luther," Appendix, Rudolf Bultmann, Martin Heidegger, *Briefwechsel, 1925–1975*, 271.

20. *"Was für ästhetische Phänomene angemessener Ansatz sein kann, kann für andere Phänomene gerade das Gegenteil einer Aufklärung und Interpretation bewirken."* Martin Heidegger, *Prolegomena zur Geschichte des Zeitbegriffs, Gesamtausgabe*, vol. 20 (Frankfurt am Main, Germany: Klostermann, 1979), 276–77.

21. *"Entschiedenheit des wirklichen, einzelnen Daseins [. . .] alle olympische und aufgeplusterte Allerweltsobjektivität wird schattenhaft und ein flüchtiger Genuss für die Aestheten des Betriebs."* Martin Heidegger to Karl Löwith, September 3, 1929. Martin Heidegger, Karl Löwith, *Briefwechsel* 1919–73 (Freiburg/Munich, Germany: Karl Alber, 2017), p. 168.

22. Ernst Cassirer, *'Geist' und 'Leben,' Zur Metaphysik der symbolischen Formen*, ed. John Michael Krois, Ernst Cassirer, *Nachgelassene Manuskripte und Texte*, vol. 1 (Hamburg, Germany: Meiner, 1995), 219–24.

23. *"Wir sind alle zum Tode gefordert und wird keiner für den anderen sterben [. . .] es muss ein jeglicher auf seine Schanze selbst sehen und sich mit den Feinden, mit dem Teufel und Tode selbst einlegen und allein im Kampf liegen. Ich werde dann nicht bei Dir sein noch Du bei mir."* Martin Luther, *Acht Sermone*, quoted in Ernst Cassirer, "Heidegger-Vorlesung," *Davoser Vorträge. Vorträge über Hermann Cohen. Mit einem Anhang: Briefe Hermann und Martha Cohens an Ernst und Toni Cassirer, 1901–1929*, 55–57.

24. Ibid., 65–67.

25. Ibid., 57; Ernst Cassirer, Martin Heidegger, "Davoser Disputation," Heidegger, *Kant und das Problem der Metaphysik*, Anhang (Frankfurt am Main, Germany: Klostermann, 1973), 253–54.

26. Ernst Cassirer, *Die Philosophie der Aufklärung* (Tübingen, Germany: Mohr, 1932), 319f.

27. One need only recall in this context the decisionist political theories of the 1920s and 1930s in Germany, notably propounded by Carl Schmitt, that sought to revive and radicalize Hobbes's absolutist doctrine by seizing on the traditional analogy between the sovereign and God to reinforce the idea of absolute sovereign power. Well beyond the limits of Hobbes's own thinking, Schmitt, in his work *Political Theology* (1922), emphasized that the sovereign's decisions can in no way be limited by natural right or any other preexisting norms, for the norm depends, according to Schmitt's phrase, on the absolute sovereign's decision, born "out of nothingness" (*aus einem Nichts geboren*) (Carl Schmitt, *Politische Theologie. Vier Kapitel zur Lehre von der Souveränität* [Berlin, Germany: Duncker und Humblot, 1985], 42). Carl Schmitt's questioning of both the traditional and rational basis of norms and his insistence that decision arises in the face of nothingness anticipates in a striking manner the philosophy of existence of Heidegger. In 1933, both Heidegger and Schmitt, who were in contact with each other at the time, joined the Nazi Party and pledged allegiance to the Hitler regime. Although the argument has been recently advanced that Schmitt's attitude toward the Weimar regime was ambiguous during the last years of its existence, the doctrine of political decisionism, coupled with his implacable hostility to parliamentary democracy, were hardly compatible with the fundamental principles of the Weimar Republic.

28. Ernst Cassirer, "The Myth of the State : Its Origin and Its Meaning, Third Part: The Myth of the Twentieth Century," *Nachgelassene Manuskripte und Texte*, vol. 9, *Zu Philosophie und Politik* (Hamburg, Germany: Meiner, 2008), 195.

# Is Progress a Category of Consolation?
## *Kant, Blumenberg, and the Politics of the Moderns*

MICHAËL FOESSEL

*Translation by Patrick Eldridge*

Blumenberg claims that "[t]he modern age was the first and only age that understood itself as an epoch and, in so doing, simultaneously created the other epochs."[1] If an epoch is inaugurated by an interruption (*epochè*), one thought to be irrevocable, then this term perfectly suits the perception that modernity has of itself: an historic event, marked by a rupture with tradition and the opening of a new era. More important than the concrete realization of this project is its novel ambition. This plays a key role in defining how one ought to interpret the themes of modernity. For a phenomenology of the history of meanings—as Blumenberg practices it—understanding modernity consists in placing concepts back into the horizon of their appearance. This assumes reason's self-affirmation, to which the historian does not naively adhere, but which he must consider in order to describe the physiognomy of the object under study. From this standpoint, the secularization thesis is incorrect, not because it relates modernity to its Christian past, but because it amounts to falling back into the natural attitude, which consists in explaining the new by reference to the old, thus suppressing the appearance of its novelty. However, "the modern age does not have recourse to what went before it [i.e., the explanatory concepts of theology], so much as it opposes [them] and takes a stand against the challenge [they pose]."[2]

Defined as an epoch, modernity often recurs to the category of progress to make its novelty manifest. Thus, we find ourselves confronted by a paradox, namely, a rupture that also simultaneously claims to be the announcement of a great, enduring historic accomplishment. It is precisely this paradox that engulfs secularization theory. In the punctuality of this progressivist announcement ("from now on, we live under the sign of the future"), how can we fail to see the transposition of the religious categories of creation (the past), revelation (the present), and redemption (the future) into human history? This model of transposition is present in theories that, from Hegel to Karl Löwith, via Schelling and, to a certain extent, Nietzsche, emphasize the debt that the philosophy of history owes to Christianity's view of the time of history.[3] Here, secularization is a transfer of meanings, as well as experiences, from the religious sphere to the profane. The suspicion of the grammar of modernity begins with this transfer; it is a grammar that claims autonomy but turns out to be dependent on a system of meaning the syntax of which it has not mastered.

It is not so much progress as progressivism—the great modern narrative—that comes to the fore in a discussion of modernity's legitimacy. How are we to understand the logic behind the elevation of progress to the status of modernity's quintessential category for understanding itself? It is possible that this logic is much less triumphal than the paradigm of secularization would lead us to believe. The concept of progress assumes that history is the product of human volition, but this attribution does not yet inspire any confidence in the future. That humanity makes history is not the gauge of its ethical or juridical value; indeed, a form of pessimism generally accompanies the insistence on God's absence. So we must first consider progress as a simple hypothesis, destined to save an historical temporality that no longer has a transcendent guarantor.

We can see the extreme caution that marks the theme of progress's entrance into Enlightenment philosophy in a passage from Kant's *The Idea of a Universal History from a Cosmopolitan Point of View*, which will serve as a guiding thread for this study.[4] After having noted the "strange" and even the seemingly "absurd" character of the project of composing a history according to an "idea of a path that the world ought to follow," an ideal history that has all the markings of a "novel," Kant claims that it is nevertheless possible to discover

> a guiding thread that can serve not only to clarify the thoroughly confused play of human affairs, or to aid in the political art of prophesying future changes [...]. It will also clear the way for (what, without presupposing a plan of nature, one cannot reasonably hope for) a comforting view [*eine tröstende Aussicht in die*

*Zukunft*], one in which we represent from afar how the human species finally works its way up to that state where all the seeds nature has planted in it can be developed fully and in which the species' vocation here on earth can be fulfilled.[5]

To begin, we will hold onto only one aspect of this very dense text: Kant presents the hypothesis of progress—understood here as a heuristic principle that enables one to approach the history of the human species as the historical development of the law—as a consoling thought. We are far removed from the triumphal progressivism that we often attribute to Enlightenment thinkers, and we are even further removed from the assimilation of the philosophy of history to a theodicy, since progress is meant to console us over the future (and not the past or the present). One could call this prudence properly Kantian. It focuses exclusively on the juridical (and not the moral) character of progress, which can justifiably be expected from the conflict between the species' tendencies. Further, this modesty is linked to the reflective judgment's epistemological status, which Kant associates with the cosmopolitan perspective on history: everything happens *as if* the advent of a society universally ruled by law constitutes the horizon of the human species' attempts to preserve itself.

We will nevertheless suppose that there is no reason to restrict the link between historical progress and consolation solely to Kantian philosophy, precisely because one can interpret the modern age as the age of consolation.[6] Born from the deterioration of old normative orders, modernity is saturated with the need to find a supplement for the metaphysical and religious paradigms that enabled us to grasp history as a whole. There is no consolation without desolation, namely, without the loss of a certitude that gives an integral meaning to experience. It is necessary then to ask, what desolation constitutes the consoling hypothesis of juridical progress and what loss solicits this response?

## THE IMPOSSIBLE SECULARIZATION OF ESCHATOLOGY

In *Meaning in History*, Karl Löwith systematically develops the theory that the modern concept of progress is the result of secularization.[7] Löwith introduces the secularization thesis in the context of a polemical goal; it consists in demonstrating the harmful effects of the Christian separation of nature and freedom (along with the linear conception of time implicit in it) by juxtaposing it with the ancient worldview (which is founded on a cyclical conception of time). Unlike Stoicism and its doctrine of the eternal return, a rupture with nature marks Christianity, and modern philosophies would be nothing other than the inevitable consequence of this. From this perspective, the "theological implications of the philosophy of history" are legible in Hegel, Marx, Proudhon, or Auguste Comte's philosophies of history. The concept of historical progress would be the distant heir of the theology of history, which is at work in philosophical Christianity, present in a line that can be traced from Augustine's *City of God* to Bossuet's sermons. Löwith speaks of "*Verweltlichung*" ("mundanization") to designate this process of immanentizing theological principles concerning the completion of time and of justice, that is, their conclusion and their achievement. The philosophy of history, considered as the attempt to "realize the kingdom of heaven in world history," would be a covert theodicy, and this especially includes its most rationalist formulations.

What objections does Blumenberg address to this type of interpretation? Chapter three of *The Legitimacy of the Modern Age*, titled "Progress Exposed as Fate," presents Löwith's book as the perfect example of what is invalid about the secularization thesis. The title of the chapter is already an indication of the kind of criticism it contains: talk of "fate" obscures what this theme owes to the valorization of human liberty. Löwith would then be a dialectical thinker in spite of himself, and even the defender of a negative dialectic. According to Löwith, the modern concept of emancipation imperceptibly slides into the category of destiny, namely, the destiny of a humanity held captive by theological pre-decisions concerning the nature of time. Blumenberg's use of the theme of unconcealment is almost certainly borrowed from Heidegger. It functions as a rallying point for all of those antimodern attitudes found in philosophies that champion the dawn of thinking in Greece (*aletheia*), against its corruption in modernity.

Beyond their diverging attitudes toward modernity, Blumenberg's critique strikes at the heart of Löwith's argument, namely, the possibility of translating eschatological schemes into the framework of intraworldly progress. Blumenberg, who continued to ponder apocalyptic doctrines, shows that Christian eschatology cannot form the basis of a conception of hope, since it is rooted in something beyond this world. The rapprochement of eschatology and progress ignores the fundamental differences in the conceptions of time at stake in the two notions. While the idea of progress is based on time as a factor in the enhancement of mankind's knowledge and power, religious eschatologies either hope for or fear the acceleration of time toward its end. As such, there is no possible eschatological hope for the future of *this* world: "when the time had come for the emergence of the idea of progress, it was more nearly an aggregate of terror and dread."⁸ Strictly speaking, it is impossible to "mundanize" eschatology, because it brings together fundamentally hostile attitudes toward the world, which place hope beyond the reach of all secular experience. The philosophy of history cannot take inspiration from an attitude that ruins its premise, that is, a belief in the normative powers of human time. According to Blumenberg, religious eschatologies reject cosmological interests, without which there is no possible philosophy of history.

If there is secularization (in the sense of a transfer of meaning to the immanent sphere), then it already happened in the transition from eschatology to the doctrine of divine providence. This transition took place in Christianity's reception of Stoic motifs, among which providence plays a leading role. This secularization is premodern and is due to the delay of the *parousia*, which forces the church to cordon off its cosmological beliefs that it held due to the imminent end of the world. The modern theme of progress bestows value on the world in a way completely unknown to monotheistic eschatologies. It is an important point in the difference between Blumenberg and the partisans of secularization. The latter emphasize the glorification of the future that the idea of progress entails—generally in order to condemn it. Progress, however, does not just involve the condemnation of the past in the name of the future; progress also involves elevating the present on behalf of the future that it announces. According to its complete formulation, "the idea of progress is [...] the continuous self-justification of the present, by means of the future that it gives itself, before the past, with which it compares itself."⁹

How to situate Kant in this analysis of the specificities in the concept of progress? While Löwith strangely says nothing about Kant in his genealogy of theories of history, Bultmann, on the other hand, does not hesitate to claim that "Kant's view of history is a moralistic secularizing of the Christian teleology of history and its eschatology."¹⁰ In support of this argument, one could cite, in addition to the references to providence peppering the texts on history, the passage from *The Idea of a Universal History* where, having already evoked the "hidden plan of nature," Kant concludes that "philosophy also has its chiliastic vision [millenarianism]."¹¹ But then how could one account for the passage that immediately follows, while staying within the secularization theory's interpretive framework: "one whose occurrence can be promoted by its idea [i.e., of millenarianism], though only from afar"? Do we not find something completely different from secularization here, that is, human liberty reclaiming what had been, up until now, illusorily attributed to God?

At any rate this is Blumenberg's thesis. In his review of Bultmann's book, he observes that

> Kant does the exact opposite of secularization when he believes he can show that specific theologumena are apt to be presented in philosophical arguments, since, for him, this means that those contents can only reach adequate expression in this way.[12]

According to Kant, critical reason allows us to translate a certain number of religious themes that predate it into an adequate lexicon. Thus, the expectation of the end of days, providence, and grace are all motifs that philosophy retroactively qualifies as metaphors, insofar as they had yet to receive adequate rational explanation.[13] In this sense, the Enlightenment, interpreted as the unveiling of reason to itself, is the moment when the religious symbols in use receive their authentic meaning. Far from secularization, with Kant (though already with the Lessing of *Education of the Human Race*) we are assisting in a correction of course. Religious expressions become symbolic approximations of what human reason, having reached maturity, learns to think through its own means.

### THE GENESIS OF THE IDEA OF PROGRESS

This critique of the secularization model would be incomplete without presenting an alternative genealogy of the idea of progress that lies at the heart of modern philosophies of history. Blumenberg is aware of this and he presents a different genesis of modern concepts, unlike the one presented in the secularization-transfer hypothesis. This counterproposal refers back to the historical method at work in *The Legitimacy of the Modern Age* and many of his other works. "Even when it writes its own history [philosophy] describes the appearance of its 'phenomena,' and there is no other way of 'preparing' them than this history itself."[14] The phenomena that philosophy studies are concepts, which not only assumes that they have a history, but above all that their conditions of appearance determine their meaning. Thus, studying the conditions under which the concept of progress emerged at the same time amounts to critically establishing its meaning.

What, then, of the theme of progress? *Instances* of progress have certainly "always occurred [...] as results of experience."[15] However, it is only at the beginning of the modern era that that philosophy projects progress, *singular*, on to the whole of history in order to describe its course. In this regard, the invention of certain technological instruments has played a decisive role: with the telescope we have opened an unlimited horizon of discovery, which can never close again. Since Galileo space has become an immense field of exploration for the mathematical knowledge of nature. From there, to believe that knowledge would meet no further limit than what space offers, is a step that the modern idea of progress could be expected to take.

Still, this idea rests on a conception of space and of time that is hardly comforting. The scientific discovery of the infinity of space, before permitting us a few consoling beliefs about the possibility of other habitable worlds, gave rise to more anxiety than hope. The Freudian thesis concerning the "narcissistic humiliation" that humanity suffered following the Copernican revolution is but one among many expressions of how the modern drive for science did not produce a particularly optimistic atmosphere.[16] If the ancient sage found a consolation for earthly life in contemplating the stars, it is because the heavenly vault was supposed to reflect the *finite* order of the world. Nature, as the cosmos in which each event and each individual destiny can be seen as necessary parts of the whole, provided the primary form of consolation. Next to this soothing conception of belonging, the infinity of the moderns is "more a predicate of indefiniteness than of fulfilling dignity, more an expression of disappointment than of presumption."[17] Although it can be mathematized, the moderns paid for the infinity of the universe by the loss of knowledge concerning the cosmic hierarchy, where each person could claim a choice place.

What holds true of space equally holds true of time, and we may guess what importance this has for the idea of progress. Before we reach any certitude regarding the final state toward which history necessarily tends, this idea necessarily entails the indeterminacy of the future. The linear and vectorial time of modern physics eludes the cyclical temporality in which premodern beliefs had placed the world. Of course, this time progress is open to human action. As we have already suggested, however, the belief that humanity makes history still does not inspire any hope in the future. Rather, at this level, we face the typically modern rift between individuals' desires to see their aspirations realized in their lifetimes, and the fact that this realization is incessantly deferred into the future.[18] Thus, we can see why Blumenberg suggests that the moderns began speaking of *infinite* progress as a result of the initially disappointed expectations that science opened to them. The need to postpone the satisfaction of a desire is all the more disappointing when nothing can guarantee that you will even be present at the moment of its accomplishment.

When applied to progress, infinity does not so much refer to people's appropriation of an attribute that, until now humanity reserved just for God, but on the contrary it means "a form of resignation."[19] The question of knowing whether we can bear something can only be seriously posed once it becomes possible to conceive that this something is endless. Far from any triumphal affirmation of the future's meaning, the idea of progress to infinity thus has the goal of making a history that has no fixed end humanly bearable.

The way that Kant brings the idea of progress and the modest-looking theme of consolation together is now more explicable. Remaining with Kant first, it is clear that he introduces the thesis of historical progress on the ruins of the metaphysical knowledge concerning the essence of time. One could show, following Lyotard, that "historical propositions" are caught in the antinomies of the series of human time, which echo the cosmological antinomies of the infinite temporality of the world.[20] The idea of progress to infinity in time rests on reason's inability to determine the world by purely conceptual means. This explains why the consoling perspective, offered by adopting a cosmopolitan point of view on history pertains to the future and not the past: the temporal series that the future opens remains untotalizable, *in specie*.

Friedrich Schlegel would later establish the link between the incompleteness of time and practical command in his Jena lectures, held precisely on the topic of transcendental philosophy.

> This proposition, that the world is still unfinished, is extremely important in every respect. If we think of the world as complete, then all our doings are nothing. But if we know that the world is unfinished, then no doubt our vocation is to cooperate in completing it.[21]

The world's imperfection becomes a metaphor for its political transformation, but only on the condition that human beings, in their transcendental freedom, are responsible for perfecting existence itself. On this topic we could cite a passage from *The Conflict of the Faculties*, where Kant associates the predictability of history with the identity between the subject and the agent of history: "But how is an a priori history possible? Answer: When the soothsayer himself causes and contrives the events that he proclaims in advance."[22] The progressivist hope that Kant articulates here not only concerns this world, but it rests on a typically modern axiom, according to which human beings cannot truly understand anything except for what has its origin in them. In this sense, the classic formulation of transcendental criticism, according to which we cannot find anything a priori–valid in nature other than what we ourselves have put there, also applies to universal history.

## MODERNITY AND CONSOLATION

For which loss and which desolation does the concept of progress console us? To answer this question, we should note how Hegel did not fail to notice how modestly Kant introduced the hypothesis of historical progress. The former, as we know, conceives of a secularization (*Verweltlichung*) of the spirit, which manifests itself in the progressive advent of figures of freedom in history. For Hegel, is the philosophy of history a simple matter of consolation? This would amount to approving of the finitude in modernity, even though Hegel's project is to precisely go beyond Enlightenment philosophy's finite perspective. This is why, after having recalled that the modern philosophy of history constitutes the "true theodicy" (i.e., the one that demonstrates God's immanence in the world), Hegel insists on the limits of consolation.

> Consolation is merely something received in compensation for a misfortune which ought never to have happened in the first place, and it belongs to the world of finite things. Philosophy, therefore, is not really a means of consolation. It is more than that, for it transfigures reality with all its apparent injustices and reconciles it with the rational; it shows that it is based upon the Idea itself, and that reason is fulfilled in it.[23]

This opposition between consolation (*Trost*) and reconciliation (*Versöhnung*) is crucial because it lays bare the ambition of Hegelian philosophy of history: not to produce a heart-warming narrative about the past, but to demonstrate the actual power of reason in time. Spirit is the true agent of history because it imposes itself on and is needed by *its other*, that is, nature and human passions. In this sense, the philosophy of history is much more than a consolation: far from being the complaint of victims, it uncovers the identity between the real and the rational. As Ricoeur has shown, Hegelian history opposes itself to narrative because it marks the abolition of any narrativity in speculative knowledge.[24] Reconciliation approaches historical reality from the standpoint of the idea that it manifests, while consolation is never anything but a narrative that organizes the past around a precarious meaning and orders the future around a possible schematization of the rational demands of the law. While reconciliation is the abolition of contingency, consolation is an interpretation of contingency, following the guiding thread of juridical progress.

What does this Hegelian critique of Kant reveal about the theme of progress? Although it is not clear whether Hegel is a thinker of progress (he prefers rather to speak of the development of the concept in time), it is, however, clear that he opposes the Kantian theme of progress *to infinity*. For Hegel this is the symbol of the bad infinity, which paradoxically approves of finitude by always pushing the moment of reconciliation further and further back. This critique brings out the theme of secularization again. This term is often understood to mean the transfer of a divine attribute to mundane reality. For instance, this holds true of attributing "omnipotence" to a sovereign state, or, quite rightly, attributing infinity to progress. However, Blumenberg warns against the secularizing interpretation of this "migration of concepts": when Hobbes establishes the omnipotence of the state, he is not deifying it because the very meaning of the attribute changes by virtue of its migration. This is why even the Leviathan can be nothing more than a mortal God.

What then of history's progress to infinity? How does it offer a consoling perspective on the future? The elevation of the concept of progress to infinity was most certainly the result of the first disappointments that accompanied the desire for the accomplishments of reason to be realized within the individual's own lifetime. Kant transferred the hope for fulfillment from the individual to the species and to the open continuum of the future, having deemed it no longer possible to be attained in the span of one lifetime. As Blumenberg once again observes, the idea of progress must confront "the necessary disappointment of each individual in the context of history, doing work in his particular situation for a future whose enjoyment he cannot inherit."[25] Progress to infinity is consoling to the extent that it makes history bearable, to the extent that its end is not certain but only regulative. In *Science as Vocation*, Max Weber interprets infinite progress as regulative for the practice of science along the same lines: "We cannot work without hoping that others will advance further than we have. In principle, this progress goes on ad infinitum."[26] As such, this idea of progress does not necessarily entail any sort of religious belief in an absolute teleology. Thus, historical experience takes place in the fissure maintained between the realm of experience and the horizon of expectation.

This link between progress and consolation is worth recalling at a time when—partially for good reasons—we are abandoning progressivist beliefs. What lesson can we draw from the fact that, in modernity, progress and the immortality of the soul are introduced as *categories of consolation*? The disorder of the state of nature, unsocial sociability, and the violence of history demonstrate that the real can no longer be taken as an object of admiration. Thus, what Max Weber called the "disenchantment of the world" is very much a part of the Modern Age's heritage. Yet this age has attempted to produce the cure for the evil that it witnesses. With Kant, the postulates of the immortality of the soul or the indefinite progress of the human species have the precise goal of showing what is possible in spite of this chaos. We can of course interpret these themes as theological relics within modernity. This sort of interpretation, however, forgets that the idea of progress is not meant to convince us that the world should be abolished, but embraced. It is not the end of the world that justifies the means of progress, but rather the consoling fact that there are accessible ends *in* the world.

NOTES

1. Hans Blumenberg, *The Legitimacy of the Modern Age*, trans. Robert M. Wallace (Cambridge, MA: MIT Press, 1999), 116.
2. Ibid., 75.
3. Cf. Robert M. Wallace, "Progress, Secularization and Modernity: The Löwith-Blumenberg Debate," in *New German Critique* 22 (1981): 1, 63–79; Jean-Claude Monod, *La Querelle de la Sécularisation: de Hegel à Blumenberg* (Paris: Vrin, 2002).
4. For another comparative reading of Kant and Blumenberg cf.: Vida Pavesich, "The Anthropology of Hope and the Philosophy of History: Rethinking Kant's Third and Fourth Questions with Blumenberg and McCarthy," *Thesis Eleven* 104 (2011): 1, 20–39.
5. Immanuel Kant, "Idea for a Universal History with a Cosmopolitan Intent" in *Perpetual Peace and Other Essays*, ed. Ted Humphrey (Indianapolis, IN and Cambridge, MA: Hackett, 1983), 39 [AA VIII, 30].
6. This thesis is developed at length in: Michaël Fœssel, *Le Temps de la consolation*, (Paris: Seuil, 2015).
7. Karl Löwith, *Meaning in History. The Theological Implications of the Philosophy of History* (Chicago, IL: University of Chicago, 1949).
8. Blumenberg, *Legitimacy*, 31.
9. Ibid., 32.
10. Rudolf Bultmann, *History and Eschatology* (Edinburgh, UK: Edinburgh University Press, 1975), 67.
11. Kant, "Idea for a Universal History," 36 [AA VIII, 27].
12. Hans Blumenberg, "Rudolf Bultmann, *Geschichte und Eschatologie*," *Gnomon* 31, no. 2 (1959): 165 (my translation—*Tr.*).

13. On this topic, cf. Hans Blumenberg, "Kant und die Frage nach dem gnädigen Gott," *Studium Generale* 7 (1954): 554–70.

14. Hans Blumenberg, *L'Imitation de la nature*, trans. Isabelle Kalinowski and Marc de Launay (Paris: Hermann, 2010), 34–35 (my translation—*Tr.*).

15. Blumenberg, *Legitimacy*, 30.

16. Cf. Sigmund Freud, "A Difficulty in the Path of Psychoanalysis," in *Standard Edition of the Complete Psychological Works of Sigmund Freud*, vol. XVII, ed. James Strachey (London: Hogarth, 1955), 135–44.

17. Blumenberg, *Legitimacy*, 85.

18. Blumenberg later conceptualizes this divergence between our limited lifetime and our aspirations that go beyond it by distinguishing between lifetime (*Lebenszeit*) and world-time (*Weltzeit*): Hans Blumenberg, *Lebenszeit und Weltzeit* (Frankfurt am Main, Germany: Suhrkamp, 1986). For other reflections on human finitude and consolation in Blumenberg cf.: Michael Moxter, "Trost," in *Blumenberg Lesen: Ein Glossar*, eds. Robert Buch and Daniel Weidner (Berlin: Suhrkamp, 2014), 337–49; Brad Tabas, "Blumenberg, Anthropology, Politics," *Telos* 158 (2012): 2, 147; Felix Heidenreich, *Mensch und Moderne bei Blumenberg* (Berlin, Germany: Wilhelm Fink, 2005).

19. Blumenberg, *Legitimacy*, 35.

20. Cf. Jean-François Lyotard, *Enthusiasm. The Kantian Critique of History*, trans. Georges van den Abbeele (Stanford, CA: Stanford University Press, 2009).

21. Friedrich Schlegel, *Neue philosophische Schriften*, ed. Josef Körner (Frankfurt: Schulte-Bulmke, 1935), 155–56 (cited in Blumenberg, *Legitimacy*, 215).

22. Immanuel Kant, *Der Streit der Fakultäten*, II, 2 (cited in Blumenberg, *Legitimacy*, 34).

23. Georg Wilhelm Friedrich Hegel, *Lectures on the Philosophy of World History. Introduction: Reason in History*, trans. H. B. Nisbet (London, New York, and Melbourne, AU: Cambridge University Press, 1975), 67.

24. Cf. Paul Ricoeur, *Time and Narrative*, trans. Kathleen Blamey and David Pellauer (Chicago, IL and London: University of Chicago Press, 1988), 193–206.

25. Hans Blumenberg, *Legitimacy*, 35.

26. Max Weber, "Science as Vocation," in *Essays in Sociology*, eds. and trans. H. H. Gerth and C. Wright Mills (New York: Routledge, 2009), 138.

# Hannah Arendt, Secularization Theory, and the Politics of Secularism

SAMUEL MOYN

In spite of the current debate about the theory of secularization and the politics of secularism across the world, Hannah Arendt has not generally been understood as a proponent of either. But her most prominent study of the liberatory possibilities that modern politics might allow, *On Revolution*, is also an account of the struggle against a civilization grounded on religious premises in favor of one beyond their claims. It would not be too much to say that Arendt placed secularization at the very center of her analysis of the revolutionary phenomenon and secularism at the core of her political hopes. Put simply, Arendt thought that what was at stake in modernity was leaving religion behind, at least as the foundation of public coexistence; and conversely, when modernity took its most politically defective forms, it was (among other reasons) because it had failed to properly make its necessary break with the religious civilization that preceded it.[1]

In what follows, besides reconstructing the fundamentals of Arendt's case, I will also try to show that it is usefully interpreted as a kind of response to and critique of Carl Schmitt's doctrine of "political theology," as outlined in a famous 1922 book of that name. Some reasons to stress a relationship between these two major figures have been noticed before: Arendt and Schmitt were central to the revival of interest in the political as such in recent decades, both insisted on its autonomy from and irreducibility to other domains of existence, and both were deeply concerned with the founding of polities and constitutional ordering.[2] But their common interest in modernization as some sort of secularization (legitimate or not) deserves to be stressed too. Now it is true that, in spite of overwhelming circumstantial evidence, there is no direct proof that Arendt herself saw *On Revolution* as a response to Schmitt's thesis about the continuation of religion in political guise. (There is direct evidence that Arendt saw it as an intervention in a twentieth-century debate, largely Germanic, that Schmitt sparked.) But even if the case for "hidden dialogue" is rejected, there is still the heuristic use of placing the views of these two major figures in the same frame.

First, it emphasizes how far Arendt willingly assented to the descriptive claim, most familiar from Schmitt's brief but powerful presentation, that modern politics have often covertly depended on the continuation of religious premises or a religious foundation. If *On Revolution* was a response to Schmitt, it is one that incorporated the position she wanted it to overcome. Alongside the now familiar Grecophile and modernist Arendts, there was also a "medievalist" Arendt who attributed political or quasi-political functions to the Christian Church, ones that alone explain the persistence of some of the very religious figures of thought in the modern political imaginary that Schmitt had stressed in his time. This persistence could occur, the "medievalist" Arendt argued, because it was both difficult and dangerous for revolutionary modernists to substitute for those political functions that the medieval church had executed so well. The essentially *substitutional* quandary of revolution is one that, Arendt thought, could make progress and regress interpenetrate, as old religious figures of thought were not simply held over inadvertently but actively called back into service in the moment of revolutionary advance.

But second, the comparison throws into relief how far Arendt hoped to break with any normative conclusion that a full secularization of political life is an impossible goal. She could do so because of a shift in model of secularization: if she thought she needed to account for what Schmitt implied only the hypothesis of the persistence *of religion* could explain, she conceded only that the very difficulty of transcending religion made its appeal nearly irresistible precisely at the moment of possible farewell. Arendt is even willing to grant that religion persists even in its absence, since she clearly thought that it is the novel difficulty of substituting for a prior religious basis for political authority that makes the modern situation fundamentally different from the classical past she so admired—and makes the latter's exact resumption impossible. Even so, not only are modern secular politics possible for Arendt, but the revolutionary Americans—whom Schmitt had praised in *Political Theology* for recognizing the template in God's sovereignty for their own popular rule—illustrated how to achieve it. Nevertheless, there is respect for Schmitt even at the heart of Arendt's normative divergence from him. The crux of Arendt's study of political revolution is that, even if it is not a requirement, political theology is a risk. Revolution in Arendt's account is often a struggle against religion in which the latter wins. Yet she did not think it always had to.

THE PROBLEM OF AN ABSOLUTE

The baseline for appreciating the challenge of finding a secular basis for modern politics, as Arendt saw it, is a sense of the political or quasi-political functions that Christianity played in European civilization. Arendt is renowned for arguing in *The Human Condition* that "the victory of the Christian faith in the ancient world ... could not but be disastrous for the esteem and the dignity of politics."[3] But she qualifies or upends this thesis in *On Revolution* with a depiction of religion as playing a collective function that modern politics will have to inherit. Her treatment of the history of Christianity in the book, as well as in her related essay on authority, is frustratingly sketchy. But several dimensions of it are clear.

Arendt gives religion (at least Catholic Christianity of the medieval period) an *institutional* and *functional* interpretation. Far from simply extinguishing Roman politics, she argued, "Rome's political and spiritual heritage passed to the Christian Church."[4] As she stated elsewhere, the Church was a "body politic," indeed an "authentically authoritarian institution," to be typologically distinguished from both tyranny and totalitarianism.[5] Of course, Christianity is based on otherworldly claims, but *as a church* its decisive effect is to establish the authoritative ordering that is at the heart of Arendt's vision of politics, discharging burdens that modern and revolutionary politics will have to assume in their time. There is identifiable intellectual content to such otherworldly claims—Arendt insisted surprisingly often over the years on the threat of eternal damnation as Christianity's chief political doctrine—but their function is to provide an institutionally grounded warrant for political coexistence.[6] So the key to interpreting this dimension of Arendt's thought is balancing her critique of Christian antipolitics with her core view that such antipolitics could and did have political or quasi-political *effects*.

Arendt's doctrine of "authority" in *On Revolution* is essentially a statement of an enduring requirement for political ordering, identifying the ultimate basis of collective cohesion (at least after the Greeks, who avoided its claims). But she used other terms too. Her description of the core of religion's function is that it provides a "sanction" for human coexistence that modernity will not be able to do without. Like *authority*, the term *sanction* is repeatedly used by Arendt in this connection, probably in both its positive sense of providing a warrant for community as well as in its negative sense of a threat of adverse consequences for members who might stray. But the most unusual phrase Arendt chose to use in *On Revolution* to describe this core doctrine of the book is the resonant but somewhat enigmatic one of "the absolute." Secularization is precisely the attempt, not to escape from the authority and the sanction that "the absolute" provides to politics, but to find nonreligious versions of them.[7] And this attempt comes to a head in revolution, and in fact may define that phenomenon's deepest agenda as a search not just for liberty but also for secularity.

For a thinker generally believed to be uninterested in or opposed to them, Arendt thus attributes an extraordinary efficacy to religion in general and Christianity in particular in providing an "absolute" in a way that irreligious politics cannot easily rival. "The enormous significance for the political realm of the lost sanction of religion," Arendt writes in one important passage,

> is commonly neglected in the discussion of modern secularization, because the rise of the secular realm ... seems so obviously to have taken place at the expense of religion ... Yet, as a matter of fact, this separation cut both ways, and just as one speaks of an emancipation of the secular from the religious, one may, and perhaps with even more right, speak of an emancipation of religion from the demands and burdens of the secular ... [P]olitics and the state needed the sanction of religion even more urgently than religion and the churches had ever needed the support of the princes.[8]

"With even more right" and "even more urgently": one may want to interpret Arendt as a follower of Friedrich Nietzsche and Martin Heidegger in her demand for a self-contained and postmetaphysical politics that finally and truly deserves the name, but one cannot fail to register her insistence that even such politics must have continuing recourse to an absolute of the kind that metaphysics in the form of religion provided far more plausibly and efficaciously than revolution could easily succeed in doing.[9] According to Arendt, moderns tried to break with the religion of the past, but they could not leave behind the hardship of the demands and burdens it had so long borne. Of course, as the citation implies, those demands and burden were always "secular" inasmuch as their effects were in this world—but medieval civilization with its otherworldly notions and devices discharged them with no trouble. It is as if Arendt thought it was easier for religion to fulfill its necessary secular functions than a fully secularist regime could by itself.

BOUND TO APPEAR IN REVOLUTION

Arendt stressed Christianity quite specifically as the antecedent to Western modernity. Though it is not said so directly in *On Revolution*, Arendt states forthrightly elsewhere that "the separation of the public and religious spheres of life which we call secularism did not simply sever politics from religion in general but very specifically from the Christian creed."[10] This approach places her in (and may have originated as) a conversation with Carl Schmitt, who following the reactionary tradition insisted on a necessarily religious grounding to society. Arendt's "response" to Schmitt would then take the form of a critique of the premises that allows concession on the details. For Arendt, it is not religion but the more basic requirement that religion meets that necessarily will continue into modernity. The question is whether the persistence of this requirement (which she concedes at the outset) must also entail the persistence of religion. "The long alliance between religion and authority," she put it at her clearest, "does not necessarily prove that the concept of authority is itself of a religious nature."[11] If the similarity in models allowed her to concede Schmitt's findings of continuity, the difference between them also exposed the hypothetical possibility of a secular politics. And if Arendt is in dialogue and contest with Schmitt, it is no surprise that the clash between their positions will have to emerge on the ground where the latter found the religious template for modern politics still visible—political revolution, especially the American one.

Revolution is interesting to Arendt in large part because the substitutional dilemma comes to a head in it. Where Schmitt had alluded to revolution as the founding by a sovereign people on the model of God's miraculous intervention in history, for Arendt it is the moment when secularization is at stake. She began with a treatment of European revolutions as successors of absolutism. (Surprisingly and disappointingly, the Protestant Reformation is simply absent from her secularization theory.) Absolutism, Arendt says, might seem like "the first and most conspicuous consequence of what we call secularization," playing an essential task in freeing politics from religion. Rather than presenting absolutism as depending on a political theology of divine right, Arendt thought that absolutism represented a historical attempt to wrest authority from the church in the service of secular politics. "Absolute monarchy," she writes, "has been responsible ... for the rise of the secular realm with a dignity and a splendor of its own."[12]

Yet on closer inspection, Arendt continues, absolutism accomplished nothing of the sort. Its work, prior to revolution, is in retrospect simply dilatory and wholly negative, illustrating theoretically that some substitution for religion was necessary and postponing for revolutions the exclusive role of finding one. "Secularization, the emancipation of the secular realm from the tutelage of the Church, inevitably posed the problem of how to found and constitute a new authority," she writes. "Theoretically speaking, it is as though absolutism were attempting to solve this problem of authority without having recourse to the revolutionary means." In *On Revolution*, Arendt probably used the concept of "the absolute" as shorthand for a difficulty that all modern polities face, because for her it was absolutism that pioneered the experiment of discovering a secular proxy for religion.[13]

But it failed, and its failure haunts all revolutions. One might have guessed otherwise, she acknowledges. After all, the European revolutions characteristically took over after absolutist rule and might have led one to think that it is *only* revolutions following upon such regimes (rather than all revolutions by definition) that might need and therefore seek some authoritative grounding. One might have argued that revolution need not have involved the simple replacement of one secular authority (king) with another (people), but done away with the need for authority altogether. But Arendt insisted that study of the American Revolution, though it occurred in the isolated Eden of a new continent, showed that all revolutions are forced to search for some authoritative ground, of the kind absolutism tried and failed to provide. The Americans, in Arendt's words, were for all their other exceptionalisms, "not spared the most troublesome of all problems in revolutionary government, the problem of an absolute." Indeed, she says, "That the problem of an absolute is bound to appear in a revolution, that it is inherent in the revolutionary event itself, we might never have known without the American Revolution."[14] This is because absolutism itself was simply a first try and specific attempt at solving a general problem of displacing religion.

It is an interesting implication of Arendt's secularization theory that not only do revolutions of necessity face the problem of the absolute; conversely, only revolutions truly face it. Not simply absolutism, but other possible solutions (she mentions the romance of the common law in ancient constitutionalist ideology) must also fail, and for the same reasons.[15] "[I]f it is true that the revolutions did not 'invent' the perplexities of a secular political realm," she concludes summarily, "it is a fact that with their arrival, . . . former 'solutions' . . . stood now revealed as facile expedients and subterfuges." The implication is that *revolutions are the only possible successors of religion*. Absolutism emerges as an unstable and unworkable halfway house between religion and modernity, an attempt (failed but spectacular) to accomplish what revolution will try to accomplish without the trouble of revolution itself. Of course, Arendt sometimes used the term *secularization* to refer to a lengthy historical process that might involve a multitude of events and factors. But at other times she recognizes that the terms of her account meant that secularization and revolution are not separate (let alone sequential) processes. Rather, they fully coincide and completely define one another. Put differently, Arendt does not think that secularization simply prepares for revolution or that revolution outlives the era of secularization as a permanent postreligious political possibility. Instead, secularization is only possible *as* revolution; conversely, the signature modern event of politics is available only insofar as it substitutes for religion. This surprising implication of Arendt's conceptualization of the secularizing move is explicitly drawn early in the work: "[W]hat we call revolution is *precisely that transitory phase* which brings about the birth of a new, secular realm."[16] Revolution equals secularization and vice versa.

THE PARADOXICAL FACT

Since religion disposed of a quandary with no immediately obvious solution *except* religion, then the problem of "the absolute" constantly made what Schmitt called political theology a temptation. This was the reason, Arendt noted in drawing the essential inference, that revolutionaries aiming at a secular politics so often turned back to the past in their very advance—why, in Schmitt's terms, they crafted political theologies pervaded by naked or ersatz religion. Arendt's work in identifying a revolutionary dynamic of religious entanglement is, in other words, the heart of her putative response to Schmitt's theory.

The core argument is that the difficulty of substitution led revolutionaries, at the last minute, to foreswear the secularity they sought. It was, Arendt insisted, "[t]he enormous difficulties which especially the loss of religious sanction held in store for the establishment of a new authority [and] the perplexities which caused so many of the men of the revolutions to fall back upon or at least to invoke beliefs which they had discarded prior to the revolutions."[17] Similarly, in perhaps the crucial passage, she argued that "in theory and in practice, we can hardly avoid the paradoxical fact that it was precisely the revolutions, their crisis and their emergency, which drove the very 'enlightened' men of the eighteenth century to plead for some religious sanction at the very moment when they were about to emancipate the secular realm fully from the influence of the churches and to separate politics and religion once and for all."[18] In Arendt's thought, therefore, revolutions may be synonymous with secularization; but they also are the moments when it is likeliest to be derailed.

This revolutionary dynamic powerfully affected both the American and French Revolution at the heart of Arendt's comparative study, albeit in starkly different ways. But it is worth noting before turning to that comparison that Arendt's emphasis on the profound challenge that displacing religion presented for moderns could even lead her—beyond her emphasis on revolutionary difficulties—to sympathize with doubts that modern secularization was worth trying. In this regard, Arendt, whose actual references to Schmitt nearly always singled out his Nazi politics for discussion, may have her own additional reason to follow him in seeing the persistence of religion as a live option precisely at the moment of apparent modernization.[19]

In a dramatic passage, Arendt reported that there were "enormous risks inherent in the secular realm of human affairs" that made recourse to religion not simply tempting at a moment of difficulty but also morally intelligible in view of what could well follow. It is as if, in Arendt's rendition, the American Founders were only partly driven by the sheer hardship of their tasks to revive religion, because they also intelligently chose it to stave off the worst potential consequences of their enterprise. "We, who had ample opportunity to watch political crime on an unprecedented scale, committed by people who had liberated themselves from all beliefs in 'future states' and had lost the age-old fear of an 'avenging God,' are in no position, it seems, to quarrel with the political wisdom of the founders," Arendt commented.

> It was political wisdom and not religious conviction that made John Adams write the following strangely prophetic words: "Is there a possibility that the government of nations will fall into the hands of men who teach the most disconsolate of all creeds, that men are but fire flies, and this *all* is without a father? Is this the way to make man as man an object of respect? Or is it to make murder itself as indifferent as shooting plover, and the extermination of the Rohilla nation as innocent as the swallowing of mites on a morsel of cheese?"[20]

The destruction of the Jews by the Nazi regime (with which Schmitt collaborated) could make the persistence of the religious into the secular not so much a matter of necessary continuity or craven obfuscation as a matter of wise foresight before the threat of secular catastrophe. The reasons for the complex interrelation of progressive secularization and regressive theology in the revolutionary crucible were not just "metaphysical." They were moral, too.

TO FALL BACK ON OR AT LEAST TO INVOKE

Like Schmitt, Arendt is tempted to see more naked political theologies in America, whereas Europe chose more covert versions. And the most obvious holdover for Americans is divinely inspired natural law and, as a corollary, rights talk. One might say that where the European revolutions were secular on their face but religious at their core, for Arendt the American Revolution was religious on its face even if secular at its core. In spite of this difference, it is easy to read Arendt's depiction of American rights talk as a kind of exemplification of Schmitt's thesis, even in the new world that (on Arendt's more ultimate account) came close to a true secular founding.

Already in *The Origins of Totalitarianism*, Arendt had shown that she thought about rights precisely in the context of a secularizing transition. Her account in *On Revolution* candidly acknowledges the role that religious appeals played in the discourse of the American founding, as if she were willing to concede Schmitt's presentation of America as honestly advertising its politics as divine in origin. In the earlier book, she suggested that the modern attempt to state moral norms independent of religious metaphysics raised an implication of which partisans of rights were "only half aware." "The proclamation of [such] rights," Arendt observed, "was also meant to be a much-needed protection in the new era where individuals were no longer secure in the estates to which they were born or sure of their equality before God as Christians. In other words, in the new secularized and emancipated society, men were no longer sure of these social and human rights which until then had been outside the political order and guaranteed not by government and constitution, but by social, spiritual, and religious forces."[21] Already there, then, Arendt thought about rights as a secularizing attempt to make up for a function previously fulfilled by religious civilization. By *On Revolution*, Arendt saw rights talk as the major means by which Americans, having inherited the problem of the absolute from religion, more or less admitted that only some concession to religion can solve it. But here she offered a further argument about why such persistence was necessary and how it showed up in events.

Maximilien Robespierre's cult of the supreme being seemed much less comical, she wrote, when one kept in mind that the Americans were just as open about "the need for a divine principle, for some transcendent sanction in the political realm." The reason for this need, Arendt contends, is that America like Europe inherited from Christianity not just a general religious background but also a transformation in the concept of lawfulness that made law's authority dependent on its source: monotheism utterly transformed the notion of lawfulness in between classical and modern times and made a command model inescapable. Positivistic theories of law—which Arendt says actually cover natural law theories that are unfailingly rooted in some divine source even in the most deistic articulations—are open or covertly religious to the core. The impossibility of thinking of law except by positing some suprahuman source, however antediluvian or covert, made it almost inescapable that religion persist. This mutation provided another reason for interpreting America, too, in the backwash of the "long centuries when no secular realm existed in the Occident that was not ultimately rooted in the sanction given to it by the Church, and when therefore secular laws were understood as the mundane expression of a divinely ordained law." The genealogical entanglement of lawfulness itself in religion meant that even the American attempt to found a new order had "to put the law above man" (in Jean-Jacques Rousseau's words) for its derivative laws to be authoritative; Rousseau's conclusion that *il faudrait des dieux*—one would seem to need gods—for law to be legitimate applied with full force to the American scene.[22]

Arendt was therefore not surprised to find that, even when they did not explicitly refer to the divine origin of their proclaimed absolutes, American appeals to inalienable rights as a constraining higher law remained theological or cryptotheological. "[T]here was no avoiding the problem of the absolute—even though none of the country's institutions and constituted bodies could be traced back to the factual development of absolutism—because it proved to be inherent in the traditional concept of law," she put it. "If the essence of secular law was a command, then a divinity, not nature but nature's God, not reason but divinely informed reason, was needed to bestow validity on it." It is true that in Arendt's final view rights were merely a necessary rhetoric masking what was truly novel about the American founding. After all, Arendt also clearly thought that their nakedly or covertly religious origin made "the proclamation of human rights or the guarantee of civil rights" simply unviable as "the aim or content of revolution." Yet they surely persisted as rhetorical necessity—what the founders needed to "plead" at the very acme of their secular ambitions.[23] Rights talk is the specifically American form of political theology.

PLEADING FOR SOME RELIGIOUS SANCTION

Alas, European revolutions involved far more profound and dangerous political theology than the supposedly merely "invoked" rights of the American scene. And in fact, Arendt's depiction of European political theologies is much less original and may well have been simply read off Schmitt's earlier account, insofar as she saw European revolutions as reassigning to the people, after the stopgap intermediation of absolutism, god's sovereign will. If her account of American political theology of rights is more original, and if she wanted to exempt America from Schmitt's exemplification of political theology in the shift from *vox dei* to *vox populi*, it was only to assign that very exemplification to European revolutions. Of course, Arendt's dissatisfaction with the concept of sovereignty is well-established and usefully studied in different sectors of the literature. Yet it bears insisting that the concept's religious origins and not just its normative confusions or practical effects were what troubled her.

In *On Revolution*, Arendt's genealogical suggestions of this sort are simply pervasive, from her tracing of the word sovereignty back through Jean Bodin to the notion of divine majesty, through her analysis of absolutist experiment as one that made the Word flesh, to her depiction of a French Revolution in which God's will is merely transformed into that of people and nation. And she happily used Schmitt's rhetoric of obfuscation or disguise to explain the putatively new forms that the absolute took while remaining derivative of its original theological model, with simple "deification of the people" the sad result. In particular, her focus on sovereign will as the key site of continuity between Christianity and modernity is an exact replica of Schmitt's earlier claims. Not surprisingly, it is this material that provides the firmest textual or historical link between Arendt and Schmitt on these matters, since in a note to one of her essays she explicitly praised Schmitt for being "the most able defender of the notion of sovereignty" who "recognizes clearly that the root of sovereignty is the will."[24] In *On Revolution*, she engaged the Schmitt-inflected thesis of Ernst Kantorowicz that "[w]hen finally the Nation stepped into the pontifical shoes of the Prince, the modern *absolute state*, even without a Prince, was enabled to make claims like a Church." Given what Arendt took to be the singular isolation of the American version of political theology compared to the triumphant and eventually globalized rival pattern of European sovereignty, one might go so far as to say that Arendt implicitly gave Schmitt credit for discerning a connection that established the model for modern history: "[T]oday it is no longer of great relevance," she wrote, "whether the new absolute to be put into the place of the absolute sovereign was Sieyès's nation from the beginnings of the French Revolution or whether it became with Robespierre, after four years of revolutionary history, the revolution itself. For what eventually set the world on fire was precisely a combination of these two."[25]

Arguably, therefore, *On Revolution* is among other things a distinctive if neglected alternative account of what Raymond Aron and Eric Voegelin variously called "secular religion" or "political religion"—terms they introduced in the late 1930s to characterize and to explain totalitarianism and which in the last decade or so have made impressive inroads in the attempt to understand various historical regimes of the twentieth century.[26] If Arendt rejected and avoided theses terms when she encountered them in Cold War debates, it is because she insisted—unlike the original advocates of the label and their contemporary descendants—that such secular commitments as atheism and secular movements as communism were not simply religions that dared not speak their name (in Voegelin's view, for instance, they were previously suppressed heresies). For Arendt, the current theories of "political religion," ranging their objects amongst historical faiths as if they were simple additions, had failed to develop a theory of their significance as *the outcome of a dynamic* she identified. Their secularism might seem like simple camouflage, but only the modern agenda of substituting for religion could make sense of whatever theistic character there may have been to totalitarian ideologies and regimes.[27]

IN PRINCIPLE INDEPENDENT OF
RELIGIOUS SANCTION

Yet if Arendt went so far with Schmitt to document the political theologies of the moderns, it seems to have been with the ultimate intent of denying the necessity and thus the outcome of his nostalgic analysis. In spite of her view of rights, it is of the essence, in reviewing her unorthodox reinterpretation of the American colonies and the revolution they spawned, to emphasize the absolute priority she gave to vindicating its achievement as transcending theological or cryptotheological continuity. Conceptually, she could do so because of her claim that "the absolute" came before religion, and could explain both its force in its time and its supersession in the end: "The long alliance between religion and authority," to repeat the clearest formulation, "does not necessarily prove that the concept of authority is itself of a religious nature."[28] Nevertheless, even here, Arendt wanted to take Schmitt's allegation seriously. It seems that she knew she was herself coming close enough to articulating a political theology that she wanted to defend in advance against the possible charge that she failed to see it.

It is well-known that Arendt located the essence of the American achievement in settler covenants and "mutual promises." From the shipboard compact of the Mayflower colonists to the Fundamental Orders of Connecticut to the Declaration of Independence, Americans created a political realm of nonsovereign freedom and mutual equality. In this way the earliest Americans stumbled into a practice (never theorized) of action in concert, bringing them out of solitude into common worldliness, that no other modern polity discovered. When the American Revolution came, it simply continued this inchoate tradition, the conflict with the mother country leading to explicit clarification of the prior basis of politics on new shores. "[I]t was as though the Revolution liberated the power of covenant and constitution-making as it had shown itself in the earliest days of colonization," Arendt proposed. In saying so, she had undoubtedly been inspired by Perry Miller's major investigations of New England covenants; but she leaned most heavily on a then-recent article by Merrill Jensen suggesting that it was these covenants that informed the American belief that simple agreement to join together for common ends created valid government, a belief rooted in practice that underwrote the Declaration of Independence—if not its peripheral and dispensable natural rights language then its mutual pledge of Americans to one another in a common cause.[29]

Yet, one might immediately think, the notion of the covenant is one of the hoariest theological concepts there is. Originally introduced to describe God's compact (*b'rit*) with Noah after the flood, the heart of his relationship with Israel from Abraham through Moses, and renewed by Jesus (on Paul's interpretation at any rate), the covenant in biblical literature is divine in initiative, derivation, membership, and terms.[30] It is somehow rather shocking that *the very concept* by which Arendt hoped to see Americans transcending political theology is one fully religious in its lineage. Almost unbelievably, of course, Arendt reads the activity of covenants (most often in her sources explicitly framed in God's company) as independent not simply of overseas monarchs but also of divine superintendence of any sort. The occasional remarks in her corpus suggest that she even thought this way about Jesus himself—as a worldly actor whose basic contribution swung free of his happenstance divinity—but

*On Revolution* rests its case on his American colonial followers pursuing their errand in the wilderness.[31] "[T]he colonial compacts had been made without any reference to king or prince," Arendt wrote, stressing their invention the later claim of colonial autonomy from the monarchy. It is as if the page before she had not herself noted that the compacts were made "in the Presence of God" not just "one another," or failed to master the obvious fact that the very final paragraph of the Declaration of Independence that features the mutual pledge language also appeals both to "the Supreme Judge of the world" and "the protection of divine providence."[32] How could covenants be an answer to Schmitt when, as a matter of historical fact, they would seem to perfectly exemplify his claims?

Before reaching any conclusion, it is at least worth seeing that Arendt anticipated the objection that the covenant is continuous with religion too, ultimately as dependent as natural rights on some theistic lineage. Though she only briefly mentions its distant origins in *On Revolution*, she of course knew what its background was. But what stands out for her is the revolution in meaning by the time of the colonists. "The Biblical covenant ... was a compact between God and Israel by virtue of which God gave the law and Israel consented to keep it," Arendt remarked, "while this [i.e., the colonial] covenant implied government by consent, ... where actually the whole principle of rulership no longer applied." Or, as she told the American Society for Christian Ethics in 1973, "There is no doubt that the notion of covenant itself somehow is Biblical in origin ... [but a] covenant of mutuality—this covenant which relies only on *mutuality*—cannot possibly be compared to covenants in which one party is God, to whom we owe existence, creation, and so on, also law and [in which] we only pledge our *obedience*." It is this shift in its content, she concluded in *On Revolution*, made "the act of mutual promise ... *in principle independent of religious sanction*."[33] Thus, she hoped to shield her presentation of colonial secularism, precisely at the moment of its maximum apparent vulnerability, from the force of the thesis of continuity.

How so? Theoretically, she says, it looks as if John Locke—though she could and perhaps should have mentioned earlier figures—cemented the shift of covenant from a divinely initiated contract to a purely human agreement among equals. But, on the one hand, Arendt says, Locke may well have drawn on the American experience in imagining a compact of free and equal men as the foundation of government. On the other hand, he presented a model in which the outcome of the political bargain is consensual hierarchy in a model not of free and equal citizens but a one to one relation between private right holder and public sovereign (the latter, she noted again, liable to be thought about on analogy with divine power—as a mortal god). Thus, the common image of Locke as America's philosopher either mistook the source for the recipient or else missed the difference between promissory equality and consensual hierarchy. The key for Arendt is that the Americans "had no notion of any theory," for the rise of promissory action is not "a theory or a tradition" but "an event"; "[n]o theory, theological or political or philosophical, but their own decision to leave the Old World behind and to venture forth into an enterprise entirely of their own led into a sequence of acts and occurrences in which they would have perished, had not they turned to the matter long and intensely enough to discover, almost by inadvertence, the elementary grammar of political action."[34]

At the stage of the actual revolutionaries, Arendt continued, the practical inheritance of Puritan covenants may have led to, or blended with, the avowed theoretical recovery of classical politics to lead America to the intentional striving for a secular order. Of course, neither Greek nor Roman law featured the premise of a lawgiver outside the law; their concept of law mooted any search for an absolute. So no simple return was available, modernity able to retrieve classical wisdom only within the context of its enduring monotheistic legacy—what I called earlier religion's presence in its absence—of the need for an absolute.[35] Thus, where the ancient world had reconstitutions (with no absolutes) the modern world has revolutions (with absolutes).[36] And in retrieving Virgil's Fourth Eclogue and updating its key line from *magnus ordo saeclorum* to *novus ordo saeclorum*—the later motto of the dollar bill—the Americans at once rehabilitated what classical wisdom they could but also did so in the new and unparalleled circumstance of a postreligious founding. Curiously, the wisdom they saved has been much commented on before—with its analogy between natality and foundation and its emphasis on the double meaning of *arché* as beginning and principle. But the *essentially postreligious* character of the new context has been neglected.[37]

A preliminary word on the Fourth Eclogue is needed to put Arendt's discussion in its proper context. The poem's afterlife over the centuries has not been told in any comprehensive history, but its prophecy of a sempiternal regime had major resonance in Germany in the interwar period—an era whose discussions Arendt's own treatment references and with which she engages. As Theodore Ziolkowski explains, there was a "remarkable turn" to the Fourth Eclogue in Weimar Germany, one centered, essentially, on whether to read it in a theological and proto-Christian way or in the secular spirit of classical politics. But Arendt's interpretation, in examining the transformation from the Virgilian poetry to the American slogan, focused precisely on the shift in meaning of one of the poem's key words: *saeculum* (pl. gen., *saeculorum*, shortened in the poem for metric reasons). A strictly temporal concept it was initially, the term Americans inherited could now mean something else. Substituting for Virgil's "great order of the ages (or centuries)" with their own "*new* order," Americans signaled that they were forced to begin anew. More important, Arendt insists, the new covenantal source of authority is one they implicitly chose *against* any "transcendent, transmundane" alternative, hence the need for the claim of secular novelty.

The American formula transforms classical wisdom, in other words, to stress not just the novelty but also the secularity of the modern enterprise. Coming to denote a domain outside religion (from its medieval legal usage to mean appropriation of church property by irreligious powers), it is no accident that Arendt, under whose pen the word *secular* in its fully contemporary acceptation appears constantly, singled out the American order as a secular one. Arendt uses the expression "transcendent, transmundane" in describing a religious foundation the American founders somehow avoid, but also, significantly, in her repudiation of the standard Christian interpretation of Virgil's poem as a prophecy of Christ's reign. The American founders, it seems, had already shown the limits of the millennial Christian appropriation of the poem— still defended in Weimar Germany, in Eduard Norden's best-selling essay that Arendt specifically singled out for criticism. Her reading of how the Americans updated Virgil (a shift to which she returned in *The Life of the Mind*, in some of the last pages she wrote) thus provides in miniature Arendt's overall interpretation of the place of revolution in modern politics: a classical revival at its best, to be sure, but one in new and changed circumstances that were crucially post- and anti- or at least nonreligious. So it is that for Arendt the American Revolution (unlike any classical polity and holdover formulae aside) equals secularization and vice versa.[38]

ONLY IMMANENT CATEGORIES

It goes almost without saying that Arendt's depiction of the egalitarian political content and the putative secular basis of covenants—America's incidentally religious colonists and its purely worldly founding—bears little relation to historical fact.[39] It is not clear how complete her failure was, however, for two essential reasons. One is that historians might be prepared to reinvent Arendt's argument by rethinking its historical details—and indeed, this reinvention has already occurred. When "the republican thesis" cast America's secular achievement as flowing from a different lineage, it no longer relied on (indeed, specifically criticized) the linkage between covenants and democracy, replacing it with a Euro-American neo-Roman tradition with deep roots. Largely unknown to Arendt herself, even if she inspired its discovery, this heritage obviated the need to posit the immaculate conception of secularism on American shores; but breaking completely with Arendt's empirical claims in order to reclaim her normative impulses, J. G. A. Pocock's reconstruction of the republican tradition premised the movement precisely on a replacement of medieval *homo credens* with modern *homo politicus*, so that it is fundamentally a postreligious and secular phenomenon.[40]

The other, more meaningful reason is that it is the theoretical option Arendt carved out that matters, not whether any historical case vindicates it (yet). Arendt aimed to identify an alternative to political theology and a model of human coexistence genuinely independent of religious premises: what she called "a purely secular, worldly realm."[41] More important, in her discussion of covenants, Arendt designed her argument, whatever its historical validity, with an eye to *warding off* the allegation that all modern politics are in straightforward or encrypted continuity with the religious past. One could then say that Arendt's crucial theoretical gambit is her alternative model of modernization—one that licenses the hypothetical possibility of secularization—even if her association of it with a particular place and time in history turns out to be specious.

If so, then Schmitt's presence in Arendt's mind (or at least over her reader's shoulder) helps disengage very important but generally neglected features of her text. He helps, to sum up, in identifying a fascinating dynamic in her argumentation. By defining religion as a powerful version of authority, but only one of its possible forms, Arendt allowed herself to travel a great distance in Schmitt's company, but in order to reach an alternative—the alternative—destination. She incorporated a version of his argument to her own but in the service of escaping it. In short, if it was Schmitt's firm position that "there are no 'immanent' categories to which a political order could appeal for its legitimacy," then Arendt, without gainsaying the potential appeal of the transcendent, just as firmly wanted to take the reverse position.[42] The religious past affects the revolutionary project and makes an exact return to the classics impossible; the intractable problem of the absolute, she thinks, forbids it. But even so, it does not follow that religion is interminable.

CODA: SEPARATING POLITICS AND
RELIGION ONCE AND FOR ALL

Arendt strove to find the possibility of transcending Christianity in the name of a truly irreligious order, a possibility widely denied today, for two reasons—one critical and one positive. The first involves properly appraising the novelty of secularization as something that *happened* to Christianity rather than as something it did to itself. After all, Schmitt's allegation of continuity, like contemporary postcolonial critique of secularism, denies how radical the changes were that secularization brought about. But given that revolutions are precisely modern rather than Christian, she continued, "the best one can say in favor" of continuity is that Christianity

> needed modernity to liberate the revolutionary germs in the Christian faith, which is obviously begging the question.... Secularization, the separation of religion from politics and the rise of a secular realm with a dignity of its own, is certainly a crucial factor in the phenomenon of revolution.... But if this is true, then it is secularization itself, and not the contents of Christian teachings, which constitutes the origins of revolution.

Even if it were true, in other words, that one found "spilt religion" (T. E. Hulme) in modern politics, it was the "spilling" that had to be explained.[43]

Now, it is ironic that Arendt herself in the same book went on to make claims about persistence that did not really take her own directive to heart. It is true that she tried to unearth the revolutionary dynamic that might explain why, at the moment of secularization, Christianity survived in overt or covert forms. But she did not really consider in the book—or anywhere else, to my knowledge—what sparked secularization (and thus revolution), unless she thought it was simply entailed by the failure of stopgap absolutism all by itself. But that argument only begs the question. And in her own understanding, it would not explain the American case anyway. All the same, her directive stands as a challenge to the claim—Schmittian in form if not substance—that secularism is Christianity in dissimulated form. That position, she might say, does not explain why the move to the covert transpired, and may not acknowledge the major transformations that occurred in that process. Just as a modernization that liberates revolution from Christianity has to be seen as a modernization *against* Christianity, so a transformation that produces secularism from Christianity has to be seen as a transformation *against* Christianity, in spite of whatever continuities remain.

No doubt, that critical argument does not finally decide the balance between break and persistence in transitions as complex as the rise of secular modernity. Yet there is another, positive argument one might imagine Arendt offering, in the space opened by the critical one. For there is no reason to reduce the process of secularization and the politics of secularism to the forms they have so far taken. Arendt's claim is that secularization is *precisely that process that risks its own subversion*, and is enormously likely to lead to its interruption and even its falsification. If so, then the persistence of Christianity in the name of secularism is not a phenomenon she would have been surprised to find, since in some versions she insisted on it herself. But, far from spelling the bankruptcy of secularism, Arendt thought this result only redoubled the need to advance it. The contemporary critique of secularism confuses history and possibility, allowing the historical investigation of the masks Christianity assumes to distract from philosophical contention that secularism can have a true face. Arendt strove mightily—in some ways this is the point of her study of revolutions—to avoid the confusion between these two outcomes. Arendt argued in effect that it is possible to concede the critique's interpretive claims while disputing its analytic framework and normative consequences. The persistence of religion, when found, does not preclude its obsolescence, and a political life beyond its powerful claims.

Still, Arendt's efforts are at best early struggles to lay out what a secularist perspective might look like. And the risk of political theology that she emphasized—but not enough—in the end still swamped not only the modern project of revolution but also her own project as an author. For even more troubling than the infirm and hypothetical version in which one can salvage any plausible secularist alternative from *On Revolution* is a final harsh reality: that Arendt herself occasionally used theological language to describe precisely the secular politics she advocated. It is legendary that in *The Human Condition* she referred to the possibility of new beginnings involved in political action as miraculous.[44] But the religious idea of miracles as a model of political revolution is precisely the case Schmitt himself cited as the best evidence for political theology! And at the very climax of *On Revolution*, Arendt's rhetoric lapsed into the theological—blatantly so. While repudiating the traditional

Christian interpretation of Virgil's Fourth Eclogue as a prediction of Jesus's birth, Arendt, for her part, wanted to read the poem as an "affirm[ation of] the divinity of birth as such"—a prophecy of the enigmatic natality that would provide the ground of secular coexistence.[45] Arendt found something religious, one might say, in the very secularity she prized. Like the language of political miracle that Schmitt had specifically targeted, this appeal to the divinity of birth fits ambiguously, and perhaps conflicts flagrantly, with Arendt's more basic attempt to strive for a purely secular politics.

Does this last fact then wreck any attempt to present Arendt as a secularist?[46] Might it even show that whatever her fervent hopes of transcending political theology, the latter must always—as Schmitt originally suggested—have the final word? There would seem to be only one way to respond to these questions in the negative: to contend that, far from contradicting her argument about the difficulty of overcoming political theology, Arendt *performed* it, unwittingly no doubt but perhaps more convincingly, in the very course of framing it most strenuously. If the move to the secular was difficult as a matter of theory, it had to be just as difficult as matter of the practice of theory. At the very moment of propounding a secular vision of the political realm, Arendt fell back on or at least invoked religion; but in her own view of revolutions, this troubling dynamic did not foreclose, and at worst concealed or postponed, the secular. The persistence of political theology could be a prelude to its end.

NOTES

This essay appeared earlier as "Hannah Arendt on the Secular," *New German Critique* 105 (Fall 2008): 71–96, but this version supersedes the original, and is updated to respond to several criticisms.

1. For Arendt's youthful flirtation with theology and later turn to the secular in moral philosophy (as opposed to political theory, the subject of this paper), see my *Origins of the Other: Emmanuel Levinas between Revelation and Ethics* (Ithaca, NY: Cornell University Press, 2005), chap. 2 and *passim*.

2. For prior attempts to relate the two, see Martin Jay, "The Political Existentialism of Hannah Arendt," now in Jay, *Permanent Exiles: Essays on the Intellectual Migration from Europe to America* (New York: Columbia University Press, 1986); William Scheuerman, "Revolutions and Constitutions: Hannah Arendt's Challenge to Carl Schmitt," in David Dyzenhaus, ed., *Law as Politics: Carl Schmitt's Critique of Liberalism* (Durham, NC: Duke University Press,

1998); and Andreas Kalyvas, *Democracy and the Politics of the Extraordinary: Max Weber, Carl Schmitt, Hannah Arendt* (New York: Cambridge University Press, 2009).

3. Hannah Arendt, *The Human Condition* (Chicago, IL: University of Chicago Press, 1958), 314; cf. Arendt, *On Revolution*, rev. ed. (New York: Viking, 1965 [1963]), 284.

4. Arendt, "What Is Authority?," in *Between Past and Future: Six Exercises in Political Thought* (New York: Viking Press, 1961), 125. This could happen, she stated, because Roman politics (from which the concept of authority derived) were based throughout their history on "the sacredness of foundation," which made the transition to Christian politics possible. Ibid., 104.

5. Arendt, "Authority in the Twentieth Century," *Review of Politics* 18 (1956): 4, 405.

6. She constantly attached specific importance to hell and eternal damnation as "the only political element in traditional religion." Arendt, "What Is Authority?," 129–35 at 132; see also Arendt, "Religion and Politics," in *Essays in Understanding, 1930–1954*, ed. Jerome Kohn (New York, 1994), 380–84 and *On Revolution*, 191, where she emphasizes that even American state constitutions all included promises of future punishments. Similarly, late in life at a conference on her work, Arendt responded to remarks by Hans Jonas by saying: "I am perfectly sure that the whole totalitarian catastrophe would not have happened if people had still believed in God—or hell rather—that is, if there were still any ultimates." Colloquy in Melvyn A. Hill, ed., *Hannah Arendt, the Recovery of the Public World* (New York: St. Martin's Press, 1978), 313–14.

7. These commitments are marginal in most commentary on Arendt, probably because theorists who place weight on authority as necessary feature of social coherence have typically argued from a conservative (frequently Catholic) or reactionary position. See, for example, Yves R. Simon, *Nature and Functions of Authority* (Milwaukee, WI: Marquette University Press, 1940) and Jesús Fueyo, "Die Idee der 'auctoritas': Genesis und Entwicklung," in Hans Barion et al., eds., *Epirrhosis: Festgabe für Carl Schmitt* (Berlin, Germany: Duncker und Humblot, 1968). Arendt's main essay on authority first appeared in Carl J. Friedrich, ed., *Authority (Nomos I)* (Cambridge, MA: Harvard University Press, 1958), in which the editor noted that the concept remained interesting in spite of its typical associations.

8. Arendt, *On Revolution*, 159–60. Cf. Arendt, "What Is Authority?," 135: "Under these circumstances [of secularity—her word], religion was bound to lose

its political element, just as public life was bound to lose the religious sanction of transcendent authority."

9. The important postmodernist interpretations of Arendt omitted or were uneasy with the fact that Arendt insisted that, for all the waning of old forms of authority, the American Revolution illustrated the persisting need of absolutes. See esp. Bonnie Honig, "Declarations of Independence: Arendt and Derrida on Founding a Republic," *American Political Science Review* 85 (1991) 1, 97–113 and Dana R. Villa, *Arendt and Heidegger: The Fate of the Political* (Princeton, NJ: Princeton University Press, 1996), esp. 157–65.

10. Arendt, "Religion and Politics," 379.

11. Arendt, "Religion and Politics," 372.

12. Arendt, *On Revolution*, 156.

13. Ibid., 157–58. There is a second association in an early lecture on the subject, in which Arendt suggested that Plato and monotheism shared in the attempt to establish a "transcendent source of authority" that "tried to impose something absolute on a realm where everything is relative." Arendt, "Breakdown of Authority," New York University, November 1953, Hannah Arendt Collection, Library of Congress Manuscript Division, Essays and Lectures.

14. Ibid., 156.

15. Ibid., 161.

16. Ibid., 18–19 (my emphasis).

17. Ibid., 114.

18. Ibid., 186.

19. She mentioned him first in a review of Max Weinreich's indictment of "Hitler's professors" and returned to him in a footnote of *The Origins of Totalitarianism* in a similar context. In the first, Schmitt is counted amongst those "outstanding scholars" who volunteered to serve the regime, and in the second is credited with "very ingenious theories about the end of democracy and legal government [that] still make arresting reading" (even as she emphasized that though he volunteered to serve the Nazis, their interest in him proved short-lived). Max Weinreich, *Hitler's Professors: The Part of Scholarship in Germany's Crimes against the Jewish People* (New York: YIVO Institute, 1946); Hannah Arendt, review in *Commentary* 2 (1946): 3, rpt. as "The Image of Hell," in Arendt, *Essays in Understanding*, 201; Arendt, *The Origins of Totalitarianism*, new ed. (New York, 1958), 339n65. See also Arendt, "Waldemar Gurian," in *Men in Dark Times* (New York: Harcourt, Brace, 1968), 252.

20. Arendt, *On Revolution*, 192, citing John Adams, *Works*, 10 vols. (Boston: Little, Brown, 1850–56), 6: 281. But Arendt made clear, in an exchange with Eric Voegelin, that while "[i]t is true that a Christian cannot become a follower of either Hitler or Stalin [and] morality as such is in jeopardy whenever the faith in God who gave the Ten Commandments is no longer secure," it is nevertheless mistaken to "conclude from the frightening events of our times that we have got to go back to religion and faith for political reasons." Arendt, "Reply [to Eric Voegelin on Arendt's *Origins of Totalitarianism*]," *Review of Politics* 15 (1953) 1, 76–84 at 82. The Rohilla were a South Asian people at first targeted by the rival Marathas and then by their British allies—in what became one of the imperial scandals of Warren Hastings et al.—who hunted them down and decimated them as insurgents.

21. Arendt, *The Origins of Totalitarianism*, 291.

22. Arendt, *On Revolution*, 186, 189, 184.

23. Ibid., 196, 148; cf. 207. Arendt seems to have been most influenced to emphasize the natural law dimension of the American founding by Edward S. Corwin's well-known works.

24. Arendt, "What Is Freedom?," in *Between Past and Future*, 240n21.

25. Arendt, *On Revolution*, 16 (Bodin), 154–55, 158–59 (Bodin to the French Revolution), 159, 195 ("Word became flesh"), 160 ("different disguises"), 195–96 (the nation as "the cheapest and most dangerous disguise the absolute ever took"), 183 ("deification"), 154 (Kantorowicz), and 157 ("world on fire"). The Kantorowicz citation is from Kantorowicz, "Mysteries of State: An Absolutist Concept and Its Late Mediaeval Origins," *Harvard Theological Review* 48, no. 1 (January 1955): 91. This was a precursor essay for Kantorowicz's *The King's Two Bodies: A Study in Mediaeval Political Theology* (Princeton, NJ: Princeton University Press, 1957), in which Schmitt's notion figures in the subtitle, and which Arendt also cites in her *On Revolution* endnotes (306). (It is probably insignificant that when she does, she mistakenly omits the word *political* from his subtitle.) In her essay on authority, Arendt mentions the premier Weimar-era critic of Schmitt's pamphlet, Erik Peterson. Combined, these two pieces of evidence make certain Arendt's awareness of Schmitt's original theses.

26. See Erich Voegelin, *Political Religions*, trans. T. J. DiNapoli (Lewiston, NY: Edwin Mellen, 1986) and Raymond Aron, "The Future of the Secular Religions," in Aron, *The Dawn of Universal History: Selected Essays from a Witness to the Twentieth Century*, trans. Barbara Bray (New York: Basic Books, 2002). The journal *Totalitarian Movements and Political Religions*, and the historical works of

its former editor Michael Burleigh, have been the main recent sites in English for this discussion; see also Emilio Gentile, *Politics as Religion*, trans. George Staunton (Princeton, NJ: Princeton University Press, 2006).

27. See esp. Arendt, "A Reply," 81–82; "Religion and Politics," *passim*; and Arendt, *Denktagebuch*, 2 vols., eds. Ursula Ludz and Ingeborg Nordmann (Munich, Germany: Piper, 2002), 1: 363–64.

28. Arendt, "Religion and Politics," 372.

29. Arendt, *On Revolution*, 165–78 *passim*, 167 for her words and 308–9n for her citation of Jensen's article. Perry Miller, *The New England Mind*, 2 vols. (Cambridge, MA: Harvard University Press, 1939, 1954); Merrill Jensen, "Democracy and the American Revolution," *Huntington Library Quarterly* 20, 1/4 (1956–57): 321–41. Arendt affirms elsewhere in the work that the "greatness" of the Declaration "owes nothing to its natural law philosophy" but rather flows from the fact that it was "the perfect way for an action to appear in words" (126–27).

30. See, for example, Delbert R. Hillers, *Covenant: The History of a Biblical Idea* (Baltimore, MD: Johns Hopkins University Press, 1969), which studies the idea in the context of ancient Near Eastern legal concepts from which it may have been derived.

31. See esp. Arendt, *The Human Condition*, 238–40, 246–47.

32. Arendt, *On Revolution*, 166–67.

33. Ibid., 172, 170. Arendt, "Remarks at the American Society for Christian Ethics, January 21, 1973," Hannah Arendt Collection.

34. Ibid., 170–73 and 308–9n. Of course, it is far from incidental, if Jeremy Waldron is right, that the Americans insisted that promissory equality required God's presence. See Waldron, *God, Locke, and Equality: Christian Foundations of Locke's Political Thought* (Cambridge, UK: Cambridge University Press, 2002).

35. Ibid., 186–89. Somehow, on Arendt's account, Montesquieu alone amongst theorists escapes the modern necessity of an absolute, but however he did so does not allow for revolutions to dispense with it. This crucial point is, I believe, missed in the very subtle article by Patchen Markell dealing with the themes in this paragraph. See Markell, "The Rule of the People: Arendt, *Arché*, and Democracy," *American Political Science Review* 100 (2006): 1, 1–14.

36. Ibid., 209 on reconstructions, and the "silence" of the "classical archive" for moderns.

37. Ibid., 211–15.

38. Ibid., 196, 200, 205 (internal absolute), 205 ("transcendent, transmundane"), 211 (Eclogue), 317nn (on Norden: "I doubt the religious significance of the

poem"). Theodore Ziolkowski, *Virgil and the Moderns* (Princeton, NJ: Princeton University Press, 1993), 79–89 at 88, which includes a discussion of Norden, *Die Geburt des Kindes: Geschichte einer religiösen Idee* (Leipzig, Germany: B. G. Teubner, 1924) in the context of Weimar intellectual history. An important article assembling all of Arendt's appeals to Virgil and stressing her neglected interest in Roman political thought generally nevertheless devotes only the briefest attention to the Fourth Eclogue and misses the issue of the secular at stake in the poem. Dean Hammer, "Hannah Arendt and Roman Political Thought: The Practice of Theory," *Political Theory* 30 (2002) 1, 124–49. On the semantic drift of *saeculum*, see Otto Brunner et al., eds., *Geschichtliche Grundbegriffe* (Stuttgart, Germany: E. Klett, 1972–1997), s.v. "Säkularisation, Säkularisierung." For what little is known about the origins of the dollar-bill motto, see J. Edwin Hendricks, "Charles Thomson and the Creation of 'A New Order of the Ages,'" in John B. Boles, ed., *America, The Middle Period: Essays in Honor of Bernard Mayo* (Charlottesville: University of Virginia Press, 1973). See later Arendt, *The Life of the Mind* (New York: Harcourt, Brace, 1981), 2: 207.

39. The major student of covenants in New England after Perry Miller, though apparently unaware that he is refuting Arendt's argument, concludes that "seventeenth century New England continued to have a deep sense of hierarchy, and ... none of the civil or church covenants are cast as contracts. God, Christ, king, the central colonial government, and the local town council were superiors in civil covenants, and God, Christ, clergy, and elders were the superiors in church covenants.... The inferiors ... submitted themselves to their covenantal superiors." David A. Weir, *Early New England: A Covenanted Society* (Grand Rapids, MI: Wm. B. Eerdmans, 2005), 227–28.

40. J. G. A. Pocock, *The Machiavellian Moment: Florentine Political Thought and the Atlantic Republican Tradition* (Princeton, NJ: Princeton University Press, 1975), Part I, passim, and 550.

41. Arendt, *On Revolution*, 226. The expression is essentially a pleonasm given the relation in Arendt's German between *säkular* and *weltlich* and *Säkularisierung* and *Verweltlichung*, unless one interprets the apparent redundancy as only further highlighting the irreligious basis of worldly politics in her thought.

42. This description is from the editorial material in Jacob Taubes, *The Political Theology of Paul*, trans. Dana Hollander (Stanford, CA: Stanford University Press, 2004), 139. Taubes wanted against Schmitt to develop a political theology of covenant putatively more faithful to the Jewish tradition that did not insist on political representation of God but still located him in the background of human commu-

nity; obviously, Arendt's attempt to move beyond Schmitt is much more radical since Taubes still agreed with Schmitt that the autonomy of human politics is impossible and thus that a political theology of some sort is still necessary.

43. Arendt, *On Revolution*, 18–19 (my emphasis).

44. See, for example, Arendt, *The Human Condition*, 247. For a different view than I advance here, see James W. Bernauer, S.J., ed., *Amor Mundi: Explorations in the Faith and Thought of Hannah Arendt* (Boston, MA: Martinus Nijhoff, 1987), as well as many recent interpretations placing Arendt in a putative tradition of "German-Jewish messianism."

45. Arendt, *On Revolution*, 212.

46. In response to this essay, several critics have observed that Arendt's affiliation with Christianity, and admiration for several features of it, make my case partial at best. See, for example, Gil Anidjar, "The Meaning of Life," 37, no. 4 (Summer 2011): 697–723 at 714–18 and esp. 714n46.

# Part III
# Jacob Taubes
## Secularization, Heresy, and Democracy

# Secularization and the Symbols of Democracy
## *Jacob Taubes's Critique of Carl Schmitt*

MARTIN TREML

*Les extrêmes se touchent*

For many years Jacob Taubes (1923-1987) and Carl Schmitt (1888-1985) have been among the most disputed and fascinating intellectuals of the German Federal Republic: on the one hand, a Jewish thinker and philosopher of religion who studied the history of apocalyptic ideas in Judaism, Christianity, and Gnosticism from antiquity until today;[1] on the other hand, a Catholic author and expert in constitutional law, renowned as a propagandist of political theology, as the jurist of the *Third Reich*, and as a "German public lawyer," who as with "[m]ost conservatives c[a]me from the margins."[2] Famous for being the theorist of the state of exception, Schmitt was an exceptional character himself. He taught young admirers like Nicolaus Sombart and Reinhart Koselleck to find in each text the key sentence.[3] In discussions, he often presented his arguments in an exacerbating way, thus regularly triggering conflicts. Astonishingly, Taubes shared these attitudes.

In the German Federal Republic Schmitt and his work have been heavily disputed for the obvious reason of *Vergangenheitsbewältigung* [working through the past] until now. But he was uneasy with the postcatastrophic young state, and made it the subject of frequent and relentless criticism. He stubbornly refused to distance himself from his errors and mistakes. Both the demand to repent in public and the newly developed German self-conception appeared to him as a "tyranny of values." This verdict finally became the title of one of his late essays, the contribution to a volume that was dedicated to the secularization debate, namely the 1967 *Festschrift* for Ernst Forsthoff, a former student and specialist in constitutional law.[4] Here Schmitt observed the increasing importance of values in philosophy since Nietzsche, culminating in their victory in neo-Kantianism, and their final transfer into the public realm of democracy.[5] Schmitt stated that nowadays "one deals only with the annihilator and annihilated."[6] In older systems of order, the battles of ideas would have constantly required mediation, but "what today is called values" would automatically understand itself as the expression of truth.[7] To Schmitt, the jurist, this urgent mediation must come from the sphere of law.

> In a polity, the constitution of which provides for a legislator and laws, it is the concern of the legislator and the laws given by him to ascertain the mediation through calculable and attainable rules and to prevent the terror of the direct and automatic enactment of values.[8]

But also jurisdiction may, from time to time, act against values—and, by necessity, also against those that Schmitt and others had followed during the Nazi regime. For he and his likes not only discussed ideas but put them under the malevolent sign of the new values of 1933, thus making themselves into henchmen of an openly anti-Semitic and, ultimately, murderous legislation. Gopal Balakrishnan is right, when he writes that

> Schmitt had initially supported the Nazis because he believed that they were poised to solve the problem of the 'pluralistic' disintegration of the secular state, as a neutral, higher power in an age of mass politics.[9]

The Nazis were obviously far from being neutral; they were partisans of mass murder. Certainly not all of Schmitt's ideas can be summarized under his support for the Nazis and his involvement in their activities. Especially his juridical and sociological statements concerning the problems of the Weimar Republic are still stimulating for any discussions on how a "failed state" comes into being and functions.[10] Most of his followers and students in Germany were conservatives, though some were also liberals like Koselleck, but what united them was the fact that they tried "to politicize moral questions—where the Left supposedly moralized political questions."[11]

Taubes, too, regarded the German Federal Republic in at least a skeptical way, but he did so from an opposite experience: that of a victim of Nazi terror. He survived the Holocaust outwardly undamaged, due to the fact that his father already had become the rabbi of Zurich in 1935, and moved there with his entire family. Many of his relatives had been murdered in the camps, and Taubes himself felt to be a getaway—his roots torn out and scattered across the earth.

Born a Polish citizen in Vienna, he became American in 1956.[12] Having received a call for the chair as Founding Professor of Jewish Studies at the Free University of Berlin in 1962, he reluctantly left New York City, where he had been teaching at Columbia University since 1956.[13] Initially, Germany appeared to Taubes as a dystopia, where he did not wish to stay too much or too long. But since the mid-1960s, and with the support of his second wife, Margherita von Brentano, who was also a philosophy professor, he restlessly immersed himself in activism without regard for his public image and academic position. "The Free University of Berlin is the Berkeley of Europe," Taubes wrote to the American philosopher Lynne Belaief, adding that the protests are "a cultural revolution from below."[14] In a speech held at the plenary meeting of the students of the Free University in 1967, Taubes defended their actions. It was the year when almost everything in the German Federal Republic changed and started from scratch. The great coalition of Conservatives and Social Democrats began in December 1966, as did terrorism, albeit small in size, in June 1967. Taubes stated,

> Not only the statute and ordinance of our university are most seriously in danger. The law which first of all guarantees our statute and ordinance is in danger, the law, by which we are formed up [*nach dem wir angetreten sind*], when we gave us statute and ordinance and united as a community of responsible [*mündiger*] teachers and responsible students.[15]

In his speech Taubes made use of a juridical notion, that is, law. However, this is also a vital notion in religious discourse, especially in Judaism, even if its key concept, *torah*, does not restrict itself to the function of law as such.

RELIGIOUS SPEECH AND THE
HISTORY OF RELIGION

The recent publication of the correspondence between Taubes and Schmitt, and between those who were closely connected to them, such as political essayist Armin Mohler and jurist Ernst-Wolfgang Böckenförde, documents their complex intellectual relationship—how Taubes and Schmitt took note of and gradually approached each other, until they finally started exchanging letters, and how Taubes later paid three visits to Schmitt in his remote refuge in the German provincial city of Plettenberg.[16] Their cautious approaches can also be understood in part as a personal reversal of the process of secularization *in nuce*. To both of them, scripture had become vital again. Taubes and Schmitt undertook a reevaluation of it but one that has gone through the criticism of history and philology without neglecting it. They took the Bible neither as a traditionally holy text nor as the words of the living God, nor even as the most important piece of literature of the Ancient Middle East, but rather as a manual for everyday life. Meticulous readers of the Bible, the abyss that separated them was bridged by the common inspiration they both found in it. This becomes obvious in Taubes's salutation in his first letter to Schmitt of November 1977—"with greetings, a hand reaching over an abyss."[17] Schmitt replied to it by a quotation from the Bible, Psalms 42:8, in Latin, the holy language of the Catholic Church, "*abyssus vocat abyssum* [where deep calls to deep]."[18] Everyone familiar with the Bible knows what the deep abyss here means. In the Vulgata, *abyssus* stands for the Hebrew *tehom*, which is the primordial water before creation above which the *ruah* of *Elohim*, God's spirit, hovers (Gen. 1:2). But *tehom* is also Tiamat, Babylon's female sea monster, the Leviathan of the Orient and, in the Mesopotamian epic of creation *Enuma Elish*, the archenemy of the highest god, Marduk.[19] In the final days it will reappear as a dragon with seven heads in one of the apocalyptic battles of the Book of Revelation.[20]

The fact that Taubes and Schmitt were both accurate readers and well-versed interpreters of the Bible finally broke the ice between them. Respectively, as a Jew and a Catholic, they knew how spiritual doubts and emotional pains could be healed by prayers. Taubes confessed to Schmitt, that "meanwhile I read *Ex Captivitate Salus*," Schmitt's copious but elucidating self-explication of his behavior after 1933, "for consolation from time to time."[21] Taubes and Schmitt alluded regularly to the Bible in ways that could not be discerned by more secular contemporaries. As such, they gained not only their Arcanum but also an actualization of the revelation laid down in Scripture and its tradition, now for their own individual lives, even if both were concerned with creating ideas for a better and just community.

For Taubes and Schmitt alike, the figure of the Katechon, in the Second Letter to the Thessalonians, a pseudo-Pauline epistle of the New Testament, was of central importance. It was, for them, neither a figure of speech nor a mere theological expression. Rather, this force, capable of hindering the apocalypse, postponing the revelation of the "mystery of lawlessness," and restraining the coming of the Final Judgment, possessed an existential reality to both.[22] The same is true for the Antichrist, a figure of utmost demonic power, the confusing benefactor and supposed patron of humanity who will appear during the Last Days, the *eschaton*, and who will mislead humanity into misery and destruction. These were the heated fantasies of a beset Christianity that always understands and uses religious speech in a self-therapeutic way. Today, John, "a Jewish prophet writing visions he claimed to have received on the island of Patmos" around 90 CE and the author of the Bible's Book of Revelation, which is concerned with the Last Days, appears as a dropout and denier of integration into the Roman world of Asia Minor.[23] However, his apocalyptic anger and furor are quite common, the more so today, when the West is encountering the nihilistic terror of militant Islam in the shape of bombers and assassinators in its capitals and cities.[24]

The parallel between apocalyptic theology and contemporary politics envisioned by Taubes and Schmitt is not only historical, but also systematic—stimulated by a methodological comment made by Walter Benjamin, who connected theology with critical theory bringing together systematic reflections with the interest in details.[25] In *Literary History and the Study of Literature*, an essay of 1931, he remarks on the reception of the past: "What is at stake is not to portray literary works in the context of their age, but to represent the age that perceives them—our age—in the age during which they arose."[26] Benjamin's paradoxical formulation can be understood as the attempt not only to draw the genesis of a work of the past in a historic-critical way, but also to track its content for a strong connection to the present. Only from the point of view of the present will the past be understood. Therefore, Hegel could not only perceive the conflict between family and the state in civil society as it is enacted in Sophocles's *Antigone*, but also describe the protagonist's clinging to her consanguinity, which led to bloody terror and complete destruction of herself, her family, and the *polis* alike.[27] Here, religious history serves for a better understanding of oneself and one's own time.

In a very similar vein of thought, Taubes repeatedly tried to contribute to the acknowledgment of current political conflicts "in the perspective of the history of religion."[28] As a thinker, he was positioned between Judaism and Western philosophy, which, for him, stretched from Parmenides to Marx and

Kierkegaard, to Heidegger and Benjamin, "from Ionia to Jena," as he used to say. Taubes was an existential thinker, who thought of himself as living in a postcatastrophic time that showed parallels to late antiquity and to the strife between Christ and Caesar. Bridging centuries, the history of religion became for him a rich arsenal of figures and constellations that could be used to make sense of the present.

As a thinker tinted with existentialism, Taubes knew that there were "notions which begin to trail through the streets and *cafés*—Anguish, Death, Dereliction, the Ecstasies of Time"—Paris being their eternal capital.[29] He once wrote to his Jerusalem teacher Hugo Bergman that the French metropolis "delights by its treasures, by its gardens and wide, broadly projecting and at the same time inviting avenues, by its eternally happy and cheerful youth, wholly devoted to the Goddess of Love, indeed fallen for the service of love."[30] In these years, he and his first wife Susan were certainly among this youth themselves.

Taubes hoped that a change in the present state of affairs would come about so that humanity could unite, as brothers and sisters, here on earth and not in heaven, as Christianity has always promised. He began from the message of the Hebrew prophets and continued with Paul's theology.[31] Taubes wanted to work for a community as universal and "truly catholic"—as he again wrote to Bergman in the early 1950s, considering the two alternatives of Communism and Catholicism.[32] Taubes's "catholic" and "communist" Judaism—if one may call it that—would neither be founded on Rome's authority nor acknowledge any kind of caesaropapism nor any barrier between people. Taubes followed exactly what Paul had preached in his Letter to the Galatians. "There is neither Jew nor Gentile, neither slave nor free, nor is there male and female, for you are all one in Christ Jesus."[33] In his political theology, Taubes wanted to extract the best from Judaism, Christianity, and antiquity.

TAUBES ON DEMOCRACY

Taubes's concept of democracy as the current space of living together politically is based on such considerations, as one can read in an essay of 1955, "On the Symbolic Order of Modern Democracy," first published in *Confluence*, a journal edited by Henry Kissinger and reprinted in this book. Two years earlier, Kissinger, at that time a faculty member at Harvard, had tried to convince Schmitt in a letter to participate in the journal too.

I am writing to you at the suggestion of Hans Egon Holthusen to explore the possibility of your collaboration with *Confluence*, a quarterly designed to give European and American intellectuals an opportunity to exchange views on contemporary problems in politics, philosophy and the humanities.[34]

Nothing came out of it. Yet, it is important to know that Kissinger's *agent de liaison*, Holthusen, was a controversial figure himself. As a former member of the SS (this fact being notoriously ignored until the 1960s), he became an influential literary critic and functionary of the *Kulturbetrieb* in the German Federal Republic after 1945, traveling regularly to the US, where he taught as visiting professor at several prestigious universities and, from 1961 to 1964, acted as director of the Goethe House in New York City.[35]

By and large, Taubes's essay can be read both as an investigation into the course and the practices of secularization and, at least implicitly, as a debate with Schmitt. He started by observing that important political representations have entered political discourse: "Authority, sovereignty, omnipotence, decision as *deus ex machina* belong equally to the basic vocabulary of religious as well as of political language."[36] This quotation shows a proximity to the ideas of Schmitt. As such, Taubes's text abounds with such allusions, on which I will comment after I have delineated its main content.

In his essay, Taubes was not interested in a critique of ideology, which was in vogue during those years. Instead, he tried to answer the question "whether, in short, certain tensions in the symbolic canon between religious language and political rhetoric might not indicate a critical state in the spiritual and temporal structure of our society."[37] He took the religious cult as *fundamentum in re*, designating it with the Greek loanword *liturgy* in the Bible, literally meaning "service" for God, the Lord. Taubes concluded that "the entire liturgy of the Western religions is founded on monarchic symbols."[38] Here he meant both Judaism and Christianity but did not mention Islam as the third great Western religion, which had at that time entered neither public consciousness nor the writings of a philosopher of history.

Taubes was not interested in a critique of language, as he worked on a critique of politics. Quickly reversing his observation, he asked for the effect of the epoch after 1789, which stands under the sign of the murder of the king and the equality of all, on what he called "religious consciousness" and its ability to coin religious symbols.[39] "The interrelationship between the execution of the divinely anointed king and the free association of brethren, between regicide and fraternity, could thus serve as a chapter heading of the spiritual history of Western civilization in the last two centuries."[40] Nietzsche and Freud described this in theory, Russian writers like Turgenev and Dostoevsky in literature. This leads to the question of

> whether the religious and political symbolism of traditional, theistic religions is capable of providing the symbolic canon for the democratic society; or whether on the contrary the democratic structure of modern society does not so affect the traditional theistic symbolism, that the same dogmatic nomenclature actually covers different images of the deity.[41]

For Taubes's understanding, the cardinal point lies in the consideration about human beings as the image of God, which has been raised for the first time in the biblical narrative of creation: "And God created man in His image, in the image of God He created him; male and female He created them."[42] But the likeness of creation with the Lord has been corrupted or even lost by human sinfulness, the extent of this corruption being something that religion and (Christian) churches have constantly contested and disagreed over.

> One extreme teaches the absolute corruption of man's nature, while more reconciling doctrines speak only of a weakening of human nature. But to free man's nature *entirely* from the corrupting effect of the original act of sin runs completely counter to the spirit of the theistic creeds whose basic doctrine of man's inherent sinfulness is reflected in the statement of Genesis: "for the imagination of man's heart is evil from his youth."[43]

After Taubes had stated that human beings are held sinful in all Western religions, he commenced on a critique of the discontent that, during the 1950s, had been raised against it. Any doctrine of the original or inherited sinfulness of humans was considered undemocratic—in the sense of Rousseau's optimism on the equality and originally human goodness, which has functioned as the basis of all democracies since 1789. "Democratic philosophy, therefore, not only aims at better conditions; it insists that no limit can be assigned to man's evolution, a belief clearly inconsistent with traditional religious canons."[44]

As the "corrupting effect of the original act of sin" might only be handled by authoritarian means, Taubes now aimed at concepts of authority.[45] In democracy, authority is the will of the people, thus directed against religious doctrines of sovereignty and their monarchic symbolism.[46] Religious groups have protested strongly against authoritarian or paternalistic ideas. This is not a recent phenomenon, as Taubes explains: "The logic of the protest is always the same; all the congregation is holy, every one of them—there is no need for priesthood or hierarchy."⁴⁷ Already in ancient Gnosticism, which was philosophically studied by Hans Jonas in his *Gnosticism and the Spirit of Late Antiquity* [*Gnosis und spätantiker Geist*] "under the spell of Heidegger" in 1934 for the first time, protest was put forward against the institutionalization of religion.⁴⁸ These protests were never launched by the official church and its organizations. Accordingly, Taubes claimed,

> Democracy flourished not in the orthodox tradition of Christian religions but among the mystical heretics and sectarians of the Middle Ages who renounced the Roman Catholic system of hierarchy, attacked the feudal order of medieval society, and tried to penetrate the entire population with the "egalitarian" message of the Gospel.⁴⁹

Here Taubes turned the history of religious protest in general into one of the church alone and began an *interpretatio Christiana*. If one follows his argument closely, then democracy would have been born out of the spirit of radical Christian sects like the Anabaptists and their "democratic principle of church organization," which they "were the first to put into practice."⁵⁰ The impulse for democracy would then not have come from Athens, but from Jerusalem, *urbs sancta* [holy city], or rather *caput Corporis Christiani* [capital of Christendom]. In the last two sections of his essay, Taubes localized this central thesis in religious history and related it to different theoretical positions, to those of the Danish Protestant Søren Kierkegaard and of the Spanish Catholic Juan Donoso Cortés, but also to two atheists, Karl Marx and Pierre-Joseph Proudhon.

> All four were laymen who were passionately interested in the symbolic order of religion; all four represented two sides of the same coin, for they agreed in their analysis of the function of religion in society. Each received an impetus for his analysis from the revolution of 1848 and each arrived at the same "result": dictatorship, which they unanimously favored against a balanced union of authority and general consent.⁵¹

While Taubes had been talking about democracy and equality before, his attention now shifted to dictatorship—what a breathtaking turn! But what he actually wanted to question was the concept of authority itself. The democratic concept of the innocent brotherhood collides with the idea of an ever-corrupting original. Yet, Taubes goes one step further, following Sigmund Freud, who regarded the renunciation of the son (and all brothers are sons) with the father as an ambivalent affair. In Christianity, the "endeavour of the son to put himself in place of the father god" was finally both abandoned and successful: abandoned, as there is One Father in Heaven; successful, as there is the single son with his mother, Christ and Mary, both in cradle and on the cross.[52]

Taubes's change of interest was further supported by the supposition that, in the twentieth century, God "is described as the total stranger, the totally other, with whom no communication is possible from the human side, who breaks into human life with terror and requires total obedience and blind faith."[53] In his idea of the completely otherworldly and even antiworldly god, Taubes was not only deeply influenced by Gnostic thoughts, but also by the ideas of Karl Barth, a Swiss Protestant, the intellectual leader of the German Confessing Church [Bekennende Kirche], the Protestant opposition against Hitler. Barth was the product of the collapse of liberal Protestantism after the World War I, when material needs met spiritual ones. In his commentary on Paul's Letter to the Romans, Barth put his liberating theology very close to an authoritarian one, not in the sense of politics, but in that of a system which does not know any intermediary, or go-between. His negligence can already be found in Paul.[54] In Barth every salutary event is conceived as happening vertically from above (*senkrecht von oben*).[55] Even before its decline and final fall, liberal Protestantism also had implications for German Judaism, as Taubes explained in his late lectures on Paul's Letter to the Romans.

> This was, so to speak, a joint firm (or rather, wanted to be—just think of Hermann Cohen's shameful tract on *Germanism and Judaism*; one can only avert one's face before this equation). But this firm had its major partner and a minor partner who took himself to be a partner while the other one didn't take him to be a partner at all.[56]

As a critic of rationalism, Barth marks the sharpest break possible between God and His creation. He does not even spare the notion of religion itself, which falls under the verdict of being a mere human machination. Barth also had a deep impact on Jewish thinking, especially of the first half of the twentieth century.[57]

In their radicalization of the concept of God Taubes's four protagonists, Kierkegaard and Marx, Proudhon, and Donoso Cortés, shared a common ground. The link between these thinkers, who are usually considered extremely different, was made by Taubes in bold conclusions and deductions: on the basis of Rousseau, "the father of all modern political theory," he asserted "that a state was never established without religion as its foundation."[58] But it is never "established religion" that achieves "the foundation of the polity."[59] Under the perspective of Kierkegaard and Donoso Cortés, Socialism turns into a "satanic theology," an antideistic desire.[60] Schmitt, to whom Taubes here refers explicitly, shared this opinion.

> Carl Schmitt, the apologist of the Nazi revolution in Germany, invoked Donoso Cortés and tried to read into the oratory of the Spanish Inquisitor his own nihilistic theory of decision.[61]

Following Schmitt, the democratic constitutional state possesses no principle of legitimization, "and was therefore doomed to end in a new Caesarism."[62] The question of how this is congruent with the primacy of the "participation in the community," which Taubes regarded very highly, must remain open.[63] This is also true for the end of the essay, where Taubes stated that "the deity [is] not the sanction of power, but of love."[64] It remains puzzling how all this is connected to dictatorship as the divine constitution or mode of relation of God to the human being, even if Taubes gives a last hint.

> Such a transformation of Paul's religious idea of the equality of men into a political postulate implies more than establishing a "logical" consistency between two human realms; it will involve a transformation of the basic elements of theistic religion.[65]

However, the authoritarian aspects are already present in Paul's theology itself, side by side with the liberating ones. It is not only that one witnesses here a transvaluation of values (*Umwertung der Werte*) in Nietzsche's sense and a liberation from all bounds, but also a preparation of a new order as "sons and heirs" in the name of Christ.[66]

TWO IMAGES OF DEMOCRACY

Taubes was accused of plagiarism several times.[67] In his essay "On the Symbolic Order of Modern Democracy," he followed his sources closely, although one should be careful not to judge too easily. For instance, Norman Cohn's *The Pursuit of the Millennium*, which tells an extremely similar story of the Jewish and Christian sources of religious protests, actually appeared two years after his essay, which nuances the allegation of plagiarism.[68] Some of Schmitt's texts actually do count among those with which Taubes sought discussion here, albeit not always explicitly. In addition to *The Concept of the Political*, he made use of *Political Theology*, for instance, in mentioning Rousseau's assumption of the natural goodness of people as the precondition of democracy and its critique.⁶⁹ Furthermore, not unlike Schmitt, Taubes highly esteemed Kierkegaard.⁷⁰

However, there is another text of Schmitt to which I would like to point here, *Roman Catholicism and Political Form*, a small book that came out with Hegner in Hellerau near Dresden in 1923, and in a revised form in Munich two years later. Balakrishnan writes about it and about its striking difference to *Political Theology*.

> It is hard to believe that the author had written one book right after the other. The Church's capacity to arbitrate, which was portrayed here as the office of a great "representative" institution, was based on a conception of politics almost diametrically opposed to the "political theology" of a Cortés, with its eschatological image of a counter-revolutionary civil war. [...]. An eschatological vision of catastrophe and renewal at one pole, and a more sober vision of a mediating classical political civilization at the other, formed the antipodes between which Schmitt's thinking would continue to move.⁷¹

Schmitt opens, as he often does, with a laconic and provocative sentence: "There exists an anti-Roman feeling [*Affekt*]."⁷² Sam Weber argues that this affect "is itself a response to another feeling that is often less conscious: namely, *fear*," which is directed against various forms of a *complexio oppositorum*, a union of opposites or contrasts.⁷³ This union is understood as "versatility and ambiguity" by many, as "the double face, the Janus head, the hermaphroditic (as Byron expressed himself over Rome)."⁷⁴ This "capacity to arbitrate" (Balakrishnan) is due to "the strict execution of the principle of representation. Its particularity can be brought out well through its opposition to the economic-technical mode of thought that dominates today."⁷⁵ It consists of a specifically juridical form showing a "formal superiority over the material of human life," a way of thinking that is always in opposition to forces that are dissolving and will thus lead to revolution and upheaval.⁷⁶ Without strictly formulating it, Schmitt makes clear that two antique religions are responsible for these destructive forces, Greek paganism and Jewish monotheism, both eternally fighting against Rome, be it Empire or Church.⁷⁷ Roman authority itself has been characterized by rational representation and "knew how to greatly overcome Dionysian cults of intoxication, ecstasy, and doom in contemplation."⁷⁸ Equally important is the following fact: "The Pope is not the Prophet, but the Vicar of Christ."⁷⁹ Catholicism is qualified for its political idea and its "triple great form: for the aesthetic form of the artistic, for its juridical form of law, and finally for its splendour as a form of power of world history."⁸⁰

The radical sects that Taubes wrote about were in opposition to everything Schmitt has designated positively here. According to Taubes, these sects gave rise to democracy's spirit and symbols, but found their ultimate executors in two Russian intellectuals—the Orthodox writer Dostoevsky and the anarchist Bakunin, both of whom Schmitt invokes at the beginning and the end of his book.[81]

Schmitt himself was no enemy of democracy as such, but of liberalism, and here his deep sympathy with theology is grounded: "All significant concepts of the modern theory of the state are secularized theological concepts." This is not only one of his most famous sentences, but it also his theory of secularization *in nuce*.[82] Schmitt was a passionate anti-Republican indeed, who despised all those who had made themselves comfortable in the "fauteuil of the achievements of 1789."[83] He regarded liberal democracy as unable to exert true authority. Already in the 1920s, Schmitt was more inclined toward dictatorship as the best form of government than toward the Roman Catholic Church as such. A dictator appeared to him as the only possible agent who could avoid an eschatological civil war. His ideal was the ancient Roman institute of dictatorship, proclaimed for a limited amount of time in case of emergency. This dictator stands *hors la loi*, as no law is binding him. For Schmitt, "a procedure can be either false or true, in that this determination is self-contained by the fact that the measure taken is in a factually technical sense right, that is expedient."[84] In other words, if the measure is harmful, it is wrong, if it is benevolent, it is right.

Taubes, however, drew very different conclusions from the crisis of democracy. He voted for a radical revaluation of values following both Nietzsche and Paul, in whose First Letter to the Corinthians a transposition of "everything" and "nothing" took place. Jesus's violent death on the cross has changed the course of the world once and for all by breaking the tyranny of the "rulers of the age," who are wise and mighty.[85] He made them into nothing, thus enabling the ones who have been "nothing" so far, the brethren of Corinth, Rome, and Jerusalem, to gain everything: "wisdom, justice, holiness, redemption."[86] This double turn from nothing to everything, and from everything to nothing marks the center of Paul's gospel.[87]

It is also possible to reveal the contrast between Taubes's and Schmitt's views as well as their different symbols of democracy by two images or concepts of images that both relied on. To Schmitt, the conception of Thomas Hobbes's *Leviathan* had an emblematic character, as it combines mythology, theology, political theory of both Judaism and Christianity, and is thus a product of their common secularization. "The important realization that ideas and distinctions are political weapons, in fact, specific weapons of wielding 'indirect' power, was thus made evident on the first page of the book."[88] The frontispiece in the edition of 1651 is the work of the Paris engraver Abraham Bosse. Much has been written about it.[89] It shows a giant, human creature, a "huge person," with crown, sword, and crosier, the bishop's ceremonial staff, who is keeping watch over the country, city, and fortress he is ruling.[90] The gigantic man himself is compounded of many small men who amount to several hundred in number, if one would care to count them. Now the sense of this image is not that many constitute a *single* power, but that all are under the protection of *one*, the state.

As a good Jew, Taubes had hardly any interest in images at all. In his late years, however, he became quite enthusiastic about the Dutch painter Hieronymus Bosch, who was active 150 years before Hobbes. Interestingly enough, Bosch is also mentioned in Schmitt's study of the *Leviathan*, when he reflects on the *trouvaille* that "the essentially demonic content of the image vanishes between 1500 and 1600," from Bosch to Breughel.[91] Schmitt declares that "[b]etween the demonology of Hieronymus Bosch and the hell of Breughel the notion of worldly realism [*diesseitiger Realismus*] arose."[92] Here he comes astonishingly close to the conception of Erich Auerbach, the German Jew and Romance philologist, who wrote on world literature and aimed at a history of earthly [*weltlicher*] realism.[93]

Taubes, in his turn, devoted seminaries to Bosch, which he held at the Free University of Berlin during five consecutive semesters, titled *Aesthetics of Gnostic Imagination, on the Gnostic Interpretation of Hieronymus Bosch*.[94] As usual, Taubes did not leave any papers or notes that cover these courses. There is only one letter to the editors of *Frankfurter Allgemeine Zeitung* that expressed his conviction of the importance and mysteriousness of the images of the Dutch artist.[95] Bosch's dark visions as well as his dreamlike depiction of sexual transgressions are definitely mysterious in themselves. In the 1960s, one part of the general opinion followed the interpretation of the German art historian Wilhelm Fraenger. He stated that Bosch had worked for a radical group of mystics who wanted to unite Christianity and Judaism for the benefit of greater, even perfect freedom, a liberty some of the ancient Gnostics had hoped for—an interpretation that suited a spirit like Taubes perfectly.[96]

One may assume that Bosch's phantasmagorias opened themselves to Taubes not only as the expressions of anxieties and fears he himself experienced during the episode of acute psychosis he suffered from 1975 to 1977, of which he was finally "cured" by electric shocks in a Brooklyn clinic. In the solutions Bosch found in his pictures one may definitely find symbols of democracy and its crisis *in actu*—now performed on the stage of world history in disguise—that the radical religious sects from antiquity and the Middle Ages to the present time had dreamed of. When there is punishment and destruction, there is also liberation and fulfillment revealing liberty and equality of brothers and sisters in hitherto unknown ways. Bosch's paintings must have fascinated Taubes like nothing else. It is the expression of a radical secularization that takes place beyond God and state.

NOTES

1. Cf. Martin Treml, "Reinventing the Canonical: The Radical Thinking of Jacob Taubes," in *"Escape to Life." German Intellectuals in New York: A Compendium on Exile after 1933*, eds. Eckard Goebel and Sigrid Weigel (Berlin, Germany and Boston, MA: de Gruyter, 2012), 457–78; Herbert Kopp-Oberstebrink, "Jacob Taubes," in *Neue Deutsche Biographie, Vol. 25*, ed. Historical Commission of the Bavarian Academy of Sciences (Berlin, Germany: Duncker & Humblot 2013), 803–4. Jerry Z. Muller, "Reisender in Ideen: Jacob Taubes zwischen New York, Jerusalem, Berlin und Paris," in *"Ich staune, dass Sie in dieser Luft atmen können." Jüdische Intellektuelle in Deutschland nach 1945*, eds. Monika Boll and Raphael Gross (Frankfurt am Main, Germany: Fischer TB, 2013), 40–61.

2. Jan-Werner Müller, *A Dangerous Mind: Carl Schmitt in Post-War European Thought* (New Haven, CT: Yale University Press, 2003), 15–17.

3. Cf. Nicolaus Sombart, *Jugend in Berlin, 1933–1943, Ein Bericht* (Frankfurt, Germany: Fischer TB 1986), 250. Christoph Schmidt (Jerusalem) not only informed me that Reinhart Koselleck told him once that Schmitt had given him the same advice, but also reminded me of this specific attitude itself. I want to thank him very much.

4. Carl Schmitt, "Die Tyrannei der Werte," in *Säkularisation und Utopie: Ebracher Studien: Ernst Forsthoff zum 65. Geburtstag* (Stuttgart, Germany: Kohlhammer, 1967), 32–67. I refer to the English Translation: *The Tyranny of Values*, ed. and trans. Simona Draghici (Washington, DC: Plutarch Press, 1996), 3.

5. In a similar vein of thought, the German philosopher Peter Sloterdijk has recently argued that modern democracies were being glued together by regular doses of excitation [*Erregung*]. Cf. Peter Sloterdijk, *Der starke Grund zusammen zu sein* (Frankfurt, Germany: Suhrkamp 1998).

6. Schmitt, *The Tyranny of Values*, 28 (translation modified).

7. Ibid., 30.

8. Ibid. (translation modified).

9. Gopal Balakrishnan, *The Enemy. An Intellectual Portrait of Carl Schmitt* (London and New York: Verso, 2000).

10. Cf. Ellen Kennedy, *Constitutional Failure: Carl Schmitt in Weimar*, Durham, NC: Duke University Press, 2004.

11. Müller, *Dangerous Mind*, 113 (there in allusion to Reinhard Mehring).

12. Cf. Treml, "Reinventing the Canonical," 463–64.

13. Cf. ibid., 463.

14. "Letter of Taubes to Belaief, Berlin, June 21st, 1971." The letter is kept in the Jacob Taubes Estate at the Center for Literary and Cultural Research, Berlin.

15. Jacob Taubes, "Rede von Professor Jacob Taubes auf der Vollversammlung aller Fakultäten der FU am 5. Mai 1967," *Anrisse* 58 (June 1967): 28 (my translation). I thank Herbert Kopp-Oberstebrink very much for drawing my attention to this hitherto unknown text of Taubes. We recently published the text in Jacob Taubes, *Apokalypse und Politik: Aufsätze, Kritiken und kleinere Schriften*, eds. Herbert Kopp-Oberstebrink and Martin Treml (Munich, Germany: Wilhelm Fink Verlag, 2017).

16. Cf. *Jacob Taubes/Carl Schmitt, Briefwechsel mit Materialien*, eds. and com. Herbert Kopp-Oberstebrink, Thorsten Palzhoff, and Martin Treml (Munich, Germany: Fink, 2011).

17. Ibid., 35 (my translation).

18. Ibid., 38 (my translation).

19. Cf. Enuma Elish, 137.

20. Cf. Book of Revelation, 12–13.

21. *Taubes/Schmitt, Briefwechsel,* 48 (my translation); Cf. Carl Schmitt, *Ex Captivitate Salus. Erinnerungen der Zeit 1945/47* (Cologne, Germany: Greven, 1950).

22. Second Letter to the Thessalonians 2:7.

23. Elaine Pagels, *Revelations: Visions, Prophecy, and Politics in the Book of Revelation* (New York: Viking 2012), 7.

24. "What might have angered this provincial Jewish prophet even more than the degrading picture of captive nations like his own would be to see Roman triumphs displayed not simply as imperial propaganda but as *religious devotion*." Ibid., 12. Change "Roman" with "Western," "religious devotion" with "lifestyle," and the pathos of a propagandist of Daesh (ISIS) suddenly appears in the lines of John's Book of Revelation. The prophet's furious rhetoric has proved to be capable of gathering the desperately disappointed and wretched ones for

the war against evil since almost two millennia. This is not to say that early Christianity and militant Islam would follow the same agenda (which they very obviously do not). But in a situation in which the imperial pairs the only good that is broadly acknowledged, any opposition against it might take its force only from beyond and outside, from a divine revelation appearing as a violent breaking into the world that would then explode and collapse. So did the Twin Towers of New York as well as "Babylon the great," which "is fallen, is fallen, and has become the habitation of devils, and the hold of every foul spirit, and a cage of every unclean and hateful bird" (Book of Revelation 18:2). Among many artists, poets, thinkers, Albrecht Dürer has taken from John a pictorial program to deal with the burning conflicts of his own time. Cf. Frances Carey (ed.), *The Apocalypse and the Shape of Things to Come* (Toronto, ON and Buffalo, NY: University of Toronto Press, 1999), 130–39.

25. Cf. Sigrid Weigel, *Walter Benjamin. Images, the Creaturely, and the Holy*, trans. Chadwick T. Smith (Stanford, CA: Stanford University Press 2013).

26. Walter Benjamin, "Literary History and the Study of Literature," in *Selected Writings Vol. 2, 1927–1934*, eds. Michael W. Jennings, Howard Eiland, and Gary Smith (Cambridge, MA and London: Belknap, 2005), 464.

27. Cf. G. W. F. Hegel, *Lectures on Fine Art*, trans. T. M. Knox (Oxford, UK: Clarendon, 1975), 1217–25.

28. Cf. Taubes's reply to the critique of Hans Blumenberg, in: "Dritte Sitzung: Surrealismus und Gnosis," in *Poetik und Hermeneutik, Vol. 2: Immanente Ästhetik—Ästhetische Reflexion: Lyrik als Paradigma der Moderne*, ed. Wolfgang Iser (Munich, Germany: Fink, 1966), 439 (my translation).

29. Jean Wahl, *A Short History of Existentialism*, trans. Forrest Williams and Stanley Maron (New York: Philosophical Library, 1949), 49.

30. "Letter of Taubes to Bergman, Paris, July 7, 1952" (my translation). The letter is kept in the Bergman Estate at the Manuscript Department of the Israel National Library in Jerusalem. This and related letters will be published by Nitzan Lebovic and myself in German in a volume *Taubes in Jerusalem* with Fink.

31. Cf. Christoph Schmidt, " 'Es gibt Vernichtung'—Jakob Taubes's *Die politische Theologie des Paulus*," in *Die theopolitische Stunde: Zwölf Perspektiven auf das eschatologische Problem der Moderne* (Munich, Germany: Fink 2009), 269–302.

32. Cf. an undated letter from Taubes to Bergman, not later than 1953.

33. Cf. Letter to the Galatians 3:28.

34. Cited in: Paul Noack, *Carl Schmitt. Eine Biographie* (Frankfurt and Berlin, Germany: Ullstein, 1996), 286–87.

35. Cf. Nicolas Berg, "Jean Améry und Hans Egon Holthusen: Eine *Merkur*-Debatte in den 1960er Jahren," in *Mittelweg 36. Zeitschrift des Hamburger Instituts für Sozialforschung* 21 (2012): 2, 35–36.

36. Jacob Taubes, "On the Symbolic Order of Modern Democracy," *Confluence* 4 (1955): 57. Reprinted in this book on pages 179–191.

37. Ibid.

38. Ibid.

39. Cf. ibid., 59–60.

40. Ibid., 59.

41. Ibid., 60.

42. Genesis 1:27.

43. Taubes, "Symbolic Order," 60. (Quotation of Gen. 8:21).

44. Ibid., 61.

45. Ibid., 61.

46. Cf. ibid., 61–62.

47. Ibid, 62.

48. Hans Jonas, *Memoirs*, ed. Christian Wiese and trans. Krishna Winston (Waltham, MA: Brandeis University Press, 2008), 59.

49. Taubes, "Symbolic Order," 62.

50. Ibid.

51. Ibid., 65.

52. Sigmund Freud, *Totem and Taboo. Resemblances Between the Psychic Lives of Savages and Neurotics*, ed. James Strachey (Norton: New York, 1990), 218.

53. Taubes, "Symbolic Order," 67.

54. Letter to the Galatians 3:19–20.

55. Cf. Karl Barth, *The Epistle to the Romans*, trans. E. C. Hoskyns (Oxford, UK: Oxford University Press, 1933).

56. Jacob Taubes, *The Political Theology of Paul* (Stanford, CA: Stanford University Press, 2004), 62.

57. Cf. Randy Rashkover, *Revelation and Theopolitics: Barth, Rosenzweig and the Politics of Praise* (London: T & T Clark, 2005).

58. Taubes, "Symbolic Order," 69.

59. Ibid.

60. Ibid.

61. Ibid.

62. Ibid., 70.

63. Ibid.

64. Ibid.

65. Ibid., 71.

66. Cf. Letter to the Galatians 4:7.

67. Cf. Treml, "Reinventing the Canonical," 459–60. For another possible case of Taubes's plagiarism, see Sigrid Weigel's essay, "In Paul's Mask: Jacob Taubes Reads Walter Benjamin" in this book: see page 195–216.

68. Norman Cohn, *The Pursuit of the Millennium: Revolutionary Millenarians and Mystical Anarchists of the Middle Ages* (Oxford, UK: Oxford University Press, 1957).

69. Cf. Taubes, "Symbolic Order," 61; Carl Schmitt, *Political Theology: Four Chapters on the Concept of Sovereignty*, trans. George Schwab (Chicago, IL: Chicago University Press, 2005), 56–57; *The Concept of the Political*, trans. George Schwab (Chicago, IL: Chicago University Press, 2007).

70. Cf. Taubes, "Symbolic Order," 65–66, 69; Schmitt, *Political Theology*, 15. For a discussion of Schmitt and Kierkegaard, cf. Christoph Schmidt, "Ironie und Kenosis: Von Kierkegaards zu Schmitts Kritik der romantischen Ironie," in: *Die theopolitische Stunde*, 75–94.

71. Balakrishnan, *Enemy*, 51–52.

72. Carl Schmitt, *Roman Catholicism and Political Form* (Westport, CT: Greenwood, 1996), 3. The translation here is taken from Samuel Weber, "'The Principle of Representation': Carl Schmitt's *Roman Catholicism and Political Form*," in *Targets of Opportunity. On the Militarization of Thinking* (New York: Fordham University Press, 2005), 25.

73. Weber, "Principle of Representation," 26. Cp. 29–31; Schmitt, *Roman Catholicism*, 4.

74. Schmitt, *Roman Catholicism*, 5.

75. Ibid., 8.

76. Ibid.

77. Cf. ibid., 7

78. Ibid., 23.

79. Ibid., 23–24.

80. Ibid., 36.

81. Cf. ibid., 5–6, 60–65.

82. Schmitt, *Political Theology*, 36.

83. Ibid., 20.

84. Carl Schmitt, *Dictatorship: From the Origin of the Modern Concept of Sovereignty to Proletarian Class Struggle*, trans. Michael Hoelzl and Graham Ward (Cambridge, UK: Polity, 2013), 10.

85. First Letter to the Corinthians 2:6

86. Ibid., 2:6 and 1:30.

87. Cf. Martin Treml, "Jacob Taubes und seine Lektüre der Paulinischen Briefe," in *Mitteilungen: Zur Erneuerung evangelischer Predigtkultur*, eds. Kathrin Oxen and Dietrich Sagert (Leipzig, Germany: Evangelische Verlagsanstalt, 2013), 121–28.

88. Carl Schmitt, *The Leviathan in the State Theory of Thomas Hobbes*, trans. George Schwab and Erna Hilfstein (Chicago, IL: Chicago University Press, 2008), 18.

89. Cf. Horst Bredekamp, *Der Leviathan: Das Urbild des modernen Staates und seine Gegenbilder 1651–2001*, 4th, rev. ed. (Berlin, Germany: Akademie, 2012).

90. Cf. Schmitt, *Leviathan*, 5.

91. Ibid., 24.

92. Ibid.

93. Cf. James I. Porter, "Introduction," in *Time, History, and Literature: Selected Essays of Erich Auerbach* (Princeton, NJ and Oxford, UK: Princeton University Press, 2014), xiv–xxi.

94. Cf. the first announcement of such a seminary in: FU University Calendar for the Summer Semester 1978, 262.

95. Cf. Jacob Taubes, [Letter to the Editors], *Frankfurter Allgemeine Zeitung*, November 22, 1980, 8. Also in Jacob Taubes, *Apokalypse und Politik: Aufsätze, Kritiken und kleinere Schriften*, eds. Herbert Kopp-Oberstebrink and Martin Treml (Munich: Wilhelm Fink Verlag, 2017).

96. Cf. Wilhelm Fraenger, *The Millenium of Hieronymus Bosch. Outlines of a New Interpretation*, trans. Eithne Wilkins and Ernst Kaiser (London: Faber & Faber, 1952).

# On the Symbolic Order of Modern Democracy

JACOB TAUBES

POLITICAL AND RELIGIOUS SYMBOLISM

Society establishes a common bond between its members by symbols. Language is mankind's fundamental symbolic form because the symbols of language guarantee its active participation in the life of a polity. The symbols of language may rule tacitly and only by implication, but they are nevertheless agents for social order, perhaps more powerful than the overt rules of a community. It is therefore not accidental that in many societies the word is still considered the prerogative of a citizen who actively participates in the life of the polity; while slaves, women, or children are treated as "infants" who have no right to speak since their judgment amounts to no more than an expression of arbitrary preference or animal faith.

Authority, sovereignty, omnipotence, and decision as *deus ex machina* belong equally to the basic vocabulary of religious as well as of political language. The striking similarities between religious and political language have of course been stressed frequently by sociologists and political theorists motivated by an effort to "unmask" the religious and political "ideologies." It might be more useful, however, to go beyond the polemical and inquire whether the parallelism of religious and political language could not serve as a guide for understanding the structure and history of our society; whether, in short, certain tensions in the symbolic canon between religious language and political rhetoric might not indicate a critical state in the spiritual and temporal structure of our society.

The language of religion culminates in the liturgy of the religious community. Liturgy, as the Greek term suggests, enacts the "service" of the people to their divine King; it is service as "worship." The entire liturgy of the Western religions is founded on monarchic symbols. The psalms, which contain a hymnology of the "divine enthronization" enacted yearly, serve together with the sacred symbols of the Roman Emperor cult as the basis for occidental liturgy. God is adored as the *rex coelestis*, the King Heaven; Christ is worshiped as *rex regum*, the King of Kings whose splendor eclipses all *reguli*, the earthly kings. The divine majesty is not an empty formula in the liturgy of the churches.

But what is a king in the perspective of our age? Does not the "royalist" symbolism of theistic religions stand in tension to the antihierarchical structure of modern democratic society? Is the royal symbol not reduced in a democratic society to a mere petrified allegory that has no root in the consciousness of the community? Is not, therefore, the entire realm of liturgy uprooted from its natural soil and reduced to a revered but barren piece of antique tradition? Does not the language of "spiritual" dominion stand incongruously to the language of "temporal" power? Can the religious symbols flourish if they are not rooted in man's concrete political experience?

To be sure, the language of liturgy is a symbolic language. But a symbol is not a loose "figure of speech." To be meaningful it must permit a point of comparison between the figure of speech and the set of reference. The decomposition of the symbol of divine kingship in our age is therefore related to the general waning of many of the religious archetypes and images that symbolize the structure of political society. In the case of the symbol of divine kingship, the decomposition of the symbol can be specifically connected with the developments of the social and political history of the last centuries.

The ideologists of the French Revolution were all well aware that the religious theistic pattern conflicted with the democratic ideology of the Republic. When Voltaire unmasked the life of Charlemagne, the first of the "holy" kings of the Middle Ages, as the life of a criminal and labeled him a tyrant, he not only debunked the traditional image of a king, but challenged the whole sacred order of monarchy—specifically the French *rex christianissimus*, the king who was anointed with sacred oil in the Cathedral of Rheims. Because the declaration of the "natural" right of every citizen by implication contested the "divine" right of kings, the American Declaration of Independence and the French *Declaration des droits de l'homme et du citoyen* have become the models for the democratic societies of the nineteenth and twentieth centuries. The "natural" rights of every man not only opposed the "divine" right of kings but also presupposed the basic *égalité* of all human beings, demanded the *liberté* from all feudal and patriarchal prerogatives and established the *fraternité* of all persons by executing the king, the living symbol of the divine rights of kings.

It should not be too difficult for a generation that has gone through the mills of William Robertson Smith, Frazer, and Freud to discover the connection between the killing of the patriarchal ruler and the proclamation of *fraternité* among men. For the "fatherhood of God" is not only complementary to the "brotherhood of men" (as the predominant contemporary view would like to have it), but also is antagonistic to it. The interrelationship between the execution of the divinely anointed king and the free association of brethren, between regicide and fraternity, could thus serve as a chapter heading of the spiritual history of Western civilization in the last two centuries. Indeed, Freud's interpretation comes only at the end of the long line in the development of the specifically modern perspective of the structure of society whose milestones include Turgenev's story of the antagonism between *Fathers and Sons*, Dostoevsky's tale of the killing of the "father" in *The Brothers Karamazov*, and Nietzsche's account of the "death of God." The regicide of the French Revolution was only the beginning of the deicide in the universal democratic egalitarian society. The hiatus between the symbolism of a monarchical liturgy and the self-interpretation of society therefore points to a crisis in the relation between the religious and political consciousness in our time.

DEMOCRACY AND MYSTICAL HERESY

It should be made clear at the outset that we are not talking here about religious institutions, but about religious consciousness. Institutional religions have always accommodated themselves without difficulty to various forms of government; indeed the elasticity of religious denominations in matters of political expediency is amazing. They seek the peace of the city wherein they are established and pray for the welfare of the authorities. In the course of time, the institutional religious bodies accept every form of government and try to function within it, whether the constitution is monarchical, aristocratic, or democratic. In Europe the Roman Catholic Church defends monarchies, and in the United States the same Church supports democratic institutions. Thus the relation between church and civil authority, between religious institutions and a specific form of government is not the issue at all in our analysis. What is involved is something "intangible": whether the religious and political symbolism of traditional, theistic religions is capable of providing the symbolic canon for the democratic society; or whether on the contrary the democratic structure of modem society does not so affect the traditional theistic symbolism, that the same dogmatic nomenclature actually covers different images of the deity. For the transformation of the religious idea of the equality of men before God into a political postulate implies more than establishing a logical consistency between two parts of a theory, it also involves transformation of a basic element of theistic religion: the image of man.

The theistic religions of the West envisage man in the image of God, but they judge him on the basis of the corruption of this image through sin. To be sure, different denominations stress the degree of man's sin differently. One extreme teaches the absolute corruption of man's nature, while more reconciling doctrines speak only of a weakening of human nature. But to free man's nature *entirely* from the corrupting effect of the original act of sin runs completely counter to the spirit of the theistic creeds whose basic doctrine of man's inherent sinfulness is reflected in the statement of Genesis: "for the imagination of man's heart is evil from his youth." The article of faith which asserts that man was created in the image of God is rendered preposterous if one fails to remember that it applies, according to the doctrine of Western theistic religions, to man in his perfect state before the original act of sin. If man is not seen in the light of his failure and sin, we turn his "fear and trembling" for salvation into a farce. Were it not for grace and mercy, man would be lost on the Day of Judgment—this is the refrain of all prayers of penitence.

What then becomes of the current slogan of the "optimism" of the theistic religions? No one who follows the various liturgies of penitence can see in it anything but a misunderstanding. It is one thing to be "optimistic" about God's victory over man's sin and revolt, and quite another to be "optimistic" about man's nature. On this point a democratic philosophy in the tradition of Rousseau differs radically from the theistic religions. For the philosophy of Rousseau and his disciples asserts that man is "naturally" good and not evil, even when put in its most moderate form, that over the long run, *most* men are good. Circumstances, not man's inherent nature, produce evil and, given the possibility of changing the circumstances, there is no limit to man's perfectibility. Democratic philosophy, therefore, not only aims to better conditions; it insists that no limit can be assigned to man's evolution, a belief clearly inconsistent with traditional religious canons.

But the fundamental difference between the symbolic structure of a democratic order and the royal symbolism of theistic liturgy concerns the sanction of authority. In the symbolic structure of the democratic order: the consent of the people establishes law and order: democracy implies that the people are the only sovereign, the ultimate authority. The will of the people is always right—or at least more often right than any individual will—and represents the highest law of the state. The government functions in the name of the people and has no authority of its own. In Lincoln's statement on "government of the people, by the people, for the people" the antihierarchical symbolic structure of the democratic order finds powerful expression. The authority of the government is not derived or ordained from "above" but guaranteed in a mystical equation of the *vox populi* with the *vox Dei*.

The divine law of the theistic religions of the West, on the other hand, does not derive its legitimacy from the consent of the people; it is established by decree. To be sure, the arguments for a democratic congregational order of society are not unknown to theistic authoritarian religions, but they are believed to be arguments of rebellion, and they are usually put into the mouths of rebels. For what is it but a program for democratic order, when Korah argues against Moses and Aaron, "Ye take too much upon you, seeing all the congregation are holy, every one of them and the Lord is among them: wherefore then lift ye up yourselves above the congregation of the Lord?" Korah's argument against religious hierarchies is repeated again and again, through the centuries, finally issuing in Luther's protest against the rule of the Papacy. The logic of the protest is always the same; all the congregation is holy, every one of them—there is no need for priesthood or hierarchy.

As a result, democracy flourished not in the orthodox tradition of Christian religions but among the mystical heretics and sectarians of the Middle Ages who renounced the Roman Catholic system of hierarchy, attacked the feudal order of medieval society, and tried to penetrate the entire population with the "egalitarian" message of the Gospel. The heretical sects stressed the equality of church members and insisted that elders and preachers should be elected by the local congregations. It was no accident that the Anabaptists, who emphasized the identity of the divine and the human spirit, had to deny the idea of sin. The "religious democracies" that came to birth in England in the seventeenth century felt themselves "blessed communities" in the sense that each individual was ennobled through his fellowship with kindred minds, and this same spirit carried over to some degree into the political democracies that grew out of the religious congregations. The democratic principle of church organization, which the Anabaptists were the first to put into practice and which came to the fore again in the sects of the English Commonwealth, became in the course of time the basic principle of English and American democracy. Nearly every one of the constructive principles of the sectarian movement came to be written into the Constitution of the United States.

Democracy was therefore, as Rufus M. Jones observes, inherently and intrinsically "mystical" in character. Only in terms of a mystical experience does a saying like *vox populi vox Dei* make sense without falling into banality. The will and consent of the people cannot be vested with infallible authority unless one presupposes that the people as a community are guided by the divine spirit. The individuals are fused into a living organic group so that each individual finds His wisdom and insight heightened through his group life and teamwork for common ends. Otherwise, why should the majority or even all of the people be less susceptible to error and crime than an individual? The democratic principle makes sense only if I assume that the general will of the people constitutes a quality that is not inherent in any single person. Such a political order "is at heart a mystical order. There is something more in each individual than there would be if he were operating in isolation. He becomes in a real sense *over-individual*, and transcends himself through the life of others."[1]


KIERKEGAARD AND MARX,
DONOSO CORTÉS AND PROUDHON

It was the pantheism of the sectarians that prepared the way for deism and hence for the American and French Revolutions. The impact of American ideas on France would not have been so powerful had it not been for their common basis in medieval sectarianism. The doctrine of the identity of the human and the divine spirit, the argument that the congregation as a whole is holy, provided the arsenal of ideas for both the American and the French revolts against royal authority. Tocqueville remarked that when conditions in society become more equal and each individual becomes more like every other, men get possessed by the idea of unity and are not content to believe that there is an absolute division between creation and Creator. They seek to expand and simplify their conceptions by including God and the universe in one great whole. For the deistic deity has no absolute power, but reigns over the universe like a king in a constitutional monarchy. In the seventeenth century the presuppositions of absolute monarchy still seemed so "self-evident" that Descartes could base his central philosophical thesis on the analogy of the sovereign will of the ruler: God had established the laws of nature just as a king establishes the laws in his kingdom. Descartes's argument was enough to convince his friend Mersenne that the laws of nature were indeed subject to the sovereign will of God. At the moment, however, when the divine King was in effect removed from His throne, the "self-evidence" of political monarchy collapsed as well. Mathiez, Aulard, and P. de la Gore, who have studied the religious history of the French Revolution, have proved that the cults of the French Revolution, the "Cult of Reason," the nationalist Decadal fêtes, the Cult of the Supreme Being, and the Cult of Theophilanthropism were popular illustrations of a deistic philosophy of religion.

But how does one pray to a deistic God who stands perhaps at the beginning of the world, but no longer rules it or takes any interest in man's life? How does man lift his eyes to heaven when there is no longer any "above" or "below" in the universe and everything is on an equal footing? The prayers of the theophilanthropic Manuel, composed in the summer of 1796 and actually used in 1797, give us a vivid picture of the difficulties involved in a deistic liturgy. It is the same difficulty that haunts all prayer books of modernistic religions. And just as man cannot pray to a pantheistic God, he cannot use in prayer the political symbols appropriate to that climate of belief. He cannot substitute the term *president* for the royal symbols. For even if the president's power were to exceed that of a king, it would not rest on his own personal authority. He is president only by the grace of the people, and is therefore not fit to represent the sovereignty of God in the language of faith. An earthly king, however, may be compared with or put in opposition to the divine King because the authority of power is personal in both cases. Thus, throughout the nineteenth century, the concept of a transcendent God was progressively eliminated hand in hand with the increasing trend toward political egalitarianism, and the issues of politics and religion were reduced to the alternative between authoritarian religion and atheism: either "back" to a transcendent sovereign God or "forward" to atheism. And the spiritual and political history of the last hundred years is still under the spell of this formulation.

There was considerable movement in both directions. Whereas the political implications of a transcendent deity were developed by the Protestant Kierkegaard and the Catholic Donoso Cortés, the political implications of atheism were developed in different ways by Karl Marx and Proudhon. All four were laymen who were passionately interested in the symbolic order of religion; all four represented two sides of the same coin, for they agreed in their analysis of the function of religion in society. Each received an impetus for his analysis from the revolution of 1848 and each arrived at the same "result": dictatorship, which they unanimously favored against a balanced union of authority and general consent. The Protestant theologian emerged with the dictatorship of the Martyr over the revolt of masses; the Catholic Grand Inquisitor with the dictatorship of the Church over liberal society; Marx with the "dictatorship of the proletariat" as a transition to the free atheistic society; and Proudhon, the ideologist of anarchism, wanted to destroy the last remnant of authority and elevate the emancipated man to the throne.

Kierkegaard is invoked today by Protestant, Catholic, and Jewish theology because he stressed the impassable gap between the divine and the human, and insisted that the divine is the "totally other," in no way to be compared with the human. He directed his attack against the pantheistic "distortions of God's transcendence," which had come into vogue in Europe since Hegel. But modem theologians and philosophers who hail Kierkegaard are hardly aware of the significant connection between Kierkegaard's theological meditations and his political theory of authority, of the necessary connection between a theology opposing all liberal mediation in religion and stressing "authority" and "obedience" in the political realm. Kierkegaard, who violently opposed the democratic revolution of 1848, was more consistent than his heirs, who extrapolate or eliminate the political implication of his theological assumptions. The bourgeois liberal society, according to Kierkegaard, was in no position to govern, since a rebellious antagonism to all superior authority stood at its source. Moreover, the revolt of the proletariat, first attempted in the revolution of 1848, showed that the bourgeois hope of balancing authority and consent was illusory. For with the symbols of authority invalidated by the liberalism of the bourgeoisie, no one was left—neither kings nor pope, generals nor Jesuits—to stem the revolt of the fourth estate. Only the martyr remained to establish authority against the yelling mob; only his sacrifice enabled the martyr to achieve in death what he could not attain while alive: the taming of the insurgent masses.

For Marx, too, the critique of religion was the basis for a critique of society. Man creates religion and society reproduces an image of itself in the divine hierarchy. But religion also realizes man's vision of himself, if only in fantasy. Religious consolation is only an "imaginary sun" around which man revolves as long as he does not revolve around himself. It was the 'task of history' to establish the 'truth of this earth' and dissipate the illusory divine truth. The revolt against heaven was for Marx the basis for every revolt against earthly powers, and thus the critique of theology became a prologue to a critique of politics. Atheism is a prerequisite for the revolution that will destroy the power that created all gods.

Donoso Cortés, the heir of the Spanish Inquisitors, would not have denied the accuracy of Marx's description. He would have found in it further evidence for his conviction that the germ of revolution lay in the revolt of man against God: "You will be like, the rich" was the formula of the socialist revolution, directed against the middle classes. "You will be like aristocrats" was the formula of middle-class revolution, against the aristocracy. "You will be like kings" was the formula for the aristocracy's revolt against kings. Finally: "You will be like gods"—such was the formula of the first revolt of the first man against God, and, from Adam to the last sodalist blasphemers, such has been the formula of every revolution.

Against the current semireligious ideology of progress, Donoso argued that while liberal society believed that civilization was "advancing," in reality it was taking great strides toward the constitution of the "most gigantic and destructive despotism which men have ever known."[2] For as religious authority declines, political control must increase, even to the point of tyranny. To Donoso, the revolution of 1848 proved that the choice was no longer between liberty and dictatorship, but between the dictatorship of insurrection and the dictatorship of government. He chose the dictatorship of government since it implied a less onerous and a less shameful tyranny: "The monarchy of the divine Right of Kings came to an end with Louis XVI on the scaffold; the monarchy of glory, with Napoleon on an island; hereditary monarchy, with Charles X in exile; and with Louis Philippe came to an end the last of all possible monarchies, the monarchy of prudence."[3]

If the institution of monarchy could not be preserved by divine right or legitimacy, by glory or by prudence, then the hour of dictatorship had come—as God sometimes directly manifests His sovereignty by violating the very laws which He has imposed on Himself, thus interrupting the natural course of events. When God acts in this way, could we not say—if human language can be applied to divine matters—that He acts dictatorially? The dictatorship of God was, for Donoso, the Catholic answer to the fundamental negation made by liberal democracy and socialism: the negation of sin, which could end only in nihilism. Donoso's apocalypse was thus not only the product of the events of 1848, but a consequence of his theological principle that there exists no middle course between God as Creator and Ruler of all things visible and invisible, and atheism. Since the royal symbols were dead, he resorted to the symbols of tyranny to describe the divine intervention. And, indeed, anyone concerned with theological argument in our century will notice to what an extent "dictatorial attributes" are ascribed to God in modern theology. He is described as the total stranger, the totally other, with whom no communication is possible from the human side, who breaks into human life with terror and requires total obedience and blind faith. Are these metaphors only symbols, or do they express a definite opinion about man's situation in the present age?

Donoso's vision of the tyranny of God was the reverse side of Proudhon's revolt against God. In Proudhon's antitheism Donoso saw the ancient heresy of Manicheism resurrected, and yet he was attracted by Proudhon, "this awful object of Divine wrath," since both spoke the same language: the language of theology. Just as Donoso emphasized the notion of order as eternal and innate to mankind, so Proudhon stressed the idea of revolution as innate and eternal. The Revolution did not begin in 1789, in a spot situated between the Pyrenees, the Atlantic, the Rhine and the Alps; it belonged to all ages and all countries. And because religion legitimizes governments and makes the principalities of government sacrosanct, Proudhon turned his arrows against the idea of God as the root of evil. Whereas Voltaire, the enemy of theistic religions, counseled the wise to "invent" a deity if God did not exist, Proudhon considered it "the first duty of an intelligent and free man unceasingly to drive the idea of God out of his mind and his conscience," for God, if He exists, is essentially hostile to man, and the society in no wise depends on Divine authority. "We attain knowledge without Him, our well-being without Him, and a community without Him; each one of our progressive steps is a victory in which we crush the divinity."[4] The ways of God are not inscrutable—many may fathom them. And Man reads in them proofs of God's impotence, if not of His ill will. The idea of God stands for human stupidity and cowardice, for hypocrisy and lies. "God is tyranny and misery. God is evil."[5]

Proudhon wrote his *The Philosophy of Misery* with an unheard violence of language against the deistic belief that seemed to him like slavery. If God exists, man must be His slave. Since man ought to be free, God cannot exist; and if He does, man will have to kill Him. Whereas Donoso chose the dictatorship of the Church and the authority of the sword because the sword was more noble than the dagger, Proudhon chose the dictatorship of insurrection and the authority of the dagger. Proudhon would have accepted Donoso's description of man as a rebel and chosen to risk everything in the chance of realizing man's absolute freedom on earth. And still, in Proudhon's Manicheism, Kierkegaard's authoritarian image of God is coming to life. Was not Kierkegaard insisting on the abyss that separates God and man? Did not Kierkegaard claim that

Christianity exists "because there is hatred between God and man"? Did he not call God man's "mortal enemy"?[6]

CONCLUSION

If it is true as Rousseau, the father of all modern political theory, observed, that a state was never established without religion as its foundation, then the socialist and anarchist critique rightly turned against established religion as the foundation of the polity. It was no accident that Donoso and Kierkegaard considered the socialist and anarchist critiques far more serious a threat than the prevailing liberal skepticism that "in its arrogant ignorance despises theology." For Donoso recognized "the strength of socialism" in the fact that it is "a system of theology." Socialism was destructive not because of its critical aspect but because it was above all a "satanic theology." Socialism was at one with the Roman Catholic theology in rejecting the "fundamental error" of liberalism that questions of government were alone important. The defenders of theism who affirmed that evil comes from human sin and that the sin of the first man corrupted human nature, could understand, as they abhorred, the Socialist argument that man's nature was inherently perfect and that only society made it sick. Donoso was fascinated by the appeal of socialism to humanity to rise in rebellion against all political institutions, while he despised the uncertain twilight of liberal ideology.

The dramatic element in the controversy of 1848 has fascinated political theorists in an age that has put "decision" above "consent." Carl Schmitt, the apologist of the Nazi revolution in Germany, invoked Donoso Cortés and tried to read into the oratory of the Spanish Inquisitor his own nihilistic theory of decision. The basic premise of both sides of the controversy of 1848 had been the equation "God is power, religion is authority": Donoso and Proudhon, Kierkegaard and Marx never questioned these equations. Wherever the liberal ideology shared this premise it could live only in an uncertain twilight despised by the protagonists and antagonists of religious authority and political sovereignty.

Neither the categories of Kelsen nor those of Carl Schmitt exhausted the problem, however. These dilemmas were well understood by Hans Kelsen and Carl Schmitt, two of the most perspicacious political theorists of the Weimar period, a period when Germany sought to build a liberal democracy entirely on a secular foundation. Kelsen considered a relativistic skepticism a sufficient basis for the democratic process of rule; indeed, he presented in his pure theory of law a theory of the state without a state, debunking "God and State" as mythical ghosts that only spooked in the minds of unenlightened people. In short, the divine was eliminated from secular life, which required no internal ceremony or rite to represent its mystery. It was precisely this justification of democracy that led Carl Schmitt to conclude that a democratic constitutional state had no legitimizing principle and was therefore doomed to end in a new Caesarism.

For the real source of the democratic belief lies not in these basic authoritarian equations, but in the religious and political experience of medieval and modern sects. There the image of God is not seen in the colors of power or the image of society in the colors of arbitrary sovereignty. Religion is not authority, but participation in the community; the deity not the sanction of power, but of love. The principle of association that came to the fore in the sects is still a legacy to the future, and the question is still open whether a community so conceived and so dedicated can long endure.

The principle of congregational association among men in the religious and political realms has a venerable tradition of its own: it is foreshadowed in the message of the Hebrew prophets and in the theology of Paul that prepared the way for a universal "catholic" church recognizing no barrier between Jew and Greek, slave and master. Paul's doctrine of the unity of mankind "in Christ" did not, however, directly touch the social and political stratification of the Roman Empire. The universal church of Paul remained a "mystical" body that did not "incarnate" itself into the structure of civil government. Therefore the political principalities and powers could continue to rule as ordained and established by divine authority. Paul established the religious equality of men "in Christ," but defended the status quo of political inequality in the frame of the Roman Empire.

The entire problem of the era of Christian history turns around the fulfillment of the Christian idea of man in the temporal realm. Such a transformation of Paul's religious idea of the equality of men into a political postulate implies more than establishing "logical" consistency between two human realms; it will involve a transformation of the basic elements of theistic religion. It is a cardinal point of all medieval and modern Free Spirits that the Christian image of man can only be realized and materialized by abandoning the theistic frame of reference—the idea of divine sovereignty, the concept of a divine "Kingship." The Christian man cannot achieve the state of perfection unless he becomes a part of Christ. From the English sectarians in the time of the Commonwealth who, like Henry Barrow in the sixteenth century, stated that

"Christ's ... government is not only tied to the ... whole congregation, but extendeth to everie action of every Christian,"⁷ the development leads to the philosophers and ideologists of the French and American Revolutions who tried to establish the heavenly city on earth. The religious congregation is still a *corpus mysticum*, a mystical body distinct from the social and political existence of man. In the mystical body of the Church the equality of men is transposed into "heaven." If men should, however, also become brethren "on earth," they must overcome the principle of domination that rules both the spiritual and temporal realms of the old dispensations.

NOTES

This essay originally appeared as "On the Symbolic Order of Modern Democracy," *Confluence* 4 (1955): 57–71.

1. Rufus M. Jones, *Mysticism and Democracy in the English Commonwealth* (Cambridge, MA: Harvard University Press, 2014), 35.

2. Donoso Cortés, "The Church, the State and Revolution," in *Catholic Political Thought, 1789–1848*, ed. Béla Menczer (Notre Dame, IN: University of Notre Dame Press, 1962), 170

3. Ibid., 165.

4. Pierre-Joseph Proudhon, *Système des Contradictions économiques, ou philosophie de la Misère* (Paris: Guillaumin et Cie, 1846), 1: 414.

5. Ibid., 415.

6. Søren Kierkegaard, *The Moment and Late Writings*, eds. and trans. Howard V. Hong and Edna H. Hong (Princeton, NJ: Princeton University Press, 1998), 177.

7. Henry Barrow, *Elizabethan Non-conformist Texts. The Writings of Henry Barrow: Volume III: 1587–1590*, ed. Leland H. Carlson (London: Routledge, 2003), 476.

# In Paul's Mask
*Jacob Taubes Reads Walter Benjamin*

SIGRID WEIGEL
*Translation by Joel Golb*

WALTER BENJAMIN'S SPIRIT

Walter Benjamin's name and theoretical figures run like a thread through the writings of Jacob Taubes. Occasionally, they are visible, sometimes surfacing all too colorfully; often they remain underground, serving to strengthen Taubes's own thinking. One first finds the name in the correspondence from the 1950s between Jacob Taubes in Jerusalem and Susan Taubes in New York (and other places she stayed and traveled during his years in Jerusalem).[1] Presumably Jacob Taubes came into contact with Benjamin's thought during his period at the Hebrew University as Gershom Scholem's assistant. In a letter to his young wife dated February 20, 1951, he suggests that on her trip to Jerusalem she take a detour: "It is worthwhile to see P[aris] as Walter Benjamin thinks Paris is the capital of 19th century and a study of the 19th century is a study of Paris." He explains the then unfamiliar name as follows: "the German translator of Perse and most intimate friend of Gerh. Scholem."[2]

It seems that this "intimate friend of Gerh. Scholem" became for Jacob Taubes a familiar author only during the 1960s—more precisely in the period of his gradual move to Berlin (following Taubes's first teaching at the Free University as a visiting professor in 1961). It happened to be earlier, however, that he felt himself aligned with Benjamin's "spirit." After his return from

Jerusalem to the United States, he wrote from Cambridge on December 6, 1953 a letter to "Verehrte Frau Doktor Arendt," in which he comments on a "*kleine Arbeit*" of his he enclosed with it: "Perhaps you'll also notice the spirit [*den Geist*] of Walter Benjamin in the last sentences."[3] Arendt is likely to have had as much difficulty discovering this spirit in Taubes's text as I have. Presumably the small manuscript was his article "The Development of the Ontological Question in Recent German Philosophy," published in 1952/53 in the journal *Review of Metaphysics*.[4] When he spoke of critical theory at that time (as in his teaching at Harvard) Taubes apparently referred mostly to Horkheimer's and Adorno's *Dialectic of the Enlightenment*, as Marcuse reports to Horkheimer in December 1954, "although," Marcuse adds, "it was indicated to him, that Horkheimer did not want this."[5] No trace of Benjamin was found at that time.

When Benjamin's influence became apparent in Taubes's work in the early 1960s, the two-volume edition of Benjamin's writings undertaken by Theodor and Gretel Adorno had already been published.[6] Although with this edition a sizable number of Benjamin's texts were now accessible, Taubes then referred almost exclusively to the theses in "On the Concept of History." This text was familiar to him already before the edition appeared; this is obvious from the correspondence between Susan and Jacob Taubes, who conversed in detail about their readings in their exchange of letters. Also, Susan Taubes's dissertation on *The Absent God: A Study of Simone Weil* (1956, submitted at Harvard in 1956 with Paul Tillich as adviser) refers to Benjamin's theory of history for comparative purposes in her discussion of Weil's critique of progress.[7] Here she cites Benjamin from a French publication in *Les Temps modernes*, where the text was published in October 1947, three years before the first German publication in the *Neue Rundschau* in 1950 (itself appearing eight years after its inclusion in the hectographed memorial number of the journal of the Institute for Social Research in 1942).

When reading Benjamin finally began to set off sparks in Jacob Taubes's writing, this initially happened in a certain characteristic mode, not by referring to Benjamin's ideas or arguments but rather by quoting single formulations and passages. For instance the much-cited thought that "all rulers are the heirs of prior conquerors"[8] is cited in slightly modified form and without indicating a source or the author's name in Taubes's essay on "Martin Buber and the Philosophy of History" (1963).

Is the eye of the philosopher or historian who reads meaning into history not dazzled by the success of the victor? Since the rulers of any time are the legitimate heirs of all those who have ever conquered before, the chain of succession of the periods of history reads as an apology of the ensuing successes throughout the ages.[9]

That very same year, Taubes ends his talk "The Intellectuals and the University" at the 1963 University Day with a long passage from Benjamin's *One-Way Street*, this time as a literal citation and indicating the source.[10] However, his historical survey, which draws a broad arc from the medieval *intelligentia spiritualis* to the intellectuals of modernity, culminates relatively abruptly in the section "To the Planetarium." Since Benjamin here—against the backdrop of a lost ecstatic relationship of humans to the cosmos—undertakes complex reflections on war and technology, Taubes's talk ends with Benjamin's insight that to engage with the question of technology does not mean to discuss the mastery of nature but to reflect on the "mastery ... of the relation between nature and man."[11] But it took some more years until Benjamin emerged from the background and entered the front stage of Taubes's writings. This actually took place in the "Notes on Surrealism" that Taubes presented in September 1964 at the second symposium of the famous *Poetik und Hermeneutik* circle.

Two main lines can be discerned in Taubes's reading of Benjamin. The first line of an obviously igneous reading runs from "Notes on Surrealism" to the essay on "Culture and Ideology" (1969), the notes to his seminar on Benjamin's "On the Concept of History" in winter 1984/85, and continuing in the essay "Walter Benjamin—A Modern Marcionite?" (1986). Benjamin appears first as the warrantor of a historical-philosophical engagement with questions that otherwise mostly pass as aesthetic in nature. Thereupon, he undergoes several metamorphoses: first appearing in the mask of the "most modern theological Marxism," then as a theorist of messianism, then as an author of political theology, and finally as a modern Marcionite. The second line starts nearly a decade later and runs along the Benjamin-Schmitt stretto, with the two authors appearing as the positive and negative poles of an electrically charged trace of thoughts. This line culminates in Taubes's lectures on Paul given in 1987, where Benjamin is presented as an exegete of the Letter to the Romans. The last mask that Taubes placed on Benjamin was Paul's.

CITATION: AMALGAMATION OF BENJAMIN'S
THEORETICAL FIGURES IN TAUBES'S WRITINGS

In his lecture at the *Poetik und Hermeneutik* meeting in 1964, Taubes undertakes a structural comparison between Gnosticism and surrealism. The title "Notes on Surrealism"[12] speaks for itself, since Adorno's *Notes on Literature* had appeared several years prior to that, in 1958. This text shows how in Taubes's writings a highly distinctive image of Benjamin takes shape by means of an adaptation of significant concepts and formulations. Close reading was not Taubes's concern, this becomes evident from Taubes's notes from his seminar on Benjamin's theses on history in the winter term of 1984/85.[13] Rather, what emerges from a linkage of individual sentences and phrases from several of Benjamin's work-complexes is a kind of palimpsest of Taubes's own theory. In his idiosyncratic practice of citation one comes across two modes of quotation, both symptoms of a fascinated, seemingly heated reading: on the one hand, the assimilation of concepts that can be identified only by connoisseurs of Benjamin's writings and thus act as a kind of shibboleth; on the other hand, programmatic formulations based on individual citations whose repetition produce the particular contours of Benjamin's image characteristic of Taubes's reading of his writings.

In the surrealism talk Taubes assimilates concepts as for example *historischer Index* ("historical index") and *Zitierbarkeit* ("becoming citable").[14] Since these are named in the vicinity of references to Benjamin, they can be assigned to the author despite the lack of source-indications. This is less the case for slightly modified or curtailed formulations such as *Abbreviatur* ("abbreviation"), *theoretische Armatur* ("theoretical tools"), and the *Interlinearversion des Textes* ("interlinear version of the text"), which derive from different texts and might be associated with the respective issues by those readers who are familiar with Benjamin's work.[15] For Benjamin, these topoi stand for highly complex connections: the "abbreviation of history," for instance, appears where Benjamin explains his term *Jetztzeit* (*now*) to be a model of messianic time.[16] The "interlinear version," however, stems from the dense final passage of Benjamin's "Task of the Translator," where he characterizes the interlinear version of holy script as a "prototype or ideal of all translation."[17] And "theoretical armature" as a topos for a kind of conceptual scaffold is an allusion to Baudelaire's verse "L' élégance sans nom de l'humaine armature" in the poem "Danse macabre."[18] In a note in *Central Park*, Benjamin refers to the poem as an indication of the "role of the skeleton in Baudelaire's erotology"[19] in order to derive from this allegory as the armature of modernism[20] and then finally to use the image of armature for theoretical scaffolding in general (in "On the Concept of History"). Since neither allegory nor translation are topics of Taubes's surrealism talk, his text does not refer to Benjamin's reflections on these themes. Rather, he takes single phrases from Benjamin's writings and inserts them in another, independent context—thus practicing a style of citation that may be indebted to Benjamin's own theory of citation: "To quote a word is to call it by its name,"[21] as Benjamin puts it in his essay on "Karl Kraus" (1931). The citation wrenches the word "destructively from its context, but precisely thereby calls it back to its origin."[22] Yet readings of this famous and frequently quoted passage often oversee that Benjamin talks here of a very specific kind of citation that he discusses by taking the example of Karl Kraus, namely, the "quotation that both saves and punishes" and in which language proves itself to be the matrix (*Mater*) of justice. These reflections concern a certain poetic kind of citing but not citation in general and much less so within a historic-theoretical analysis of Surrealism. Therefore it seems that the spirit of Benjamin has now actually taken on the form of a ghostly existence of a single Benjaminian topoi.

The second way Taubes cites Benjamin concerns single programmatic formulations referring to the authority/authorship of Benjamin. This concerns, for example, the idea of nihilism as a kind of benchmark for Taubes's picture of Benjamin, an issue to be discussed in more detail later, in connection with the lectures on Paul. It first gains programmatic character in the 1964 talk on surrealism. Here, Taubes argues that although "*politics whose method is called nihilism* (Benjamin)" can only shatter not construct anything new, both late ancient Gnosticism and Surrealism released revolutionary energies in petrified structures opening new forms of human experience.[23] The argument itself comes from Benjamin's essay on surrealism, where he describes the exponents of surrealisms as seers and astrologers who, however, recognized "how destitution—not only social but architectonic, the poverty of interiors, enslaved and enslaving objects—can be suddenly transformed into revolutionary nihilism."[24] Yet Taubes presents the argument without reference to Benjamin's discussion of surrealism. Rather, he cites the final phrase from the "Theological-Political Fragment," a text that Benjamin suddenly breaks off with the words "world politics whose method must be called nihilism," highlighting its essentially fragmentary nature. Taubes exactly connects an observation about surrealism with this phrase from Benjamin's interrupted theoretical effort that is engaged with a quite different question, namely, with the reflection on the "messianic rhythm of nature,"[25] and mobilizes it for his comparison between Gnosticism and surrealism.

TAUBES IN THE CIRCLE OF *Poetik und Hermeneutik*

Just like the first symposium of the *Poetik und Hermeneutik* group that took place in 1963 in Gießen, the home university of Hans Blumenberg, Clemens Heselhaus, and Hans Robert Jauß, the second meeting in 1964 pursued historical reflections on aesthetic topics. Focusing on art and poetry, this meeting addressed the questions how the departure from traditional objective reference has taken place and how the rise of concreteness (*Gegenständlichkeit*) could be aesthetically grasped without figurative reference. Already in his introductory remarks, Taubes calls the basic task into question: The upheaval at issue here cannot, he argues, be grasped immanently by means of aesthetics; rather, what is needed is a "historical-philosophical interpretation that determines the historical index of the poetic production as much as of the theoretical principles."[26] With this alternative perspective, Taubes moves along the lines of Benjamin's elaboration of a genuine Jewish theory of modernity—a theory that does not discuss literary and artistic phenomena in a framework of aesthetics, a tradition that stems from antique thought, to be carried forward and perfected to systematic knowledge in the European-Christian Renaissance. In Benjamin's writing philosophy of language and history replaces aesthetics. [27]

In his own talk, titled "Surrealism and Gnosis," Jacob Taubes nuances by characterizing his reflections as "religious-historical notes."[28] His discussion nevertheless remains in Benjamin's debt, albeit less to the 1929 essay on surrealism. From this essay, he cites, alongside the above-cited argument, the idea of profane illumination. He states that "the creative overcoming of religious illumination" is realized "in a profane illumination, a materialist, anthropological inspiration."[29] While identified as a citation through italics, the quotation here remains again without a proper reference. And although Taubes indicates that he agrees with Benjamin that such an overcoming is realized in surrealism, the corresponding passage in Benjamin's original reads somewhat differently. For in his "last snapshot of the European intelligentsia"—the subtitle of the Surrealism essay—Benjamin formulates the creative overcoming of religious illumination through profane illumination not as a fact but as a claim that surrealism only inadequately met: "This profane illumination did not always find the Surrealists equal to it, or to themselves; and the very writings that proclaim it most powerfully, Aragon's incomparable *Paysan de Paris* and Breton's *Nadja*, show very disturbing symptoms of deficiency."[30] In comparison to Benjamin's essay on surrealism, Taubes's talk relies more on the central concepts of Benjamin's last works, namely, Baudelaire, the aphorisms titled "Zentralpark," and the theses "On the Concept of History."

After reflecting on the structural similarities between Gnosticism and surrealism and underscoring their differences grounded in contrasting "cosmological alphabets" of protest, Taubes specifies his perspective by referring to Benjamin's theory of history.[31] He grounds his effort "to elucidate the conditions of possibility of surrealist poetry in view of the experience and doctrine of late ancient Gnosticism" on the historical index of readability: "The historical index of a mythology does not merely state that it belongs to a certain epoch. Above all, it states, as Walter Benjamin subtly notes, that it is only 'possible' or readable in a specific epoch."[32] This is a citation of a note from the N-block of Benjamin's *Arcades Project* on epistemological questions, where a "becoming possible" has been added to Benjamin's "arriving at readability."[33]

Taubes's comparison between Gnosticism and surrealism can be understood as an application of the sentence that immediately follows in Benjamin's *Arcades* notes: "Every present is determined by the images that are synchronistic with it: each Now is the Now of a certain perceptibility."[34] Since the *Arcades Project* had at the time not yet been published, Taubes here refers to unpublished material from the project that must have been circulating. Indeed, Benjamin already formulated the respective epistemological insight early on, for instance, in the key passage from his essay "Literary History and the Study of Literature" (1931), where he articulates the beautiful image of the work as a *microeon*.

> What is at stake is not to portray literary works in the context of their age but to represent the age that perceives them—our age—in the age during which they arose. It is this that makes literature an organon of history [*Geschichte*], and to achieve this, and not to reduce literature to the material of historiography [*Historie*], is the task of the literary historian.[35]

Taubes's formulation does not quote this text, but it is an almost exact citation from the notes to the *Arcades Project*.

In the controversial discussion of Taubes's talk, Siegfried Kracauer was the one who engaged with Taubes's theoretical concern of structural comparison most directly.[36] He addressed the possibilities and simultaneous problems of such a farsighted view (in the double sense of the word), namely an approach in which movements that are historically vastly separate are compared as corresponding primal situations, in this case connecting a movement from the centuries of early Christianity to one from the twentieth century. Kracauer's "methodological observation" assesses the Janus face of Taubes's procedure. The questionability of such structural comparisons, grounded in massive distance from the material, corresponds to the possibility of uncovering something in order for, similarly to aerial photos, "normally invisible configurations" to become recognizable.[37] He also remarks, alluding to Taubes's position in the academic institution—and presumably also to the position of the philosopher of religion in the circle of philosophers and literary historians forming *Poetik und Hermeneutik*: "As an aside, it would be worth a few additional considerations why it is that so often problematic conceptions become the source of durable insight."[38] Possibly, we can interpret this remark in view of its implicit counterpart as well, that is, that unproblematic conceptions often become a source of untenable insight. Taubes, in his response, brushes aside this suggestion, speaking instead of historiography's theoretical armature, again employing a series of Benjamin's concepts. In historiography, he explains, "comparable constellations crystallize out of the raw material of events. Any constructive principle tends toward abbreviation, without which no progress of insight would be possible."[39]

Taubes's interpretation of Gnosticism was the part of his talk that caused most controversy. His sharpest critic would be Hans Blumenberg, who regarded Taubes's structural comparison as static and its "inner-systematic consequence" as "trivial."[40] "The decisive structural difference between Gnosticism and surrealism," Blumenberg indicates, "ignored by J. Taubes, is the fact that Gnosticism did not know protest and revolt as forms of reaction."[41] What is at stake here is not a fact that Taubes overlooked, but rather precisely what he held dearest in his idea of Gnosticism. As a response, he sharpens the controversy to one between the perspectives of the history of philosophy and the history of religion, seconding this with the hint that the Church Fathers are a source of Blumenberg's own understanding of Gnosticism. Taubes argues that with Blumenberg's approach seeing the main problem of Gnosticism in a "demonization of the world-creator" and the resulting contradiction between redeemer and creator, the movement's revolutionary traits become of secondary relevance.

> However, from a religious-historical perspective the Gnostic revolt and provocation acquire an entirely different significance, despite the adaptation of

philosophical topoi from ancient tradition. It demonstrates a revolution in consciousness that exceeds the boundaries of ancient experience, if not *de jure*, at least *de facto*.[42]

Through Blumenberg's dismissal of what is most relevant to him in the gnosis-surrealism constellation, namely, revolt and provocation, Taubes is motivated to formulate a thesis through which he incorporates the warrantor of his theoretical armature into the comparative constellation. In supplementing the dimensions of revolt and provocation with a "representation of actualized utopia as the return of paradise," Taubes asserts that as a topos this idea is sustained up through "the modern theological Marxism"—and ascribes the latter to both Benjamin and Bloch, thus turning Benjamin without hesitation into a theological Marxist.[43] The philosopher of religion's desire not only overlooks that he thereby makes Benjamin into a partisan of surrealism, but also that in constructing a theological Marxism he undertakes a conciliation of exactly those ideas from which Benjamin's thinking emerged in a tension-filled relation. In making this argument he appeals to those designations through which Benjamin's dissimilar friends carried out their dispute about him: on the one hand, Scholem's wrestling over Benjamin's approach to theology and Judaism; on the other hand, Adorno's critique of an inadequate materialist foundation for Benjamin's theory of modernism.

BENJAMIN IN THE GUISE OF A
MARXIST AND MARCIONITE

In Taubes's subsequent texts that are now explicitly concerned with Benjamin we find an unfolding of both ingredients of the ascription "theological Marxist"—initially Marxism in line with the spirit of the time, later on the part of theology. At a sociology conference in 1969, Taubes gave a talk on "Culture and Ideology," in which he examines Benjamin's reflections on capitalism and evaluates them as an analysis of the superstructure, hence as a necessary step beyond Marx, considering Benjamin's discussion of the "phantasmagoria of capitalist culture," in particular.[44] The talk belongs to those texts of Taubes that adhere to academic convention insofar as he explains Benjamin's theses using to proper citations. In this case the citations are from the part of the *Arcades Project* made accessible through the 1955 edition of Benjamin's writings—from "Paris, Capital of the Nineteenth Century." Taubes's own propensity toward a Marxist analysis of culture is here manifest in his approving citation of Adorno's critical comments on an allegedly insufficient materialism of Benjamin's method, for instance, in the formulation that Benjamin placed himself at the "crossway of magic and positivism." However, Taubes in turn reveals proximity to Benjamin's orientation when he cites his concern from the artwork-essay "to make those insights available from extreme reactive theoreticians 'completely useless for the goals of fascism."[45] Later Taubes's judgment of the two theorists would thoroughly change when in his lectures on Paul he connects Adorno's *Minima Moralia* to an aestheticization of messianism and speaks about it almost sarcastically.

By contrast, the theological perspective of Taubes's image of Benjamin occurred only two decades later, in 1986, in the essay "Walter Benjamin—A Modern Marcionite?,"[46] written in the intellectual context of a German and French enthusiastic reception of Benjamin initiated through the publication of the *Arcades Project* the previous year. However, only a single page of Taubes's ten-page essay actually refers to Benjamin. As the subtitle announces, an inspection of Scholem's Benjamin-interpretation in the perspective of the history of religion, the essay is rather centered on an existing controversy described by Taubes as the opposition between a political sense of theocracy and an internalizing tendency. Since he argues here against drawing a demarcating line—associated with Scholem—between a "Jewish externality and Christian internality,"[47] his text is clearly a continuation of his own dissociation from Scholem in his earlier article "The Price of Messianism" (1983). There he had strongly criticized Scholem's "On the Jewish Understanding of the Messianic Idea" (1950), by arguing in particular against Scholem's strict opposition between Christianity and Judaism via the criterion of its internalization of the idea of redemption.[48]

Taubes's critique in the article on "a modern Marcionite" is now directed against what he sees as Scholem's annexation of Benjamin's "Theological-Political Fragment," interpreted "as a piece of Jewish theology." What is at stake here is to wrest the "intimate friend" Benjamin from Taubes's own former teacher, and to counter him with another Benjamin, one that supports his own position. "This lesson [*Lehrstück*] is," Taubes states, with reference to Benjamin's designation of his argument as a "lesson [*Lehrstück*] in philosophy of history," "if anything, the harshly anti-Jewish, Christian, in Scholem's sense, but actually Marcionite-Joachimite, piece [*Stück*] of theology by Bloch and Benjamin that Bloch early, Benjamin late, to end up, by means of arduous twist and turns, at a messianic Marxism."[49] In Taubes's picture of a modern Marcionite, Benjamin himself gets his say only with a few passages from the fragment: primarily the image of the two arrows with opposing directions, through which Benjamin describes the relationship between the "order of the profane" and "messianic intensity"; further the formula of the messianic intensity of the heart; the reference to a worldly *restitutio in integrum* leading to an eternity of decline; and, again, the concluding phrase about the task of world politics whose method is called nihilism.[50] What mainly concerns Taubes here is not so much a lesson in "messianic philosophy of history," but rather the outline of a " 'revolutionary gnosis' in the spirit of Marcion," who was for him the "most important interpreter of the apostle Paul," an approach he sees most clearly formulated in Bloch's work *The Spirit of Utopia*.[51]

Possibly the reading of Benjamin's "Theological-Political Fragment" as Marcionite theology went somewhat too far for Taubes himself; in any case in the essay's summary the question mark of the essay's title comes into play— with Taubes now using Benjamin's image of opposite-moving arrows for the controversial Jewish-Christian constellation he is occupied with.

> In sum, the fronts—Judaism and Christianity, political and apolitical messianism—are faltering. Reflections of higher complexity as Benjamin's theological-political theses present them, cannot be settled unambiguously. There are Marcionite vectors that determine the force field contrary to the Jewish ones. However overwrought it would be to portray Walter Benjamin as a modern Marcionite, it would equally be obscurantist to read the "task of world politics whose method must be called nihilism" without a Marcionite thorn in the flesh. [...]. I do not want to appropriate Benjamin for a specific orientation, but rather to suggest that he (with Ernst Bloch)—as a mystical Marxist—bears traits of which one hardly would have dreamt with quantities like Marxism and Jewish messianism.[52]

It is the very mixture from which the explosive stuff of thoughts emerges that constitutes Taubes's fascination with his Benjamin.

In this last paragraph, Taubes puts into question the all-too forced disambiguation of Benjamin's reflections. Perhaps it is added in debt to a critical discussion of his talk in the circle of Benjamin experts. For the remarks Benjamin himself has left us on Gnosticism are quite unambiguous, and obviously critical. After studying Gnostic sources in 1918 (in Wolfgang Schulz's edition *Dokumente der Gnosis*, 1910),[53] he initially had a mere ironical remark on the movement to offer. In the academic satire *Acta Muriensa*, which he coauthored with Scholem under the title "Athos and Atheists," the "venerating inclination towards the theological system of Gnosis" serves as a mocking characterization of a *Gelehrte*.[54] Later, in "Experience and Poverty" (1933), Benjamin counts the contemporary revival of Gnosticism among those problematic ideas that he interprets as the reverse side of a misery determined by the unfolding of technology.[55] In his studies on Kafka he assesses Kafka's writings as a "struggle against gnosis,"[56] citing at length from the conversation of Kafka with Brod, as transmitted by Brod, with Kafka's statement that we are "nihilistic thoughts, suicidal thoughts, that come into God's head." When Brod commented that this reminded him "at first of the Gnostic view of life," namely, "God as the evil demiurge, the world as his Fall," Kafka refused this as follows: "Oh no, [. . .] our world is only a bad mood of God, a bad day of his." And in response to Brod's question whether of "outside this manifestation of the world that we know" there was hope, Kafka responded, smilingly, "Oh, plenty of hope, an infinite amount of hope—but not for us."[57]

It is thus scarcely possible to derive a fascination with Gnosticism from Benjamin's remarks. Moreover, with the Kafka citation, a connection between nihilism and Gnosticism is expressly rejected. Nonetheless, Taubes stuck to his Marcionite Benjamin, for the question mark he had attached to that portrait of Benjamin seems to have quickly dissipated, as the 1987 lectures on Paul show. The interpretation he presents there of Benjamin's "Theological-Political Fragment" against the template of the Letter to the Romans, however, only gains clarity in light of the second line of Taubes's reading of Benjamin.

### CARL SCHMITT AND JACOB TAUBES: ON THE PRODUCTION OF A COMPOSITE PORTRAIT

The Schmitt-Benjamin constellation first surfaces in Taubes's lecture "Culture and Ideology" at a 1969 sociologists' conference: formally, Benjamin's critique of the concept of culture is in agreement, he argues, "with an attack on cultural history and sociology from the Right, which is simultaneously carried out by Carl Schmitt and Christoph Steding." At this point, the argument is still supplemented by the comment that Benjamin's criticism is "separated from Schmitt's and Steding's attack by an abyss"[58]—an abyss that will be bridged in the subsequent following steps of Taubes's reading. A draft of a letter to Schmitt written the following year—Taubes intended to organize a personal meeting with him—begins with an evocation of Benjamin's lines to Schmitt in December 1930, which accompanied a copy of his book *The Origin of the German Mourning Play*,[59] in order to suggest an analogy between Schmitt's thinking and Benjamin's. Guided by the rhetorical figure of "Benjamin and you as well," Taubes's letter to Schmitt develops the theme of a spiritual affinity despite "you and Benjamin having landed on different sides of the barricades" in the world civil war of the time.[60] In using Benjamin's letter as evidence that in Schmitt Benjamin had identified "a congenial species" (*eine wahlverwandte Art*), he invites Schmitt to extend him the same recognition. According to the well-known Schmittian formula that "the enemy is the figure of our own question," he poses the question: "Or were you blinded by the civil war's massive friend-enemy emplacement to discovering in him an elective affinity of spirit [*einen wahlverwandten Geist*]?" He tried to make the willingness to respond easier for the addressee through an expression of appreciation for his having been one of the first, in his 1956 book *Hamlet and Hekuba*, to assess Benjamin's book on *Mourning Play*.[61]

When due to Schmitt's bad health no initial meeting took place, Taubes took the initiative by giving contour to the asserted spiritual affinity between the two authors. As a result of this obsessively pursued project, a significant shift occurred in Taubes's system of coordinates: from an interest in Marxism and messianism to an interest in political theology. In a letter to Schmitt written in November 1977, he thus flatly states that "[e]verything that concerns me at present becomes for me a question of political theology."[62] From now on, Jacob Taubes saw Carl Schmitt in everything. For instance, he comments on the title of an announced lecture by Christian Meier on "Aeschylus and the Politics of the Greeks" in December 1978 as follows: "Already the title of the lecture by colleague Meier is tied to theses of Carl Schmitt."[63] In 1978 his project received a boost when the personal encounter with Schmitt came to fruition, so that political theology completely occupies the last decade of Taubes's activity at the FU Berlin. One example is the working group on "Political Theology and Hermeneutics" he initiated in 1980 as a sort of secession group of *Poetik und Hermeneutik*. For Taubes, a structural comparison between theological and juridical concepts and the Schmitt-Benjamin constellation is in the crosshairs of a study of the history and present of political theology.

A remarkable blind spot within this project is Taubes's evident failure to grapple with Benjamin's essay *Critique of Violence* (1921), although Benjamin here considers the relationship between theological and juridical concepts in a fundamental way. Taubes would have encountered here an insurmountable limit of the analogy between theological and juridical concepts. For toward the end, when Benjamin discusses divine violence as a model of "pure violence by human beings," he observes that in distinction to the latter sort of violence (by humans), the divine sort cannot be recognized as such "with certainty."[64] The limitation of human knowledge regarding divine violence reflects on the qualitative difference, which Benjamin discusses in leitmotif form, between biblical or sacral concepts, on the one hand, and the register of human concepts, on the other hand. For Benjamin, precisely this marks a limit to secularizing theological concepts to those at work in politics.[65]

Benjamin likewise does not think in terms of eons. In distinction to the Schmittian idea of the "Katechon," a concept of central importance for Taubes that he described in the commentary to his colloquium as a historical force "able to *arrest* the appearance of the Antichrist and the end of the present eon,"[66] Benjamin outlined his image of the *microeon*: a form of epistemology on a human scale. Additionally, the desire for deferral is conceived more as a human stance than as a historical power, for instance in the culture of narration, within which Benjamin locates hope as a worldly pendant to the messianic. He discovers this sort of small-scale messianism in the approach taken by the narrator of Goethe's *Elective Affinities*, in the novel's figures, and in Kafka's prose: "In the stories which Kafka left us, epic art regains the significance it had in the mouth of Scheherazade: its ability to postpone the future. In *Der Prozeß*, postponement is the hope of the accused man only if the proceedings do not gradually turn into the judgment."[67] This version of delay is closer to Scholem than Taubes would have liked.[68] We thus read, for example, in Scholem's essay *On Jonah and the Concept of Justice* (1919) that "deferral elevated to action is justice as a deed."[69] From the study of theological sources and from the conversations with Scholem during the Bern years, Benjamin developed his basic approach to traditional biblical figures; here theological concepts are precisely *not* transferred to a legal sphere.[70] Likewise, he sees the significance of deferral "not in the world of law, where retribution [*Vergeltung*] rules, but only where, in the moral world, it is encountered by forgiveness [*Vergebung*]"—as discussed in the essay "The Meaning of Time in the Moral World," written around the same time as Scholem's Jonah-text.[71]

A study of the "Critique of Violence" and Benjamin's reflections on the relationship between law and justice would have disturbed Taubes's Schmitt-Benjamin stretto. This remarkable blind spot in Taubes's readings of Benjamin is covered over by another text of Benjamin. For Taubes tirelessly cites Benjamin's letter to Schmitt from 1930, these lines thus receiving something like the status of a foundational document for his own project—legitimation and program at once.[72] While in Taubes's repeated evoking of the letter its function as a screen memory becomes clear, he himself tends to treat it as a kind of holy document, akin to a secret society's relic. In Taubes's project of political theology, the spirit of Benjamin has slipped in as the permanent trace of one of his letters.

> In the project's course, the interpretive patterns and linguistic conventions of the Schmitt-Benjamin constellation change imperceptibly. What began with the abyss and was continued with right and left on the barricades, what was grounded in a juxtaposition of Benjamin's "actual messianic position" with Schmitt's Christian figure of the *Katechon*[73] develops into a discourse within which the categories of right and left no longer play a role, as Taubes explicitly underscores a number of times. In the end the left-right barrier is replaced by an above-below barrier. This is the case for example in a discussion in which Jacob Taubes takes the place of Benjamin, in the appendix to the lectures on Paul, under the title "The Jacob Taubes—Carl Schmitt Story":
>
>> Schmitt thinks apocalyptically, but from above, from the powers [*Gewalten*]; I think from below. What we two have in common is that experience of time and history as term [*Frist*], as last respite [*Galgenfrist*]. Originally that is also a Christian experience of history.[74]

Taubes's project of political theology thus produces a composite portrait comprising not only features of both Walter Benjamin and Carl Schmitt but also his own. In his lectures on the Letter to the Romans, he finally superimposed the mask of Paul on this composite image.

The introduction to these lectures is concerned with "autobiographical approaches to the 'Letter to the Romans.'" Here Taubes's visit to Carl Schmitt takes on the character of a revelatory experience whose contents are inherently not communicable. "The conversations were monstrous [*ungeheuerlich*]. I cannot relate them here. In part they were conducted under a priestly seal."[75] In this way Carl Schmitt here literally takes on the figure of a priest. For through his demand related by Taubes, "now, Taubes, let us read Romans 9–11," the spiritual relative of Paul who was always already latently located within the Jewish philosopher of religion named Jacob has, as it were, come to himself: "And this is how I—a poor Job—came to the Letter to the Romans—as a Jew and not as a professor."[76] As an effect of this scene, the reading of Paul's letter turns into a confession and legacy at once; and authors who are relevant for Taubes are read into that horizon. In this way Benjamin as well, in whose writing neither the Letter to the Romans nor Paul ever play a role, becomes a spiritual relative not only of Schmitt but of Paul. [77]

## MISREADINGS: TAUBES'S CREATION OF A PAULINE BENJAMIN

The Benjamin chapter in the lecture on Paul starts with a strong statement: "Romans 8 has its closest parallel, it seems to me, in a text that is separated from it by nearly nineteen hundred years, Walter Benjamin's 'Theological-Political Fragment.'"[78] The method has in a certain sense remained the same; Taubes's "far-sightedness," to take up Kracauer's formulation, now simply focuses not on Gnosticism and surrealism but on Paul and Benjamin. In the consolidation of the two thinkers, alongside Romans 8 (on the spirit's life) he brings Romans 5 (on grace and the gift of justice), 13 (on the power of the state originating in God), and the Letter to the Corinthians into play. Taubes sees one of the parallels, for instance, in Benjamin's concept of Creation, which he calls Pauline since Benjamin regards the futility of Creation and the creature's sighing. As further evidence for his Pauline Benjamin, Taubes refers to the remarks on transience within the fragment. In light of these hints, Benjamin even becomes an "exegete of the 'nature' of Romans 8 and of Romans 13, nihilism as world politics." Taubes sees at least a distinction, however, "in the thought of the autonomy of what he [Benjamin] calls the profane." But he interprets Benjamin's reflections on the relationship between the profane and the messianic in the framework of the doctrine of the two kingdoms [*Zwei Reiche*].[79]

What is happening in this kind of reading Benjamin is more than a shift in accent and assessment. Rather, Taubes here engages in an act of *misreading* in Harold Bloom's sense,[80] by positioning Benjamin as his predecessor while at the same time reading him through the lens of his own work. In this process, Taubes reads past the basic structure of Benjamin's thinking. Within that thinking, Creation and history are as qualitatively different from each other as is biblical from profane speech; and it is only on the basis of this ineluctable separation that the reference of human action and speaking within history to biblical concepts can be illuminated in their dynamic and dialectic. For Benjamin, Creation is the world of Genesis, a site before the emergence of history, but not the inadequate world for which Gnosticism blames the demiurge, the creating God of the Hebrew Bible. Thus for Benjamin, lament that emerges only from the loss of a modest existence in the state of Creation is the language of the creature, whereas men's self-understanding as creaturely is analyzed as an effect of a counterhistorical stance: one that, for instance, confuses the suffering at an unfolding mourning play of the historical circumstances in the Baroque period with a prehistorical life in the state of Creation, as he argues in his book on *The Origin German Mourning Play* and in his essay on "Karl Kraus."[81]

Likewise, in the "Theological-Political Fragment" Benjamin does not, as Taubes paraphrases it, oppose the "order of the profane" to the "order of the messianic"; rather, Benjamin speaks of "messianic intensity." The counterstriving figure of the arrows moving in opposite directions is an image for a situation in which humanity's search for happiness as played out in the profane realm necessarily draws away from the messianic direction, while nevertheless advancing the messianic end of life. In his image, Benjamin thus understands the striving for happiness as a kind of reflection or echo of the messianic in the profane world. Here, he creates an analogy between the direction of messianic striving, oriented toward an end and completion of history, and human nature, whose goal is biological transience—or to speak with Freud, an approximation of the organic to the inorganic. In my view, Benjamin's counterstriving constellation can just as much be read against the template of Freud's similarly counterdirected economy of the *Thantos* and *Eros* than as an exposition of the Letter to the Romans.[82] Similar to Freud's definition of life as a detour on the path to assimilation of the organic to the inorganic, that is, to the end of life, Benjamin speaks of transience. In his fragment, the striving for happiness also describes a movement toward an end, in the case of earthliness the end of life, thus drawing an analogy to the messianic end of history as the end of history itself. Therefore, Benjamin can characterize nature here as being messianic: "[N]ature is messianic by reason of its eternal and total passing away."[83] In this fragment he reformulates reflections on transience that already concerned him as a young student. In the context of some of his notes on imagination (*Phantasie*) we find reflections on "eternal transience" that he connects to a certain kind of imagination, namely, in the mode of de-formation or de-figuration considered as an act of negativity: "This de-formation (*Entstaltung*) shows furthermore [...] the world caught in the process of eternal dissolution; and this mean eternal transience."[84] And in the very last, short paragraph of the "Theological-Political Fragment," before it breaks off, Benjamin tries to continue his reflections on messianic nature analogically in the context of the question of politics: "To strive for such a passing away [transience]—even the passing away of those stages of man that are nature—is the task of world politics, whose method must be called nihilism."[85] It would be presumptuous to try to interpret this in every sense cryptic sentence in a transparent manner. It is even more presumptuous to read it as Benjamin's political program.

Such an interpretation already has to be rejected in view of a number of other remarks of Benjamin on nihilism; for in no way does he emerge here as an advocate of nihilism. Rather, it is striking that Benjamin distinguishes between different varieties of nihilism. Where in the above cited passage of the surrealism essay he is concerned with the rare case of a turn taken by enslaved things into revolutionary nihilism,[86] elsewhere he speaks of a nihilism of *Weltschmerz* on the part of the Russian writer Sergei Yesenin,[87] of Goethe's nihilism of state and Humboldt's nihilism of politics,[88] he also attributes Proust with a wild form of nihilism[89] and L. F. Céline, Gottfried Benn, and Ernst Jünger with anthropological nihilism.[90] Also in the *Arcades Project*, he even assesses nihilism as the immanent core of bourgeois coziness. Other than in the time of Baudelaire, he argues, in the twentieth century nihilism has been assimilated into the apparatus of the rule of the bourgeoisie.[91] An author who treats nihilism in this manner will hardly propagate a world-political program along nihilistic lines. In addition, the idea of a world politics is alien to Benjamin's thinking—the idea never appears in his writing.

The point of Taubes's reading of Benjamin in the lectures on Paul is, on the contrary, to fix Benjamin's thinking on the plain of world politics as nihilism in order to interpret the concept of nihilism in the sentence he repeatedly cites from the "Theological-Political Fragment" as the "guiding thread also of the *hos me* the Corinthians and Romans. The world decays, the *morphē* of this world has past."[92] And again, what follows is the citation of the pathos formula of his Benjamin reading: "Here, the relationship to the world is, as the young Benjamin understands it, world politics as nihilism."[93] If one considers Taubes's formulation that links the world's decay with the dissolution of its *morphē*, as an adequate paraphrase of Paul's Letter to the Romans, it is far more likely that he arrived at this specific interpretation of Paul's epistolary writings through his reading of Benjamin and its superimposition by his fascination with Carl Schmitt's political theology than that Walter Benjamin has ever been an exegete of Paul. A similar phenomenon applies to Giorgio Agamben's otherwise fascinating *The Time That Remains: Commentary on the 'Letter to the Romans'* (2000), where constant associations with Benjamin appear by means of certain Benjaminian formulations[94]—in order to finally claim a discovery of Pauline citations in the "Concept of History" theses. But that is another story.

NOTES

1. Susan Taubes (born Feldman) was herself a philosopher; see Sigrid Weigel, "Between the Philosophy of Religion and Cultural History: Susan Taubes on the Birth of Tragedy and the Negative Theology of Modernity" *Telos* 150 (2010): 2, 115–35.

2. Susan Taubes, *Die Korrespondenz mit Jacob Taubes 1950–1951*, ed. Christina Pareigis (Munich, Germany: Fink, 2011), 245. The translation of Saint-John Perse's *Anabase* by Benjamin and Bernhard Groethuysen (first published in 1929) had at that time just been published again in "Schriftenreihe internationaler Avantgarde," in *Das Lot* (Berlin, 1950).

3. *The Hannah Arendt Papers at the Library of Congress*. General, 1938–1976, n.d.—"T" miscellaneous—1948–1975, n.d. (Series: Correspondence File, 1938–1976).

4. Jacob Taubes, "The Development of the Ontological Question in Recent German Philosophy," *Review of Metaphysics* 6 (1952/1953): 651–64.

5. Max Horkheimer, *Briefwechsel 1949–1973. Gesammelte Schriften*. Vol. 18 (Frankfurt am Main, Germany: Fischer, 1996), 287. I owe this hint to the article: Micha Brumlik, "Jacob Taubes und die Kritische Theorie," in *Abendländische Eschatologie: Ad Jacob Taubes*, eds. R. Faber, E. Goodman-Thau, Th. Macho (Würzburg, Germany: Königshausen & Neumann, 2001), 477.

6. Benjamin, *Schriften*. 2 Vols. eds. Th. W. Adorno and Gretel Adorno, assisted by Friedrich Podszus (Frankfurt am Main, Germany: Suhrkamp, 1955).

7. The dissertation includes two footnotes on Benjamin, one of them two pages long.

8. Benjamin, "On the Concept of History," in *Selected Writings, Volume 4*, eds. Howard Eiland and Michael W. Jennings (Cambridge, MA: Harvard University Press, 2006), 391.

9. Jacob Taubes, "Martin Buber and the Philosophy of History," in *From Cult to Culture: Fragments towards a Critique of Historical Reason*, eds. Charlotte Elisheva Fonrobert and Amir Engel (Stanford, CA: Stanford University Press, 2010), 10. The most precise examination on Taubes and Benjamin yet, to which I agree in many aspects, is: Günter Hartung, "Jacob Taubes und Walter Benjamin," in *Abendländische Eschatologie: Ad Jacob Taubes*.

10. Jacob Taubes, "The Intellectuals and the University," in *From Cult to Culture*, 282–301.

11. Benjamin, "One Way Street," in *Selected Writings, Volume 1*, eds. Marcus Bullock and Michael W. Jennings (Cambridge, MA: Harvard University Press, 2003), 487.

12. Jacob Taubes, "Notes on Surrealism," in *From Cult to Culture*, 98–123. The essay was first published in the proceedings of *Poetik und Hermeneutik*: Jacob Taubes, "Noten zum Surrealismus," in *Immanente Ästhetik, Ästhetische Reflexion: Lyrik als Paradigma der Moderne*, ed. Wolfgang Iser (Munich, Germany: Fink, 1966), 139–43.

13. Cf. Jacob Taubes, *Der Preis des Messianismus: Briefe von Jacob Taubes an Gershom Scholem und andere Materialien*, ed. Elettra Stimilli (Würzburg, Germany: Königshausen & Neumann, 2006), 67–92.

14. Jacob Taubes, "Notes on Surrealism," 98, 109.

15. Ibid., 112–13.

16. Benjamin, "On the Concept of History," in *Selected Writings, Volume 4*, 396.

17. Benjamin, "The Task of the Translator," in *Selected Writings, Volume 1*, 263.

18. Benjamin translated these lines: "L'élégance sans nom de l'humaine armature. / Tu réponds, grand squelette, a mon gout le plus cher!" as "des sterblichen Gerüsts erlesnen Adel. Großes Skelett! Du stimmst zu meinen liebsten Sätzen!," in Charles Baudelaire, *Tableaux Parisien*. Deutsche Übertragung mit einem Vorwort über die Aufgabe des Übersetzers von Walter Benjamin (Heidelberg, Germany: Verlag Richard Weissbach, 1923), 23.

19. Benjamin, "Central Park," in *Selected Writings, Volume 4*, 167.

20. Ibid., 183.

21. Benjamin, "Karl Kraus," in *Selected Writings, Volume 2*, eds. Michael W. Jennings, Howard Eiland, and Gary Smith (Cambridge, MA: Harvard University Press, 2003–2006), 453.

22. Ibid., 454.

23. Jacob Taubes, "Notes on Surrealism," 110.

24. Benjamin, "Surrealism," in *Selected Writings, Volume 2*, 210.

25. For an examination of this somewhat cryptic fragment as a historico-theoretical fragment informed by the reading of Freud's counterstriving constellation of Eros and Thantos in "Beyond the Pleasure Principle" and an attempt to construct a similar constellation concerning messianic hope and the transience of natural life: Sigrid Weigel, "Fidelity, Love, Eros: Benjamin's Bi-referential Concept of Life as Developed in 'Goethe's *Elective Affinities*." in *Walter Benjamin and Theology*, eds. Colby Dickinson and Stéphane Symons (New York: Fordham University Press, 2016), 75–92.

26. Taubes, "Notes on Surrealism," 134.

27. For Benjamin's alternative reference to images/pictures for examples: Sigrid Weigel, "The Flash of Knowledge and the Temporality of Images: Walter

Benjamin's Image-Based Epistemology and Its Preconditions in Visual Arts and Media History." *Critical Inquiry* 41 (2015): 1, 344–66.

28. Taubes, "Notes on Surrealism," 111.

29. Ibid., 105.

30. Benjamin, "Surrealism," in *Selected Writings, Volume 2*, 209.

31. Taubes, "Notes on Surrealism," 104.

32. Ibid., 105.

33. Benjamin, *The Arcades Project*, trans. Howard Eiland and Kevin McLaughlin (Cambridge, MA: Harvard University Press, 2004), 462 (translation modified).

34. Ibid., 462–63 (translation modified).

35. Benjamin, "Literary History and the Study of Literature," in *Selected Writings, Volume 2*. 464 (translation modified).

36. Kracauer was not a member of the circle, he just joined the symposium at *Schloss Auel* near Cologne when he was on one of his rare visits to Germany.

37. Kracauer compared this method with the way Hans Jonas acknowledged Spengler, namely "that his bird's-eye view, he made visible the phenomenon of 'pseudomorphosis' of cultures. For the same reason J. Taubes's far-sighted analogy seems to me to be very productive." Kracauer, "Notes on Surrealism," 112.

38. Ibid., 112.

39. Taubes, "Notes on Surrealism," 113.

40. Blumenberg, "Notes on Surrealism," 116.

41. Ibid., 117.

42. Jacob Taubes, "Notes on Surrealism," 119.

43. Ibid., 120.

44. Taubes, "Culture and Ideology," in *From Cult to Culture,* 250. First published in the proceedings of the 16th German Conference of Sociology *Spätkapitalismus oder Industriegesellschaft?* ed. by T. W. Adorno (Stuttgart, Germany: Enke, 1969), 117–38.

45. Jacob Taubes, "Culture and Ideology," 253.

46. Jacob Taubes, "Walter Benjamin: A modern Marcionite? Scholem's Benjamin Interpretation Reexamined," in *Benjamin and Theology*, eds. Colby Dickinson and Stéphane Symons (New York: Fordham, University Press, 2016), 164–78. First published in: Norbert Bolz, Richard Faber (ed.): *Antike und Moderne. Zu Walter Benjamins "Passagen"* (Würzburg, Germany: Königshausen & Neumann, 1986), 138–47.

47. Jacob Taubes, "Walter Benjamin: A Modern Marcionite?," 168 (translation modified).

48. Cf. Taubes, "The Price of Messianism," in *From Cult to Culture*, 3–9.

49. Taubes, "Walter Benjamin: A modern Marcionite?," 166–67 (translation modified).

50. Cf. Ibid., 169.

51. Ibid. 165–66 (translation modified).

52. Ibid., 175 (translation modified).

53. The book is part of a list of book orders in Benjamin's correspondence: Walter Benjamin, *Gesammelte Briefe*, ed. Theodor W. Adorno Archiv. 6 vols. (Frankfurt am Main, Germany: Suhrkamp, 1995–2000), 1, 430.

54. Benjamin, *Gesammelte Schriften, Band IV*, 442.

55. Benjamin, "Experience and Poverty," in *Selected Writings, Volume 2*, 732.

56. Benjamin, *Gesammelte Schriften, Band II*, 1268.

57. Benjamin, "Franz Kafka. On the Tenth Anniversary of His Death," in *Selected Writings, Volume 2*, 798.

58. Taubes, "Culture and Ideology," 252.

59. Cf. Benjamin, *Gesammelte Briefe*, 2, 558.

60. Jacob Taubes, Carl Schmitt, *Briefwechsel mit Materialien*, eds. Herbert Kopp-Oberstebrink, Thorsten Palzhoff, and Martin Treml (Munich, Germany: Fink, 2012), 28.

61. Ibid., 29.

62. Ibid., 37.

63. Ibid., 84.

64. Benjamin, "Critique of Violence," in *Selected Writings, Volume 1*, 252.

65. For a more extensive analysis, see Sigrid Weigel's other article in this volume.

66. Jacob Taubes, Carl Schmitt, *Briefwechsel*, 212.

67. Benjamin, "Franz Kafka. On the Tenth Anniversary of His Death," in *Selected Writings, Volume 2*, 807 (translation modified).

68. Many of Benjamin's knowledge of Judaism stems from the years he spent in Bern and his intense exchange with Scholem during this time.

69. Gershom Scholem, *Tagebücher nebst Aufsätzen und Entwürfen bis 1923*, eds. Karlfried Gründer and Friedrich Niewöhner (Frankfurt am Main, Germany: Jüdischer Verlag, 2000), 528. See also the chapter on Kafka in Stefano Marchesoni, *Walter Benjamins Konzept des Eingedenkens* (Berlin, Germany: Kulturverlag Kadmos, 2016).

70. Cf. the first three chapters of Sigrid Weigel, *Walter Benjamin: Images, the Creaturely, the Holy* (Stanford, CA: Stanford University Press, 2013).

71. Benjamin, "The Meaning of Time in the Moral Universe," in *Selected Writings, Volume 1*, 286.

72. There exists no correspondence between Benjamin and Schmitt, as Derrida assumed in *Force de loi: Le "Fondement mystique de l'autorité"* (1994), but just one short letter by Benjamin enclosed to the copy of his book he sent to Schmitt. In addition, the suggested affinity between Benjamin and Schmitt is not least based on mistranslations. For example, if the argument refers to Benjamin's *Critique of Violence* (1921) and to the term "state of exception"—as in Giorgio Agamben's book *State of Exception* (2003/2005)—this term is actually not to be found in Benjamin's original text. He instead talks of monstrous cases (*ungeheure Fälle*). For a more thorough analysis see the third chapter of Weigel, *Walter Benjamin*.

73. This is the announcement of the "Hermeneutic Colloquium on Political Theology" in the winter 1978-1979. Jacob Taubes, Carl Schmitt, *Briefwechsel*, 212.

74. Ibid., 249. Also see Jacob Taubes, *To Carl Schmitt: Letters and Reflections*, trans Keith Tribe (New York: Columbia University Press, 2013), 13. (Translation modified)

75. Jacob Taubes, *Die Politische Theologie des Paulus*: Lectures delivered at the Research Institute of the Protestant Student's Community in Heidelberg, February 23–27, 1987, based on recordings and revised by Aleida Assmann, ed. Aleida and Jan Assmann in collaboration with Horst Folkerts, Dietrich Hartwich, and Christoph Schulte (Munich: Fink, 1993), xx. For the English translation see: Jacob Taubes, *The Political Theology of Paul*, trans. Dana Hollander (Stanford, CA: Stanford University Press, 2004), 2 (translation modified).

76. Ibid., 3.

77. There are no traces in Benjamin's work indicating any discussion of Paul's epistolary writing itself. And the name of the philosopher who most intensely occupied himself with Paul's Letter to the Romans at that time, Karl Barth, only emerges at the margins: for example, when in 1936 Benjamin mentions that the editor of the journal *Orient und Okzident*, Fritz Lieb, for whom he was working on an article on Ljesskow, was a disciple of Karl Barth (Benjamin, *Gesammelte Briefe*, V, 275); however, from Lieb he only heard trivia of Barth, namely, on weather (V, 551); or when in his review of Adorno's work on Kierkegaard (1933) he mentions Karl Barth's *Dialectical Theology* as the last attempt to think in the line of Kierkegaard (III, 380), although in a letter in 1939 to Karl Thieme, whom he appreciated a lot, he admits not to know Karl Barth's dialectical theology, but he regrets this only because he thus misses to take the opposition of Thieme's thoughts to Barth's into consideration (V, 297).

78. Taubes, *The Political Theology of Paul*, 70.

79. Ibid., 74.

80. Harold Bloom, *A Map of Misreading* (New York: Oxford University Press, 1975).

81. Cf. the first chapter in Weigel, *Walter Benjamin*.

82. Cf. note 25.

83. Benjamin, "Theological-Political Fragment," in *Selected Writings, Volume 3*, eds. Howard Eiland and Michael W. Jennings (Cambridge, MA: Harvard University Press, 2002), 306.

84. Benjamin, "Imagination," in *Selected Writings, Volume 1*, 281 (translation modified).

85. Benjamin, "Theological-Political Fragment," in *Selected Writings, Volume 3*, 306.

86. Benjamin, "Surrealism," in *Selected Writings, Volume 2*, 210.

87. Benjamin, "Neue Dichtung in Rußland," in *Gesammelte Schriften, Band II*, 760.

88. Benjamin, "Goethe," in *Selected Writings, Volume 2*, 170.

89. Benjamin, "Moskauer Tagebuch," in *Gesammelte Schriften, Band VI*, 381.

90. Benjamin, "Benjamin an Scholem. San Remo. 2.7.1937," in *Gesammelte Schriften, Band V*, 1161.

91. Benjamin, *The Arcades Project*, 216, 385.

92. Taubes, *The Political Theology of Paul*, 72.

93. Ibid., 100.

94. Giorgio Agamben, *The Time That Remains: A Commentary on the Letter of the Romans*, trans. Patricia Dailey (Stanford, CA: Stanford University Press, 2005). The most significant example is the way how in his reading he circumscribes Pauline ideas by using Benjamin's term of now-time (*Jetztzeit*) and its description as homogeneous and empty time.

# Part IV.
# Jan Assmann
## A Late Voice in the German Secularization Debate

# Secularization and Theologization
## Introduction to Jan Assmann's *Monotheism*

DANIEL STEINMETZ-JENKINS

Scholarly works devoted to the so-called German secularization debate often begin with Hegel and typically end with the Hans Blumenberg's dispute over the "legitimacy of the modern age."[1] This would seem to suggest that theoretical debates in Germany today concerning secularization—specifically to what extent modern secular concepts have either broken or remained indebted to theological sources and inspirations—are no longer of significant interest. There can be no doubt that the dispute over secularization has waned in Germany since the 1980s; Jacob Taubes and Carl Schmitt died and Odo Marquard and Blumenberg's work no longer really addressed the topic. In spite of this there are a number of ways in which the German quarrel over secularization lives on. The post-9/11 claims of Jürgen Habermas regarding the "Judeo-Christian" origins of liberal democracy and human rights have rekindled memories of a long-standing scholarly debate in Germany.[2] In addition, since the late 1990s there has been increased interest in the topic in the United States, France, and elsewhere.[3] In the United States, in particular, a substantial literature now exists devoted to pinpointing the Christian origins of international relations theory, human rights, and secularism. Clearly political Islam is the main motivating factor behind this inquiry. In this sense the German secularization debate of the twentieth century proves highly relevant for understanding contemporary debates outside of Germany regarding the nature of secularization.

Much of the recent American literature, however, flatfootedly views the origins of secularism as a mere byproduct—and nothing more—of early modern Catholicism or Protestantism.[4] What if the origins of secularism, however, are much older than the Enlightenment, and actually preceded the birth of the Christian West? Might this possibility force scholars to reconsider the now oft-repeated claim that the origins of democracy, human rights, and secularism are to be found in Christianity? A shining example of such a counternarrative is on ful display in the writings the Egyptologist Jan Assmann, who can perhaps be considered the last great thinker of the German secularization debate.

Assmann's groundbreaking work on the history of Egyptian religion, his understanding of biblical monotheism as the defining psychohistorical event of the West, and his call for a new perspective on Moses have all contributed to pushing him into the center of much scholarly debate and inquiry.[5] Assmann has played a significant role in reviving interest in Freud's *Moses and Monotheism*, and he is perhaps best known in the US for his writings on cultural memory.

My aim in this piece is to provide a brief explanation of Assmann's unique understanding of secularization, and specifically his attempt to reorient the terms of the German debate. As such it serves as introduction to Assmann's essay "Monotheism," which this book makes available for the first time English. The small article is in fact, a condensed version of a much larger argument Assmann's makes concerning the theological origins of modernity in his still untranslated book, *Herrschaft und Heil*.[6] Much of my analysis, then, will make reference to this book, yet the crux of Assmann's thesis on secularization is on full display in "Monotheism."[7] The conclusion to this introduction will argue that Assmann's argument can be viewed as an attempt to overcome the German secularization debate.

THEOLOGIZATION: OVERCOMING CARL SCHMITT

In order to grasp Assmann's understanding of secularization, it is essential to recognize the main factor motivating it: to overcome the political theology of Carl Schmitt. Assmann pursues this by trying to undo Schmitt's famous dictum "that all significant concepts of the modern state theory are secularized theological concepts."[8] What did Schmitt specifically mean by this assertion? Schmitt understood the political to be structured according to a monotheistic and omnipotent conception of God. Assmann believes that this view of

God, which forms the basis of Schmitt's secularization thesis, is the product of the biblical conception of mosaic monotheism, or what he describes as the Mosaic distinction.

Ancient Egypt established a political order entirely this-worldly, immanent, and legitimated through visible religious representations. The Mosaic distinction initiated a political revolution by associating such representations with idolatry. The biblical figure of Moses inaugurates a new conception of the political by rooting the legitimacy of political order onto a nonworldly, transcendent, and nonrepresentable reality. Assmann describes the shift from political order being secured by worldly representations in Egypt to political legitimacy being derived from a monotheistic God that refuses all representations as theologization. Assmann states this thesis as follows:

> Political concepts ... have never left the realm of the political. They are political concepts even in the theological context. Such concepts pertain to the theology of a God, who engages in politics, either occasionally, when he is invited to—as with the 'heathens'—or the God does so 'full-time,' insofar as he forms an alliance with his people and directs their destiny—as with the Old Testament. Before constitutional law took these concepts over from theology, theology took these concepts over from the political sphere of the early great civilizations. I call this process 'theologization'; it aims to show the becoming-theological of central political concepts, just like Carl Schmitt aimed to show the becoming-political of central theological concepts. If Schmitt asserted that the 'origin of modern constitutional law lies in the spirit of theology,' then I am turning the tables and postulating that the 'origin of (monotheistic) theology lies in the spirit of politics.'[9]

In something of a polemic manner, Assmann, arguing in the vein of Schmitt but with cross-purposes, is suggesting that theologization means in principle that there are no legitimate theological-political concepts. Alois Halbmayr, one of Assmann's German critics, remarks that this actually entails that theological concepts "before they became theological concepts were political concepts and even as theological concepts they are still political."[10] It is in this manner that Assmann attempts to counter Schmitt not by appealing to the legitimacy of modernity,[11] but the illegitimacy of political theology by using Schmitt against himself.[12] Nevertheless, on Assmann's own terms, what does it mean to say that theological concepts are really political concepts? The answer to this question is inseparable from Assmann's theory of religion and politics in ancient Egypt.

THE BIRTH OF POLITICAL THEOLOGY

The tenor of Egyptian religion, according to Assmann, is inclusivity, integration, compatibility, reciprocity, and plurality. These notions are the product of a cosmo-theistic worldview by which the divine does not stand in opposition between the world, human beings, or society, but instead constitutes a principle that permeates and arranges them.[13] This is a world of continually developing synergistic processes. The sources of legitimacy that facilitate these processes are the pantheon of deities that represent and maintain political and religious order in the world. As Assmann states,

> In the political-religious dimension, a polytheistic world structured the political arrangement of society. It determined the membership of each to a city, festival and religious community. It decided the relationship of settlements to states, states to districts and districts to residency and defined in this manner the political identity of the land and all of its subdivisions down to the individual citizen.[14]

In *Moses the Egyptian*, Assmann argues that cosmo-theism not only ordered society down to the lowest sum of its parts, but also allowed for the "ecumen" of interconnected nations. This affirms that not the names or shapes of deities, but their similar functions allowed for their translation between disparate cultures. "Thus they functioned as a means of intercultural translatability. The gods were international because they were cosmic. The different people worshiped different gods, but nobody contested the reality of foreign gods and the legitimacy of foreign forms of worship."[15] Translation is made possible by a commensurability of function that allows for an overlapping consensus amongst the gods. The basic premises of this commensurability are guaranteed by cosmo-theism. This is to affirm that contained within the various comprehensive doctrines of democratic societies are functional equivalents than can be translated into a public conception of reason allowing for, in Rawlsian language, an overlapping consensus.

Theologization takes place "when concepts that had previously belonged in the sphere of justice are now inscribed theologically in this process of de-differentiation."[16] Out of the inscription of the political within the theological emerges the birth of a law-giving deity.[17] The Mosaic distinction derives its semantics from the rejection of Egypt. By juxtaposing Egypt with true religion, it "cut the umbilical cord which connected [Moses's] people and his religious ideas to their cultural and natural context."[18] Assmann describes this as semantic relocation by which the concepts and rhetoric of loyalty were transferred from the political to the divine sphere, where they acted as models between the relationship of god and man.

> Relocation means that something is withdrawn from one sphere and transferred to another. Thus, protection was no longer sought on the "mundane" plane, from kings and patrons, but on the divine plane, from a deity ... It means the transfer of the political institutions of alliance, treaty and vasseldom from the mundane sphere of politics to the transcendental sphere of religion. In Israel we are dealing with the "semiological divinization" or theologization of Egyptian, Hittite, Babylonian, and especially Assyrian foreign politics.[19]

This passage suggests that at the heart of semantic relocation is the emergence of political theology. The carrying out of this relocation is most clearly seen in the prohibition of images and idols. The prohibition against idols must be construed as a rival political alternative counterpolitic that sets itself directly against the very core of Egyptian political authority. As such, Egypt offers not a false religion but a false politics. On this basis Assmann is able to argue that as a result of the prohibition against idols the discourse between true and false religion first emerges since loyalty to the one true God affirms not denying the existence of other deities, but denying loyalty and allegiance to a false politic.[20]

In "Monotheism," he asks the question of what this distinction has meant for the history of political theology. This question is raised in light of Assmann's assertion that semantic relocation is sufficient but does not necessitate the potential for violence. The propensity toward violence arises not from the idea of the One God nor with distinction between truth and untruth. It instead is linked with the persecution of untruth when the distinction between true and false is conflated between "us" and "them," and thus construed in terms of friends and enemies. It is at this juncture that he suggests Carl Schmitt's conception of friends and enemies can be accounted for within the semantic field of the Mosaic distinction, and specifically the ban on images.

> Is there a correlation between the distinction of true and false and that between friends and enemies? This relationship is obvious and connected with the prohibition of images. The prohibition of images directed the theological distinction between truth and untruth, god and gods, into the political and interpreted it in the sense of friends and enemies. It defines who God's enemies are and where they stand. With the banning of images it is a matter of defining an enemy in light of the distinction between true and false.[21]

## ANTI-SEMITIC?

What might present itself at this moment is one particular charge against Assmann suggesting that his argument is potentially anti-Semitic.[22] From this angle the leveling of anti-Semitism at Assmann involves the claim that Judaism is ultimately responsible for establishing a turn not for the better, but for the worst by abolishing the golden age of primary religion.[23] It seems Assmann has responded to this charge in a variety of ways. The following interaction focuses on two of his responses to this criticism. Foremost, Assmann argues that of the three Abrahamitic religions, "Judaism is the only one that has never turned the implications of violence and intolerance into historical reality precisely because it has relegated the final universalizing of truth to eschatology and not to history."[24]

In light of this statement, it should be asked how Assmann views the modern state of Israel. It is interesting that in *Herrschaft und Heil* Assmann suggests that the very identity of ancient Israel was predicated as being against the Egyptian state in a manner analogous to Pierre Clastres's notions of *Société contre l'État*.[25] This could suggest that Assmann makes a direct link between the monotheistic revolution and a rejection of the state. Assmann further remarks that, though Judaism constitutes a culture established fundamentally on difference historically, this distinction has not been predicated on a division between friends and enemies.

> God is truth; the gods of others are lies. That is the theological basis of the distinction between friend and enemy. Only on this ground and in this semantic context has political theology actually become dangerous. The political theology of Carl Schmitt also stands in this tradition of revelational theology's propensity towards violence. Here lies, in my opinion, the actual "political problem" of monotheism.[26]

Judaism draws and maintains this boundary in the form of self-exclusion. Self-exclusion, concludes Assmann, necessitates no violence and is to be contrasted with Islam and Christianity, which historically have not recognized a boundary of this nature.

## ASSMANN AND THE END OF THE GERMAN SECULARIZATION DEBATE

As previously mentioned, the question of the legitimacy of the modern age is much more debated now in the United States than it is in Germany. Scholarship on all sides of the American political spectrum seem to be more open to the idea that Christianity is most responsible for providing the conditions for what Charles Taylor has described as the Secular Age.[27] Gone is the dominant scholarly viewpoint that the Enlightenment and Scientific Revolution ushered in today's secular societies. Whether out of nostalgia for an older European Catholic political order or due to Leftist-inspired frustrations over limitations of contemporary liberalism, it is now commonplace for US scholars to argue that the secular West emerged out of a Christian political-theological matrix.[28]

The German secularization debate of the twentieth century provides key resources for enriching the American debate over secularism. Like with the current debate in the US, the chapters in this volume have singled out Christianity or Judaism as the key factors for understanding the nature and legitimacy of modernity. The question is whether the rush to correct a secular bias has led scholars to embrace a theological one. Jan Assmann's intervention into the debate is to be found exactly here.

For him the question of the legitimacy of the modern age cannot be reduced to the question of whether modernity is a secularized form of Christianity or Judaism. Rather, we must go back to great ancient civilizations from which monotheism emerged if we truly are to understand the current age. In this sense Assmann's idea of the Mosaic distinction seems to radically reconceptualize the terms of the secularization debate. The legitimacy of modernity is no longer a debate regarding Christianity and the Enlightenment, but rather monotheism versus polytheism. The former represents to some degree political exclusivity and intolerance, while the latter contains the seedbeds for political inclusivity and tolerance. "Monotheism," Assmann affirms, "derives its crucial semantic elements from a construction of the rejected other ... it depends on the preservation of what it opposes for its own definition."[29] Assmann's new perspective on Moses is an attempt to recall a cultural memory and thus an alternative tradition that remains present but in a theologized form. This "simultaneity makes it possible to identify with the forms of expression of a past going back thousands of years."[30] This would suggest that Assmann appears to be advancing not simply a remembrance, but rather a possible recovery of political legitimacy. By invoking an alternative memory of the past, Assmann's project is ultimately attempting to revive an alternative political tradition. In doing so he has attempted to overcome political theology, and to redirect the general terms of the German secularization debate.

## NOTES

1. See, for instance, the following book-length studies: Hermann Lübbe, *Säkularisierung: Geschichte eines ideenpolitischen Begriffs* (Freiberg, Germany: Karl Alber, 1965); Giacomo Marramao, *Cielo e terra* (Rome, Italy: Laterza, 1994), Jean-Claude Monod, *La querelle de la sécularisation: théologie politique et philosophies de l'histoire de Hegel à Blumenberg* (Paris: Vrin), 2002. Strangely, a major study devoted to the German secularization debate–running from Hegel to Blumenberg or beyond—has yet to appear in English.

2. See, most obviously, his debate with then-Cardinal Joseph Ratzinger in: *The Dialectics of Socialization: On Reason and Religion* (San Francisco, CA: Ignatius Press, 2007).

3. For some of the main figures involved in the US see the following forum: *New German Critique*, special issue on "Secularization and Disenchantment," eds. Peter Eli Gordon and Jonathan Skolnik, 92 (Winter 2005). For an attempt to explain the political reasons behind the French reception see: Daniel Steinmetz-Jenkins, "French Laïcité and the Recent Reception of the German Secularization Debate into France," *Journal of Politics, Religion and Ideology* 12, no. 4 (2011): 433–47. Some of the best work today on the topic comes by way of Belgium. In addition to some of the contributors to this book see the edited volume: *Radical Secularization? An Inquiry into the Religious Roots of Secular Culture*, eds. Stijn Latré and Walter Van Herck (London: Bloomsbury, 2014). With a few exceptions there has been very little interest among British scholars in the German debate; the subject has basically been ignored by the Cambridge School of political thought, who have generally remained uninterested in the question of the theological origins of modernity.

4. See for instance: Josef Massad, *Islam and Liberalism* (Chicago, IL: University of Chicago Press, 2015); Saba Mahmood, *Religious Difference in a Secular Age: A Minority Report* (Princeton, NJ: Princeton University Press, 2015); Elizabeth Shakman Hurd, *Beyond Religious Freedom: The New Global Politics of Religion* (Princeton, NJ: Princeton University Press, 2015).

5. This debate has primarily taken place in Germany where his book *Moses the Egyptian* was met with fierce criticism, especially by German theologians. For reactions to the book see *Politsche Theologie*, ed. Jürgen Manemann, Band 4 (Berlin, Germany: Lit Verlag, 2002); Klaus Muller, "Gewalt und Wahrheit: Zu Jan Assmanns Monotheismuskritik," in *Das Gewalt Potential des Monotheismus und der dreieine Gott*, ed. Peter Walter (Freiberg, Germany: Herder, 2005), 74–83; Peter Schäfer, "Das jüdische Monopol: Jan Assmann und der Monotheismus," *Süddeutsche Zeitung*, August 8, 2004; Jan Assmann, *Die Mosaische Unterscheidung*.

*Oder der Preis des Monotheismus* (Munich, Germany: Carl Hanser Verlag, 2003), 145–273.

6. Jan Assmann, *Herrschaft und Heil: Politische Theologie in Altägypten, Israel und Europa* (Munich, Germany: Fischer Verlag, 2000). Herrschaft and Heil in this instance designates politics (Herrschaft) and theology (Heil).

7. This article draws in part on a much larger discussion I have previously devoted to Assmann's understanding of secularization: Daniel Steinmetz-Jenkins, "Jan Assmann and the Theologization of the Political," *Political Theology* 12 (2011): 4, 511–30.

8. Carl Schmitt, *Political Theology: Four Chapters on the Concept of Sovereignty* (Chicago, IL: University of Chicago Press, 2006), 36.

9. See page 232.

10. Alois Halbmayr, "Monotheismus als theologisch-politisches Problem: Kommentare," *Politsche Theologie*, ed. Jürgen Manemann Band 4 (Berlin, Germany: Lit Verlag, 2002), 135.

11. This, of course, is a reference to Hans Blumenberg, who nevertheless argues that Schmitt's political theology was itself a product of a secularized eschatology carried out as the ancient Church became more institutionalized. See Hans Blumenberg, *The Legitimacy of the Modern Age* (Cambridge, MA: MIT Press, 1983), 37–51.

12. Clearly Assmann's acceptance of Schmitt's conception of modernity is inseparable from his critique of biblical monotheism. The connection of Schmitt to the Mosaic distinction is confirmed by Assmann's acknowledged acceptance of Heinrich Meier's thesis of Schmitt being a political theologian, especially with the revelation of Schmitt's Glossarium. In his book on Carl Schmitt and the "Jewish Question," Raphael Gross singles out Assmann's acceptance of Schmitt's appraisal of political modernity as entirely problematic. Gross condemns Assmann's transfer "of an entire spectrum of Schmittian positions intertwined with the jurist's Nazi and anti-Semitic engagement." See Raphael Gross, *Carl Schmitt and the Jews: The "Jewish Question," the Holocaust, and German Legal Theory*, trans. Joel Golb (Madison: University of Wisconsin Press, 2007), 240. As Christian J. Emden in his review of Gross's book explains, "This remark refers in particular to Assmann's theory of cultural memory, which to a considerable extent rests on the notion that social groups seek to construct such cultural memory in order to stabilize their own identity. For Gross, however, this argument ultimately supports the notion of the 'homogeneity of cultures and nations' and, as such, echoes anti-Semitic conceptions of a German Volk." See Christian J. Emden, "How to Fall into Carl Schmitt's Trap," H-Net Reviews, July 2009, http://www.hnet.org/reviews/ show rev.php ?id =24782.

13. For a philosophical engagement with Assmann's notion of cosmo-theism see Jürgen Werbik, "Absolutistsicher Eingottglaube? Befreiende Vielfalt des Polytheismus," in *Ist der Glaube Feind der Freiheit?: Die neue Debatte um den Monotheismus*, ed. Thomas Söding (Breisgau, Germany: Herder, 2003), 142–75.

14. See page 234.

15. Jan Assmann, *Moses the Egyptian: The Memory of Egypt in Western Monotheism* (Cambridge, MA: Harvard University Press, 1997), 3.

16. Assmann, *Religion and Cultural Memory*, 36.

17. Jan Assmann, *The Price of Monotheism*, trans. Robert Savage (Stanford, CA: Stanford University Press, 2009), 48–56.

18. Assmann, *Moses the Egyptian*, 209.

19. Jan Assmann, "Axial Breakthroughs and Semantic Relocations in Ancient Egypt and Israel," in *Religion and Politics: Cultural Perspectives*, ed. Bernhard Giesen (London: Brill Academic, 2005), 44, 45.

20. "The political meaning of monotheism in its early stage does not deny the existence of other gods. On the contrary, without the existence of other gods the request to stay faithful to the lord would be pointless." Assmann, "Axial Breakthroughs," 50. They are false not because they are nonexistent but rather because they signify an oppressive political alternative. Of course this conception of the political is inseparable from a sharp distinction between God and the world. In *The Price of Monotheism*, Assmann makes the interesting argument that Karl Barth's dialectic theology and its radical transcendence vis-à-vis the liberal Protestant culture of its day is analogous to the Mosaic distinction and Egyptian culture and religion. *The Price of Monotheism*, 31–35.

21. See page ...

22. For Assmann's reaction to this charge, see *The Price of Monotheism*, 12–15.

23. Although this controversy has primarily taken place in Germany, the intellectual historian Richard Wolin recently made similar accusations against Assmann. See: "Biblical Blame Shift: Is the Egyptologist Jan Assmann Fueling Anti-Semitism," *Chronicle of Higher Education*, April, 15 2015. Strangely, Wolin does not seem aware of Assmann's numerous refutations of these charges, or that he was a student of Jacob Taubes, both of whom were trying to overcome Schmitt's political theology. In Assmann's case, it is quite clear that he is trying to overcome the friend/enemy distinction, which the Mosaic distinction does not necessarily entail.

24. Assmann, *God and Gods*, 111.

25. See *Herrschaft und Heil*, 49.

26. Assmann has responded in a number of other ways to this charge as well by suggesting that he interprets Moses not as a figure of history, whose existence is questionable, but rather as a figure of memory. Constructing how Moses is remembered is part of Assmann's project of mnemohistory, which "analyzes the importance which a present ascribes to the past ... The task of mnemohistory consists in analyzing the mythical elements in tradition and discovering their hidden agenda." Assmann, *Moses the Egyptian*, 11.

27. Charles Taylor, *A Secular Age* (Cambridge, MA: Belknap Press, 2007).

28. For a Catholic perspective that sees the roots of modern secularism—and its disorders—as a consequence of the Protestant Reformations see Brad Gregory, *The Unintended Reformation: How a Religious Revolution Secularized Society* (Cambridge, MA: Harvard University Press, 2012). For a perspective that ardently defends secularism yet nevertheless sees much of the secular modernity to be heavily indebted to conservative Christian ideas see Samuel Moyn, *Christian Human Rights* (Philadelphia: University of Pennsylvania Press, 2015).

29. Assmann, Moses the Egyptian, 211.

30. Assmann, *Religion and Cultural Memory*, 28. Assmann discusses the notion of the "theologizing of cultural memory" in the same book. See: 37–42.

# Monotheism

JAN ASSMANN

TRANSLATION BY PATRICK ELDRIDGE

SECULARIZATION AND THEOLOGIZATION

I am almost tempted to apologize for making use of Carl Schmitt once again, an author who is not so readily quotable and who is certainly overcited on the theme of "political theology."[1] Still, there is no easier way for me to clarify what I mean by "theologization" than by a critical reflection on Schmitt's work *Political Theology* from 1922, which opens with the sentence: "Sovereign is he who decides on the exception."[2] Schmitt holds that the concepts of sovereignty and of the state of exception are borrowed from theology: "All significant concepts of the modern theory of the state are secularized theological concepts."[3] In theological terms, "exception" means nothing other than "miracle," a kind of cosmological exception brought about by a repeal of the laws of nature; and "sovereignty" means the omnipotence of a God, who, as the creator of the world and its laws, also has the power to repeal these laws, from case to case.

Schmitt's rather witty and seductive reconstruction is wide off the mark, albeit in a revealing manner. The analogy between miracle and exception is anachronistic since it presupposes a concept of the laws of nature that is foreign to ancient thought. The exception, considered theologically, is not the miracle, but rather it has exactly the same meaning as in the political sphere. The sovereign God is not just lord of nature, but also, and above all, the lord of history. He is the one who decides on the state of exception, namely, on war.

This not only holds for biblical religions, but also for the pagan religions that are older than the Bible. Even in pagan religions, God is sovereign and decides on the state of exception. Typically, before beginning a war, an oracle would be consulted and the decision between war and peace was left to the divinity. The decision over the state of exception was always a matter that man happily allocated to a sphere that was inaccessible to humans, that is, the divine, which, incidentally, is opposed to the miracle, which evidently belonged to the magical, that is, priestly domain.

The political concepts, which Schmitt wants to derive from theology, have never left the realm of the political. They are political concepts even in the theological context. Such concepts pertain to the theology of a God, who engages in politics, either occasionally, when he is invited to—as with the pagans—or the God does so full-time, insofar as he forms an alliance with his people and directs their destiny—as with the Old Testament. Before constitutional law took these concepts over from theology, theology took these concepts over from the political sphere of the early great civilizations. I call this process "theologization"; it aims to show the becoming-theological of central political concepts, just like Carl Schmitt aimed to show the becoming-political of central theological concepts.[4] If Schmitt asserted that the "origin of modern constitutional law lies in the spirit of theology," then I am turning the tables and postulating that the "origin of (monotheistic) theology lies in the spirit of politics."

I understand the *origin of theology* in the same sense that Christian Meier speaks of the origin of the political (also so we can now proceed to an authority who is in no way suspect).[5] In my view, it is possible to show that Israel was the birthplace of theology in a way that completely corresponds to Athens being the birthplace of a certain type of political thought. What Christian Meier calls "the political" is not simply a political order. Rather, it is a sort of Archimedean point from which one can reflect on political organization and strive for the best one, on the basis of a consideration of alternatives. Likewise, what originated in Israel is not just religion in the Egyptian, Mesopotamian, or Roman sense. Here too, there is the discovery of an Archimedean point, from which one can discard religions as idolatry, paganism, and superstition, and accept the best or true religion. We must therefore distinguish between religion, which belongs to the basic conditions of human existence, and theology, which arose reflexively and in critical contrast to other religions as a form of worshiping the true God in Israel and elsewhere. Theology in this sense is the mark of a secondary religion.[6] The concept of the "origin of theology" thus does not refer to origin of religion in general, but rather the origin of *secondary* religion, which has become reflexive and exclusionary.

Secondary religion originates when one makes a distinction between true and false, and has introduced it into the sphere of religion. Only on this basis does it become possible to contrast oneself polemically with all previous religions, and to build the new edifice of a secondary religion on the ruins of the excluded, false, primary religion. The decisive and defining criterion of secondary religion is the iconoclastic or theoclastic antagonism directed against the primary religion. Whenever this antagonism appears in the guise of secondary religion, it has political consequences. This does not, however, entail that political theology is specific to secondary religions. Primary religions too know the most diverse forms of connection between authority and the sacred [*Herrschaft und Heil*]. Secondary religions, however, intervene in the existing political order and reshape it in ways that are unthinkable within the scope of primary religions. The Archimedean point of a religiously founded truth—which is foreign to primary religions—enables them to make these political changes.

There is also theology within the horizons of primary or polytheistic religions. There it does not so much concern questions of orthodoxy, or the distinction between true and false, or even, ultimately, the distinction between God and world; rather, quite to the contrary, it revolves around questions of the divine's inner-worldly appearance and the relation between God and the pantheon. The typical form of pagan theology is the *theologia tripartita*, which focuses on how the divine appears in three dimensions: the cosmic, the political, and the mythical.[7] The pantheon does not stand over and against the world (in the sense of cosmos, humans, and society); rather, it is a principle that permeates the world, giving it sense, structure, and order. A pantheon constitutes the *cosmos* first, which is thought to be a synergetic process made up of cooperating and opposing forces. At any rate, for the Egyptians, the cosmos was not so much a well-ordered space as it was a process that worked well, resulting each day anew from the gods' handiwork. Thus, it is clear that—and, for that matter, how—the principle of multiplicity is inherently inscribed into this worldview. The cosmic process would lose its synergetic character if it were thought of as the activity of a single God. A pantheon then constitutes the *state* and *society* second, insofar as the gods exert an earthly authority. All great divinities are gods of the city [*Stadtgötter*], and all significant settlements are cities of the gods [*Gottesstädte*]. The cult is nothing other than the service owed to the gods, as lords of the city. In the political-cultic dimension, a pantheon constitutes society's political structure: it determines belongingness to any fixed, civic, and cultic community, it determines the relationship between the settlements and the cities, between the cities and the regions, between region and residence, and thus defines the political identity of the country in all of its subdivisions, down to the last subject. Here too the principle of multiplicity shows its significance and absolute necessity. This richly nuanced sociopolitical identity would become an indistinct gray mass, if one single God were to replace the many gods. A pantheon constitutes, thirdly, the world of human fate [*Schicksalwelt*] (and this is perhaps the function of polytheism that is most difficult to comprehend). It is a world that mythically presents, as a meaningful whole, the gods' joys and sorrows, their crises and resolutions, their stages of life and transitions. The myths tell of the gods and thus establish and organize the forms of human life. Even this meaning-bestowing, foundational function stands or falls with the principle of multiplicity. The fates of the gods only unfold in relation to one another. Thus a pantheon articulates itself as a cosmic, political, and mythical theology, and the divine finds linguistic expression in a discourse on the cosmos, on state and cultic structures, and on mythical fates.[8] This is the theology that monotheism sets itself against.

THE POLITICAL MEANING OF BANNING IMAGES:
ICONOCLASM AS POLITICAL THEOLOGY

The contrastive, exclusionary character of monotheism finds its clearest expression in the prohibition of images.[9] The diverse motives of lawgivers, and the founders of peoples and religions unite in the prohibition of images. Here, Moses appears as a political theologian. The book of Exodus is not about the destruction of the Egyptian religion and, further, iconoclasm is not directed at the Egyptians, but against Moses's own people. One could perhaps even say it is directed against the inner Egyptian, which everyone carries in his heart as a temptation or longing.

The original scene of biblical iconoclasm is the episode of the golden calf.[10] The golden calf was not intended to stand in for the Egyptian Apis bull, but rather as a replacement for Moses, whom the Israelites thought dead, since he had not come back down from Mount Sinai. They wanted to replace the vanished representative of God with a representation of God, and they asked Aaron "to make Elohim for us, who shall go before us." Aaron cast for them the image of a bull, which the Israelites immediately acknowledged as their God: "This is your God, Israel, who led you out of Egypt." This image of God then is not some other God, if one looks at it in the subjectively meant sense, but is rather an image of Yahweh.[11] But there can be no image of Yahweh, and this is why, regardless of all good intentions, any image is automatically the image of another God, and thus becomes a sin (1 Kgs. 12:30). Moses's iconoclasm is directed against this image. First, however, he destroyed the tablets of the Ten Commandments in a rage. Wherever this image stands, the divine tablets do not belong, and so they must be immediately destroyed in order to avoid any contamination. The image is thereafter destroyed and not in a rage but quite methodically. He melts it down in the fire, grinds it into a fine powder, mixes it with water, and then gives it to the people to drink. The meaning of this practice becomes clear if we substitute image for holy animal. Namely, it is absolutely forbidden to consume holy animals. Thus, the Israelites were compelled to commit a severe breach of taboo in the eyes of pagan—indeed, Egyptian—religion, insofar as they relapsed back into worship of the calf. This image was subjectively intended to be an image of the Lord, however it became the image of the Apis bull, which they now must consume. In this way Moses sought to deaden the Egyptian within them, or at least one can symbolically interpret the practice as such.

All images, or—at once more precisely and more generally—all representations presuppose absence. In Egypt this is evidently the case. The gods are distant and hidden, and precisely for this reason they are present in their cult images in temples. Images of the divine also include sacred animals and the king. Egypt is a world full of representations of the divine, a world where the gods' presence is represented, which precisely for this reason presupposes the gods' absence. The Bible gives expression to this dynamic through concepts of life and death. The representations are dead in comparison with the living God. In order for the living God to dwell among his people, the images must disappear. The Egyptians take the exact opposite view. In order for the gods to bind men into a community, they must be manifest in images, kings, and sacred animals. No other means than representation can establish contact with the pantheon. If the images are destroyed, then the gods retreat from the world once again.

God is present and will suffer no representation. Whoever makes an image thereby presumes God's absence. So long as Moses was present as God's representative, no representation was necessary. But as soon as the people began to assume Moses was dead, a representation was inevitable. History teaches us that the inevitability of images stems from the experience of absence, above all from the experience of death and the desire to establish contact with the one who disappeared, beyond the boundaries of absence.[12]

Here is a revealing reflection on this theme, taken from the apocryphal Wisdom of Solomon (*Sapientia Salomonis*):

> For a father, consumed with grief at an untimely bereavement,
> made an image of his child who had suddenly been taken from him;
> he now honoured as a god what was once a dead human being,
> and handed on to his dependents secret rites and initiations.
> Then the ungodly custom, grown strong with time, was kept as a law,
> and at the command of monarchs carved images were worshipped.
> When people could not honour monarchs in their presence,
> for they lived at a distance
> they imagined their appearance far away,
> and made a visible image of the king whom they honoured,
> so that by their zeal they might flatter the absent one as though present.
>
> Then the ambition of the artisan impelled
> even those who did not know the king to intensify their worship.
> For he, perhaps wishing to please his ruler,
> skillfully forced the likeness to take more beautiful form,
> and the multitude, attracted by the charm of his work,
> now regarded as an object of worship the one whom shortly
>     before they had
> honoured as a human being. (Wisdom of Solomon, 14:15–20)

According to this theory, the origin of the cult of images lies in the cults of death and of the ruler, in sepulchral art and in political representation. At the time when this text was written, the world was full of statues of Roman emperors. The reverence shown to these statues acted as a test of loyalty for the subjected peoples, who were allowed to keep their own cults, customs, and laws, so long as they were only loyal to the Roman Empire, and this loyalty was publicly manifest in their veneration of images of the emperor. Images originate, on the one hand, from below—from the wish of those left behind to make contact with the one who is absent—and, on the other hand, from above—from the governing institutions' need for representations, that is, a presence in the whole area it governs, mediated by images. The two basic functions of images that the Book of Wisdom singled out have astonishingly prevailed in the age of photography. There is hardly a home that does not display absent and, especially, deceased family members, and there is not a single authoritarian or totalitarian state without images of the leader hanging in offices or classrooms.

Both basic functions of the image seem to lie at the heart of the biblical prohibition of images. For his worship, God wants neither death-cult nor ruler-cult. His living, albeit invisible, presence will not suffer any representation. Representation presupposes absence: the absence of the deceased or of the tyrant, who wants to exist everywhere and control everything, who, however, is a human being and thus can only be in one place at a time, and must therefore be resigned to an indirect presence through media. Images of God, insofar as they do not aim to present other gods, but rather God himself, assume that God is either dead or, like the Roman emperor, is subject to human limitations. Images are incompatible with the real presence that God claims, and that the covenants founds, that is, they are incompatible with the living and political form of divine involvement in the world. Only gods who are dead or are removed from the world need images. The living God does not need them; they are an abhorrence to him because they stand in the way of his specific engagement in the world.

One key feature of the prohibition of images is political and stems from the Jewish people's abhorrence for the coercive Hellenistic and Roman cult of the ruler. Banning images promotes a political theology of immediacy, which brooks no representation. God does not rule through images and surrogates; rather he lives among his people and announces his will in directives written by his own hand by speaking through his prophets and letting his spirit envelop his people. In this image-free space of God's immediate rule, images cannot be tolerated insofar as they present a foreign form of rule.

## THE BAN ON IMAGES AS DENUNCIATION OF COSMO-THEISTIC SYMBIOSES

The other key feature of the prohibition of images is directed against the symbiotic world-relation that lies at the basis of polytheistic, or better, cosmo-theistic religions. Cosmo-theism concerns the immanent divinity of the world [*Göttlichkeit der Welt*], which is manifest as a pantheon [*Götterwelt*]. Monotheism emancipates God from this immanence and juxtaposes him with the world, considered as an independent mass. Monotheism's emancipatory impulse achieves its most acute expression in the prohibition of images. This clearly concerns the radical detachment of God from all visible and sensory forms, the forms through which the divine appears in the cosmo-theistic, symbiotic world-relation. The ban on images not only forbids the depiction of God, but also of idols

> in the form of any figure—the likeness of male or female, the likeness of any animal that is on the earth, the likeness of any winged bird that flies in the air, the likeness of anything the creeps on the ground, the likeness of any fish that is in the water under the earth. And when you look up to the heavens and see the sun, the moon, and the stars, all the host of heaven, do not be led astray and bow down to them and serve them, things that the Lord your God has allotted to all the peoples everywhere under heaven. But the Lord has taken you and brought out of the iron-smelter, out of Egypt, to become a people of his very own possession, as you are now. (Dt. 4: 16–20)

This speaks to something that also plays a role in another place in the Bible, which connects the concept of image and the enumeration of creatures. Man is made in the image of God in order to rule over animals. "Then God said, 'Let us make humankind in our image, according to our likeness; and let them have dominion over the fish of the sea, and over the birds of the air, and over the cattle, and over all the wild animals of the earth, and over every creeping thing that creeps upon the earth" (Gen. 1:26). Man is placed above creation, not within it. Man should not worship animals, feeling weak, or dependent on them, but should rather freely and independently govern them. It is freedom, independence, and responsibility that make man an image of God. Man must not entangle himself in the world, believing that he must tend to them, worship them, or reconcile himself to them; he is set over them, which does not mean that he should exploit them, but rather that he takes up a free, independent, distanced, and yet also responsible and caring relationship to them. This freedom and independence become compromised when man begins to make images. Creating images is a form of entanglement in the world. The prohibition of images, just like the *dominium terrae*, aims to efface the sphere of the divine from the world, that is, the world unavailable to humans. Man should be able to avail of the world: hence, he acknowledges its nondivinity, or, more precisely, only acknowledges the divinity of the extra-worldly God. Ruling over something is the opposite of worshiping it. This applies to images too. Man should rule over matter, not worship it. Man should not worship images, for that would imply worship of the world.

Insofar as one God replaces a pantheon, the symbiotic relation to the world transforms into the relation between a subject and an object. In the cosmic dimension, the world becomes an object of divine creation and preservation; in the political dimension, society, and the state (now constituted anew as the community of the chosen people) become the objects and allies of God's rule; and in the mythical dimension God becomes lord of history, which is no longer the history of the gods, but world history. Cosmic theology is now creation theology, political theology is now theocracy, and mythical theology is now *historia sacra*. All three theologies describe forms of divinity's relationship to the world. If monotheism initially makes a strict division between God and world, this does not mean that God has nothing more to do with the world. On the contrary, monotheism can say that God not only created the world, but loves it so much that he gave up his only son, and further—in the context of Christian religion—his engagement in the world can take the form of incarnation while still preserving the distinction between world and God, as in the dialogical form of Martin Buber's "I and Thou."

## MONOTHEISM'S POTENTIAL FOR VIOLENCE

The name and the concept Moses stands for an authority that unfolds in time and history. These are not legends affixed to a great man, but rather themes, that Western humanity continually breathes new life into and employs. Moses is the symbolic figure of a turning point in human history, a change that cannot be located in either the historical period of the bronze age, or in the historical effect of one personage. This turning point is exclusively connected to monotheism, which promotes the worship of one single God who alone is the true God, and denounces all other gods as idols, as lies and deceptions. With this new type of religion, the distinction between truth and falsehood takes its place in the history of religion [*Religionsgeschichte*].

What does this turning point mean for the history of political theology? Is there a connection between the distinction of truth and falsehood, and the distinction between friend and enemy? The connection is plain and it is tied to the prohibition of images. The prohibition of images transforms the theological distinction between truth and falsehood, God and idols, into a political one, and interprets it in terms of friend and enemy. It defines who the enemies of Gods are, and where they stand. The prohibition of images defines the enemy in the light of the distinction between the true and the false. The enemy of God is whoever adheres to lies and worships idols.

In fact, the texts of the Old Testament employ a vocabulary of violence when it comes to excising the idol-worshipers. During the Enlightenment, writers repeatedly denounced the Old Testament as a text that glorified violence, pointing to the Levites's gruesome punishment, who, following the scene of the golden calf, marched through the camp and indiscriminately killed three thousand people (Ex. 32:25–35). Elias's revenge on the priests of Baal (1 Kgs. 18:40) and the implementation of Josiah's cult reforms (2 Kgs. 23:4–20) are hardly less violent. According to the Old Testament's presentation, monotheism was brought about through massacres. While the violence of biblical semantics is undeniable, it is also undeniably the case that of the three Abrahamic religions connected to this vocabulary, it was never the Jews but exclusively the Christians and Muslims who translated this violence into action. Judaism is a culture of difference. For Judaism, it is obvious that monotheism establishes a border or limit and that the Jewish people must preserve it. The border between Israel and other nations is not the border between friend and enemy. One only becomes an enemy by not respecting that border. Judaism then establishes the border and preserves it in the form of self-delimitation or self-exclusion. Self-exclusion does not require any violence. Christianity and Islam, on the other hand, do not acknowledge this border and for precisely this reason have had violent histories. The violence of their God against the other gods gives them the right to use violence against people who, in their eyes, remain devoted to other gods. Behind this lies the distinction between (religious) truth and lies, which is the distinguishing mark of monotheistic religion alone. God is the truth, and other peoples' gods are lies. That is the theological basis of the distinction between friend and enemy. It is only on this ground and in this semantic context that the political theology of violence became truly dangerous. Carl Schmitt's political theology also stands in this revelation-theological tradition of readiness for violence. In my view, the true "political problem" of monotheism lies here. If one wants to save the idea of monotheism, then one will have to divest it of its inherent violence.

NOTES

1. This paper is based on chapters I.2 and XI.3 of my book: Jan Assmann, *Herrschaft und Heil: Politische Theologie in Altägypten, Israel und Europa* (Munich, Germany: Carl Hanser, 2000).

2. Carl Schmitt, *Political Theology: Four Chapters on the Concept of Sovereignty*, trans. George Schwab (Chicago, IL and London: University of Chicago Press, 2005), 5.

3. Ibid., 36.

4. Schmitt's secularization theory (and above all that of Blumenberg) does not solely concern demonstrating how concepts migrate from one sphere to the other. The constancy of the structure should become clear through the shake-up of the positions. According to Blumenberg the "legitimacy of the modern age" rests on this constancy. On this basis, however, not only does the state presuppose theology but also replaces it. Cf. Hans Blumenberg, *The Legitimacy of the Modern Age*, trans. Robert Wallace (Cambridge, MA: MIT Press, 1983); Wolfgang Hübener, "Carl Schmitt und Hans Blumenberg oder über Kette und Schuß in der historischen Textur der Moderne," in *Der Fürst dieser Welt und die Folgen: Religionstheorie und die politische Theologie, vol. I*, ed. J. Taubes (Munich, Germany: Wilhelm Fink, 1983), 57–76; Pini Ifergan, "Cutting to the Chase: Carl Schmitt and Hans Blumenberg on Political Theology and Secularization," *New German Critique* 37 (2010): 149–71.

5. Christian Meier, *The Greek Discovery of Politics*, trans. David McLintock (Cambridge, MA: Harvard University Press, 1990).

6. On this distinction, cf. Theo Sundermeier, "Religion, Religionen," in *Lexikon missionstheologischer Grundbegriffe*, eds. Karl Müller and Theo Sundermeier (Berlin, Germany: Reimer, 1987); Jan Assmann, *Ma'at. Gerechtigkeit und Unsterblichkeit im Alten* (Munich, Germany: Beck, 1990), 19f.; 279–83; Jan Assmann, *The Price of Monotheism*, trans. Robert Savage (Stanford, CA: Stanford University Press, 2009). I prefer this neutral terminology over Max Weber's distinction between salvation- and world- or culture-religions. Cf. Wolfgang Schluchter, *Max Webers Studie über Konfuzianismus und Taoismus* (Frankfurt, Germany: Suhrkamp, 1983), 17–19; Wolfgang Schluchter, *Rationalism, Religion and Domination: A Weberian Perspective The Rise of Western Rationalism: Max Weber's developmental History*, trans. Neil Solomon (Berkeley: University of California Press, 1989). Of course, not all secondary religions are salvation-based religions, although the inverse is true.

7. On ancient conceptual history [*Begriffsgeschichte*], see: Ernst Feil, "Von der 'politischen Theologie' zur 'Theologie der Revolution'?" in *Diskussion zur Theologie der Revolution*, eds. Ernst Feil, Rudolf Weth (Munich, Germany: Christian Kaiser, 1969), 113ff. On *theologia tripartita*, cf. Godo Lieberg, "Die theologia tripartita als Formprinzip antiken Denkens," *Rheinische Museum* 125 (1982): 25–53; Wilhelm Geerlings, "Die theologia mythica des M. Terentius Varro," in *Mythos. Erzählende Weltdeutung im Spannungsfeld von Ritual, Geschichte und Rationalität: Bochumer altertumswissenschaftlicher Colloquium vol. II*, eds. Gerhard Binder and Bernd Effe (Trier, Germany: Wissenschaftlicher Verlag, 1990), 205–22. On *theologia civilis* specifically, cf. Hubert Cancik, "Augustinus als constantinisher Theologe," in *Der*

*Fürst dieser Welt und die Folgen: Religionstheorie und die politische Theologie vol. I*, ed. J. Taubes (Munich, Germany: Wilhelm Fink, 1983), 136–52; Albrecht Dihle, "Die Theologie tripartita bei Augustin" in *Geschichte—Tradition—Reflexion. Festschrift für Martin Hengel*, ed. Hubrecht Cancik (Tübingen, Germany: Mohr Siebeck, 1996), 183–202.

8. For a presentation of Egyptian religion according to these categories, see my book: Jan Assmann, *The Search for God in Ancient Egypt* (Ithaca, NY: Cornell University Press, 2001).

9. For literature on the biblical prohibition of images, see: Christoph Dohmen, *Das Bilderverbot: Bonner Biblische Beiträge 62*, 2nd ed. (Frankfurt, Germany: Athenäum, 1987); Trygvve Mettinger, *No Graven Image? Israelite Aniconism in Its Near Eastern Context: Coniectanea Biblica OT Series 42* (Stockholm, Sweden: Almqvist and Wiksell, 1995); Christoph Uehlinger, "Du culte des images à son interdit," *Le monde de la bible* 110 (April 1998): 52–63; Angelika Berlejung, *Die Theologie der Bilder: Herstellung und Einwehung von Kultbildern in Mesopotamien und die alttestamentliche Bilderpolemik. Orbis Biblicus et Orientalis 162* (Freiburg, Switzerland: Universitätsverlag, 1998); Michael B. Dick, "Prophetic Parodies of Making the Cult Image," in *Born in Heaven, Made on Earth. The Making of the Cult Image in the Ancient Near East*, ed. Michael B. Dick (Winona Lake, PA: Eisenbrauns, 1999), 1–54; Michael J. Rainer and Hans-Gerd Janßen eds., *Bilderverbot. Jahrbuch für politische Theologie vol. II* (Münster, Germany: LIT, 1997); Christian Scheib and Sabine Sanio eds., Bilder—Verbot und Verlangen in Kunst und Musick (Saarbrücken, Germany: PFAU, 2000); Jan Assmann, *The Price of Monotheism*, trans. Robert Savage (Stanford, CA: Stanford University Press, 2009), 97–103.

10. On this, see: Pier Cesare Bori, *The Golden Calf and the Origins of the Anti-Jewish Controversy* (Atlanta, GA: Scholars Press, 1990).

11. Cf. also 1 Kgs. 12:28ff. Jeroboam makes two golden calves and installs them in Bethel and Dan, which were meant as cultic installation for lords and masters, not for foreign gods. Nevertheless, this "became a sin." [Henceforth all passages from the Bible are taken from the *New Oxford Annotated Bible*, 4th ed.—*Tr.*]

12. On this theme, see the encompassing essay by: Hans Belting, "Aus dem Schatten des Todes: Bild und Körper in den Anfängen," in *Der Tod in den Weltkulturen und Weltreligionen*, ed. Constantin von Barloewen (Munich, Germany: Diedrichs 1996), 92–136; cf. also Hans Belting, *An Anthropology of Images: Picture, Medium, Body*, trans. Thomas Dunlap (Princeton, NJ: Princeton University Press, 2014), 84–123; Thomas Macho, "Tod und Trauer im kulturwissenschaftlichen Vergleich," in *Der Tod als Thema der Kulturtheorie*, auth. Jan Assmann, ed. Thomas Macho (Frankfurt, Germany: Suhrkamp, 2000), 91–120, 99–105.

CONTRIBUTORS

JAN ASSMANN is professor emeritus at the University of Heidelberg, where he held the chair of Egyptology between 1976 and 2003. He is also Honorary Professor of Cultural Studies at the University of Constance. Assmann has published on a wide range of topics in Egyptology, religious studies, memory studies, and cultural studies. His books in English translation include *Moses the Egyptian: The Memory of Egypt in Western Monotheism* (Harvard University Press, 1997), *Of God and Gods: Egypt, Israel and the Rise of Monotheism* (University of Wisconsin Press, 2008), *The Mosaic Distinction or the Price of Monotheism* (Stanford University Press, 2009). His most recent book is *Exodus: Die Revolution der Alten Welt* (Beck, 2015).

JEFFREY ANDREW BARASH is professor emeritus of philosophy at the Univeristé de Picardie in Amiens. His research concerns twentieth-century continental philosophy, with a specific focus on history, memory, and myth. He has published many books in French and English including *Martin Heidegger and the Problem of Historical Meaning* (Fordham University Press, 2003), *Politiques de l'histoire. L'historicisme comme promesse et comme mythe* (PUF 2004), and most recently, *Collective Memory and the Historical Past* (Chicago University Press, 2016).

AGATA BIELIK-ROBSON works as the professor of Jewish Studies at the University of Nottingham and at the Institute of Philosophy and Sociology, Polish Academy of Sciences in Warsaw. She has published articles in English, Polish, Russian, and German on philosophical aspects of psychoanalysis, romantic subjectivity, theory of literature, and philosophy of religion (especially Judaism and its crossings with modern philosophical thought). Her publications include books: *The Saving Lie: Harold Bloom and Deconstruction*

243

(Northwestern University Press, 2011), *Judaism in Contemporary Thought: Traces and Influence* (Routledge, 2014), and *Jewish Cryptotheologies of Late Modernity: Philosophical Marranos* (Routledge, 2014). She is also a coeditor of *Bamidbar: The Journal for Jewish Thought and Philosophy*, which appears in English in Passagen Verlag, in Vienna. Her new project, the book called *Another Finitude*, deals with the issue of the "finite life" and its peculiar messianic interpretation that can be found mostly in the late writings of Jacques Derrida.

PATRICK ELDRIDGE is assistant professor of philosophy at the University of New Brunswick, Saint John. He works and has published on different topics in phenomenology and continental philosophy.

MICHAËL FOESSEL is professor of philosophy at the Ecole Polytechnique in Paris. His academic work focuses on the philosophy of Immanuel Kant: *Kant et L'équivoque du Monde* (CNRS, 2008), but he also publishes on a wide range of philosophical and political topics: *La Privation de l'intime* (Seuil, 2008), *Après la fin du monde: Critique de la raison apocalyptique* (Seuil, 2012), *Le Temps de la Consolation* (Seuil, 2015), and he coedited *Modernité et Sécularisation: Hans Blumenberg, Karl Löwith, Carl Schmitt, Leo Strauss* (CNRS, 2007). Foessel also writes regularly for French newspapers *Le Monde* and *Libération*.

SAMUEL MOYN is professor of law and professor of history at Yale University. He has written several books in his fields of European intellectual history and human rights history, including *The Last Utopia: Human Rights in History* (Harvard University Press, 2010) and *Christian Human Rights* (University of Pennsylvania Press, 2015), based on Mellon Distinguished Lectures at the University of Pennsylvania in fall 2014. He also edited or coedited a number of others. His most recent and final book of human rights history is *Not Enough: Human Rights in an Unequal World* (Harvard University Press, 2018). Over the years he has written in venues such as *Boston Review*, the *Chronicle of Higher Education*, *Dissent*, *The Nation*, the *New Republic*, the *New York Times*, and the *Wall Street Journal*.

DANIEL STEINMETZ-JENKINS is a lecturer at Yale University's Jackson Institute for Global Affairs. He is writing a book for Columbia University Press titled *The Crisis of Secularism since 1989: A Global Perspective*.

Willem Styfhals is a postdoctoral fellow of the Research Foundation Flanders (FWO) at the Institute of Philosophy, KU Leuven. He is the author of *No Spiritual Investment in the World: Gnosticism and Postwar German Philosophy* (Cornell University Press, 2019).

STÉPHANE SYMONS is an associate professor at the Institute of Philosophy, KU Leuven. He is the author of *Walter Benjamin. Presence of Mind, Failure to Comprehend* (Brill, 2013), *More than Life: Georg Simmel and Walter Benjamin on Art* (Northwestern University Press, 2017), and *The Work of Forgetting, Or How Can We Make the Future Possible?* (Rowman and Littlefield International, 2018).

JACOB TAUBES (1923–1987) was a German philosopher of religion and professor of Jewish Studies and Hermeneutics at the Freie Universität Berlin. He has also taught at Harvard, Columbia, and Princeton University. His books include: *The Political Theology of Paul* (Stanford University Press, 2004), *Occidental Eschatology* (Stanford University Press, 2009), and the essay collections *From Cult to Culture* (Stanford University Press, 2009), and *Apokalypse und Politik* (Fink, 2017).

MARTIN TREML is researcher at the Zentrum für Literatur- und Kulturforschung in Berlin (ZfL) and head of the projects Aby Warburg and Cultures of Religion and Jacob Taubes in Context. He is the editor of Taubes's correspondences with Carl Schmitt (Fink, 2011) and Hans Blumenberg (Fink, 2013), as well as the collection of Taubes's essays, *Apokalypse und Politik* (Fink, 2017). He has also edited many books on issues in religious and cultural studies, among others *Nachleben der Religionen: Kulturwissenschaftliche Untersuchungen zur Dialektik der Säkularisierung* (Fink, 2007), *Heiliges Grab—Heilige Gräber: Aktualität und Nachleben von Pilgerorten* (Lukas, 2014), and *Warburgs Denkraum: Formen, Motive, Materialien* (Fink, 2014).

SIGRID WEIGEL is emeritus professor and former director of the Zentrum für Literatur- und Kulturforschung in Berlin (ZfL). She is also permanent visiting professor at Princeton University's German Department and honorary doctor at KU Leuven (Belgium). Her work concerns a wide range of topics in the humanities. Among her many books and edited volumes, the following appear in English: *Body-and Image-Space: Re-Reading Walter Benjamin* (Routledge, 1996), *Walter Benjamin: Images, the Creaturely, and the Holy* (Stanford University Press, 2013), *Escape to Life: German Intellectuals in New York: A Compendium on Exile after 1933* (De Gruyter, 2012). Her most recent monographs are: *Genea-Logik: Generation, Tradition und Evolution zwischen Kultur- und Naturwissenschaften* (Fink, 2006), *Grammatologie der Bilder* (Suhrkamp, 2015), *Geld und Genealogie* (Fink, 2019).

KIRK WETTERS is a professor in Yale University's Department of Germanic Languages and Literature. His current work pursues questions of legitimacy, illegitimacy, and legitimation in a wide range of literary and theoretical authors. His two monographs are *Demonic History from Goethe to the Present* (Northwestern University Press, 2014) and *The Opinion System: Impasses of the Public Sphere from Hobbes to Habermas* (Fordham University Press, 2008); coedited volumes: *Das Dämonische: Schicksale einer Kategorie der Zweideutigkeit* (Fink, 2014), and *Hans Blumenberg* (*Telos* 158, 2012).

# INDEX

absolutism, 169; Agamben on, 41; Arendt on, 133–43; Blumenberg on, 53; Hobbes on, 113, 118n27
Adorno, Theodor, 194; Bloch and, 69; *Dialectic of Enlightenment*, 35, 194; on Mannheim, 21–22, 26; *Minima Moralia*, 202; *Notes on Literature*, 196; on Weber, 21–22
afterlife (*Nachleben*), 4–5, 71n1, 87, 88, 95
Agamben, Giorgio, 38–41; Derrida on, 38, 48n43, 49n46; *The Kingdom and the Glory*, 15–16, 17n5, 31, 38–44; on *oikonomia*, 1, 40–44; *The Signature of All Things*, 39, 44n2, 48n43, 49n46; *State of Exception*, 215n72; on theological genealogy, 1, 7, 38; *The Time That Remains*, 15–16, 210, 216n94
Altizer, Thomas, 53
American Revolution, 136–37, 139–47, 184, 191
Anabaptists, 167, 183
Anders, Günther, 101
Anidjar, Gil, 15–16
anti-Semitism, 160, 161, 224, 227n12
Arendt, Hannah: Heidegger and, 101, 134; *The Human Condition*, 133, 149; *The Life of the Mind*, 146; on Locke, 144–45; marriage of, 101; Moyn on, 12, 131–50; *On Revolution*, 12, 131–44, 149; *The Origins of Totalitarianism*, 139; Schmitt and, 7, 131–50; Taubes and, 194

Aron, Raymond, 142
Assmann, Jan, 231–40, 243; *Herrschaft und Heil*, 14–15, 233; *The Price of Monotheism*, 228n20; on theologization, 7, 219–25
atheism, 53–54; Nancy on, 70–71; "pious," 52
Auerbach, Erich, 172
*Aufgabe* versus *Forderung* (exaction versus task), 94
Augustine of Hippo, 103, 117n16, 122

Bacon, Roger, 79n50
Bakunin, Mikhail, 171
Balakrishnan, Gopal, 160, 170
Barash, Jeffrey Andrew, 11–12, 101–15, 243
Barrow, Henry, 190–91
Barth, Karl, 107, 168, 215n77, 228n20
Baudelaire, Charles, 196–97, 199, 210, 212n18
Beckett, Samuel, 62, 63
Bekennende Kirche, 168
Benedict XVI (pope), 226n2
Benjamin, Walter, 4, 89–97, 193–210; *Arcades Project*, 199, 201–2, 210; *Critique of Violence*, 95, 98n2, 205–6, 215n72; *Doctrine of the Similar*, 89–90; "Experience and Poetry," 204; "Karl Kraus," 91–92, 197, 209; language theory of, 83–86, 88–90; on Last Judgment, 85, 91, 92; *Literary History and the Study of Literature*, 163, 199;

247

Benjamin, Walter *(cont'd)*
  *On Language*, 89, 90; *On the Concept of History*, 84–86, 195, 197, 199; "On the Role of Language in Mourning Play and Tragedy," 85; *One-Way Street*, 195; *The Origin of the German Mourning Play*, 204–5, 209; Schmitt and, 7, 195, 206–7, 215n72; Scholem and, 214n68; "The Task of the Translator," 83–86, 196; Taubes and, 13–14, 193–210; "Theological-Political Fragment," 197, 202–4, 208–10; on translation, 67, 83–86, 92–93, 97, 98n5; Weigel on, 11, 83–97, 193–210
Benn, Gottfried, 210
Berman, Hugo, 164
Berman, Marshall, 76n41
Bielik-Robson, Agata, 10–11, 51–71, 243–44
Bismarck, Otto von, 29
Blake, William, 58
Blanchot, Maurice, 70, 71
Bloch, Ernst, 68–70, 78n50, 201, 203
Bloom, Harold, 208
Blumenberg, Hans, 198; Agamben on, 39–41; on Christianity, 33–34, 37, 63–65; on echo chambers, 36–37, 43; on *factum brutum*, 61; on Gnosticism, 53, 55, 70, 200–201; Heidegger and, 122; on history of philosophy, 124; Jünger and, 75n33; Kant and, 12, 119–29; *The Legitimacy of the Modern Age*, 23–24, 34, 53, 58–59, 63–64, 86–88; Löwith and, 6–7, 10–12, 23–44, 65, 122; "negative anthropology" of, 48n30; Nietzsche and, 66–67; on nominalism, 59–60; on progress, 128; Schmitt and, 86–88; on secularization, 3, 6–7, 24, 219; Weber and, 24, 32, 33; *Work on Myth*, 59–60, 71, 75n33
Böckenförde, Ernst-Wolfgang, 161–62
Bodin, Jean, 141
Borutta, Manuel, 17n5
Bosch, Hieronymus, 172–73
Bosse, Abraham, 172
Bossuet, Jacques-Bénigne, 122

Brentano, Margherita von, 161
Breton, André, 199
Brient, Elisabeth, 76n38
Brueghel, Pieter, 172
Bruno, Giordano, 76n38, 87
Buber, Martin, 194
Bultmann, Rudolf, 103, 107, 108, 124
Byron, Lord, 170

Calvin, John, 112–13
Cambridge School, 112
capitalism, 3, 4, 23, 24, 27
Cassirer, Ernst, 11–12, 101–15; *The Myth of the State*, 114–15; *Mythical Thought*, 103–7, 109–10; *The Philosophy of Enlightenment*, 112; *Philosophy of Symbolic Forms*, 103–5, 109; *Spirit and Life*, 110
Catholicism. *See* Christianity
Céline, Louis-Ferdinand, 210
Charlemagne, Holy Roman Emperor, 180
choice versus decision (*Wahl* versus *Entscheidung*), 95–96
Christianity, 104, 120, 189, 240; Arendt and, 132–34, 143–50; Blumenberg on, 33–34, 37, 63–65, 75n34; Heidegger on, 103, 107–8; Judaism and, 164, 170–72; Löwith on, 32–34, 37; messianism of, 69; monotheism of, 170, 224–25; Nancy on, 15–16, 55, 61–62; Neoplatonism and, 117n16; Schmitt and, 170, 171; Stoicism and, 111, 121–23; Taubes on, 164; totalitarianism and, 133. *See also* Marcionism; Paul
Clastres, Pierre, 224
Cohen, Hermann, 104–7, 168
Cohn, Norman, 169
Comte, Auguste, 122
consolation, 119–21; desolation and, 121; Hegel on, 127; modernity and, 127–29; progress and, 126; reconciliation versus, 127
Copernican turn, 67–68, 77n44, 125
Corinthians, letters to, 14, 171, 208, 210
Corwin, Edward S., 153n23
cosmo-theism, 237–39

cryptotheology, 10, 51–71; Arendt on, 140, 142–43; "spectral," 79n50; Spinoza and, 72n13

Davos Debate (1929), 11–12, 101–15
"death of God," 4, 52–59; Altizer on, 53; Derrida on, 54; Nancy on, 53, 55; Nietzsche on, 57, 58, 62, 181; Proudhon on, 188
decisionism, 27–29
*Déclaration des droits de l'homme et du citoyen*, 180–81
Declaration of Independence, 142, 144, 180–81
deism, 140, 169, 184–85, 188
Deleuze, Gilles, 52
democracy, 181–84; Agamben on, 41; authority in, 183; Habermas on, 219; patriarchy and, 46; "religious," 183; Rousseau on, 169–70; Schmitt on, 171; Taubes on, 13, 164–73, 179–91
Derrida, Jacques, 69–70, 80n60; on Agamben, 38, 48n43, 49n46; "Faith and Knowledge," 54; *Force de loi*, 215n72; *Ghostly Demarcations*, 69–70, 79n56; *Glas*, 51, 73n16; on Hegel, 58, 73n16; on Marx, 79n56; on origin of history, 51; *The Sovereign and the Beast*, 48n43; on *tsimtsum*, 56; "Ulysses Gramophone," 72n12
Descartes, René, 57, 62, 63, 74n29, 184–85
*deus absconditus* (Hidden God), 52–55, 64, 70
*deus fallax*, 57, 74n29
Deuteronomy, 238
disenchantment, 4, 7, 25, 43, 129
"divine mandate," 93–96
divine right of kings, 135–36, 180–81, 187
Donoso Cortés, Juan, 167–70, 185–89
Dostoevsky, Fyodor, 166, 171, 181
Duns Scotus, John, 52
Dürer, Albrecht, 5, 175n24
Dyzenhaus, David, 46n10, 47n15

"economic theology," 1, 40–44

Egyptian religion, 220–24, 232–35
Eldridge, Patrick, 119–29, 231–40, 244
Eliot, T. S., 61
Emden, Christian J., 227n12
*Entweltlichung*, 65
*Entzauberung*. See disenchantment
Epicureanism, 63–64, 66
eschatology, 121–24, 163; Blumenberg on, 40; Löwith on, 5, 122–23; Schmitt on, 170, 171; Taubes on, 12, 206

*factum brutum* (primal fact), 59–64, 68, 74n21; Bielik-Robson on, 11; cryptotheologies of, 70; Derrida on, 80n60
Foessel, Michaël, 12, 78n49, 79n60, 119–29, 244
*Forderung* versus *Aufgabe* (exaction versus task), 94
Forsthoff, Ernst, 160
Foucault, Michel, 8–9, 22, 23, 41
Fraenger, Wilhelm, 172
Frank, Jacob, 77n42
Frankfurt School, 27, 46n10, 194
Frazer, James George, 181
Free University of Berlin, 161, 172, 193, 205
French Revolution, 171, 180–81, 184–88, 191
Freud, Sigmund, 62, 166–68, 181, 209, 212n25; on Copernican revolution, 125; on monotheism, 220

Galatians, Letter to, 164
Galileo, 125
genealogy, 7–10; categories of, 10, 23, 25–26; Foucault on, 8–9, 22, 23; function of, 42; secularization and, 2–8, 15–16; theological, 1, 7, 38; "weak," 21–22, 30; Weber on, 22–26
Genesis, Book of, 89–91, 91, 166, 182
*genius malignus*, 57, 74n29
Gentilis, Albercius, 87, 98n10
George School, 93, 94
*Geschöpf* versus *Gebilde* (creation versus shaped form), 94–95
Geulen, Eva, 50
Gillespier, Michael, 15–16

249

Gnosticism, 40, 167, 203–4; Blumenberg on, 53, 55, 70, 200–201; Bosch and, 172; danger of, 53, 55, 56, 69, 70; overcoming of, 76n42; Strauss on, 76n42; surrealism and, 14, 196–201; Taubes on, 172

Goethe, Johann Wolfgang von, 61, 210; *Elective Affinities*, 93–96, 206; *Wilhelm Meister's Apprenticeship*, 29

Gogarten, Friedrich, 107

Golb, Joel, 193–210

Gordon, Peter Eli, 115n3

Gregory, Brad, 15–16, 17n5

Gross, Raphael, 227n12

Grotius, Hugo, 113

Gundolf, Friedrich, 93

Habermas, Jürgen, 219; on Schelling, 74n27; on Schmitt, 26–29, 46n10; on Weber, 26–29, 47n15, 49n46

Halbmayr, Alois, 221

Harnack, Adolf von, 107

Hastings, Warren, 138, 153n20

Hegel, G. W. F., 23, 54, 120, 122; on *Antigone*, 163; on consolation, 127; on "death of God religion," 52, 54, 57; Derrida on, 58, 73n16; Kant and, 127–28; *Phenomenology of Spirit*, 55; on progress, 127–28; on religion, 78n49; on secularization, 219

Heidegger, Martin, 11–12, 101–15; Arendt and, 101, 134; *Being and Time*, 101–4, 108; Cassirer on, 110; *Beiträge zur Philosophie*, 76n42; Blumenberg and, 122; influence of, 45n9; on Luther, 103, 107–8, 114; marriage of, 103; on philosophy of religion, 103, 107–8; on religious experience, 108; "The Task and the Ways of Phenomenological Research," 101

Heller-Roazen, Daniel, 45n8

Herder, Johann Gottfried von, 89, 114

heresy, 167, 181–84. *See also* Marcionism

hermeneutics, 39, 195–96, 198–201, 205

Heselhaus, Clemens, 198

Hidden God (*deus absconditus*), 52–55, 64, 70

history, 67; origin of, 51; philosophies of, 31–36, 122–27, 194–96; "task" of, 186; theology of, 122

Hobbes, Thomas, 113, 128, 171–72; Schmitt and, 118n27, 162

Holocaust, 161

Holthusen, Hans Egon, 165

Horkheimer, Max, 35, 194

Hulme, T. E., 148

humanism, 5, 32, 39, 45n8

"immanentization," 5, 52, 54–56, 67; Bielik-Robson on, 10; Nancy on, 69

infinity, 125–26, 128

intellectuals, 14, 159, 195, 198

Islam, 163, 165, 175n24, 219–20, 224, 240

Jauß, Hans Robert, 198

Jensen, Merrill, 143

Jonas, Hans, 55–56; Arendt on, 151n6; "The Concept of God after Auschwitz," 55; *Gnosticism and the Spirit of Late Antiquity*, 167; Kracauer on, 213n37; Luria and, 55, 64; *The Sacredness of the Person*, 17n5; Strauss and, 76n42, 77n42

Jones, Rufus M., 184

Joyce, James, 72n12

Judaism, 168, 240; anti-Semitism and, 160, 161, 224, 227n12; Christianity and, 164, 170–72; kabbalah of, 54, 60; messianism in, 52–54, 68, 69, 79n50, 106; monotheism of, 104–6, 170, 224–25

Jünger, Ernst, 210

kabbalah, 54, 60

Kafka, Franz, 60–61, 204, 206

Kahn, Victoria, 16

Kant, Immanuel, 66, 113, 160; Cassirer on, 111; *The Conflict of the Faculties*, 126–27; Foessel on, 12, 79n60, 119–29; Hegel and, 127–28; *The Idea of a Universal History*, 120–21, 123; on progress, 120–21, 123, 129; on religion, 78n49

Kantorowicz, Ernst, 141
Katechon, 162–63, 206, 207
Kelsen, Hans, 189–90
kenosis, 57–58, 73n16
Kepler, Johannes, 114
Kierkegaard, Søren, 103, 108, 215n77; Taubes on, 164, 167–70, 185–86, 188–89
Kissinger, Henry, 164–65
Koselleck, Reinhart, 159, 160
Kracauer, Siegfried, 199–200, 208, 213nn36–37
Kraus, Karl, 91–92, 197, 209

language, 92; Benjamin on, 83–86, 88–90; "mere," 84–86, 98n5; origin of, 83, 89–90; theories of, 83–86, 88–90
Last Judgment, 85, 91, 92, 182
Lazier, Benjamin, 76n42
Lessing, Gotthold Ephraim, 78n49, 124
Levinas, Emmanuel, 150n1
Lieb, Fritz, 215n77
Lilla, Mark, 15–16
Lincoln, Abraham, 183
liturgy, 180, 183, 185
Locke, John, 144–45
Loos, Adolf, 91
Löwith, Karl, 120; Blumenberg and, 6, 7, 10, 12, 23–44, 65, 122; on Christianity, 32–34, 37; cryptotheology and, 52–53; Heidegger and, 110; *Meaning in History*, 5, 23, 31–32, 35–37, 67; appendix to, 37; Wetters on, 78n46; on mythic narrative, 62; on progress, 121; Taubes and, 78n46; on *Verweltlichung*, 122; Wetters on, 10
Luria, Isaac, 54–60, 64. *See also* tsimtsum
Luther, Martin, 54, 61, 72n7; Bultmann on, 108; Cassirer on, 105, 110–14; *Eight Sermons*, 111; Heidegger on, 103, 107–8, 114
Lyotard, Jean-François, 126

Manicheism, 188
Mannheim, Karl, 21–22, 26
Marcionism, 14, 195, 201–4; inverted, 64, 75n34. *See also* Christianity

Marcuse, Herbert, 194
Markell, Patchen, 154n35
Marquard, Odo, 5
Marx, Karl, 31–32, 66, 122, 201–4; Derrida on, 79n56; secularization and, 23; Taubes on, 164, 167, 168, 185–87, 189
Mayflower Compact, 143, 145
McCormick, John P., 49n46
Meier, Christian, 205, 232
Meier, Heinrich, 227n12
messianism, 198, 202, 209; Christian, 69, 195, 203; Jewish, 52–54, 68, 69, 79n50, 106, 203
millenarianism, 123, 146, 169
Miller, Perry, 143, 155n39
Milton, John, 59–60, 64–67, 73n18
Mohler, Armin, 161–62
monotheism, 104–6, 170, 237–40; Arendt on, 152n13; Assmann on, 219–25, 228n20, 231–40; Freud on, 220
Montesquieu, 154n35
Moses, 143, 183, 220, 222–24, 234–35, 239
Moyn, Samuel, 12, 131–50, 229n28, 244
mystical nominalism, 79n50
myth, 60–62; Blumenberg on, 59–60, 71, 75n33; Cassirer on, 103–7, 109–10, 114–15

*Nachleben* (afterlife), 4–5, 71n1, 87, 88, 95
Nancy, Jean-Luc, 51–53, 69; on atheism, 70–71; *Corpus*, 51, 58, 62; on death of God, 53, 55; *Dis-Enclosure*, 15–16, 55, 61–62; on end of myth, 59; on instantaneous immanentization, 69; *The Sense of the World*, 61, 80n63
Napoleon Bonaparte, 187
National Socialism, 27, 112–14; Heidegger and, 112, 114; Schmitt and, 159–61, 169, 189, 190; Taubes and, 160–61
Neoplatonism, 55, 59–60, 63, 68; Cassirer on, 104–5; Christianity and, 117n16; Heidegger on, 107–8; Strauss on, 73n13

251

Newton, Isaac, 58
Nicolas of Cusa, 76n38
Nietzsche, Friedrich, 120, 166, 171; Arendt and, 134; Blumenberg and, 66–67; on "death of God," 57, 58, 62, 181; on "lies necessary for life," 59; *On the Genealogy of Morals*, 8–9, 22, 23; Schmitt and, 160; on transvaluation of values, 169
nihilism, 62, 197, 208–10
nominalism, 59–60, 63, 70; mystical, 68, 79n50
Norden, Eduard, 146
Novalis, 72n4

Ockham, William of, 79n50
*oikonomia*, 40–44

pantheism, 56–57, 185
Parmenides, 163
*parousia*, 123
Parsons, Talcott, 26–28
Pascal, Blaise, 67, 111
Paul (apostle), 14, 143; authoritarian aspects of, 169; Heidegger on, 103, 108; Taubes on, 164, 168, 169, 171, 190, 193–210. *See also* Christianity
Perse, Saint-John, 193, 211n2
Petri, Elfride, 103
Pfau, Thomas, 15–16
philology, 26, 39, 45n8
philosophy of history, 31–36, 122–27, 195–96
Platonism, 55, 104–5; Arendt on, 152n13; Heidegger on, 107–8; Stoicism and, 111–13. *See also* Neoplatonism
Pocock, J. G. A., 147
political theology, 1, 2, 7; birth of, 222–23; secularization and, 15–16
positivism, 26–27
progress, 33, 124–29; Blumenberg on, 128; consolation and, 126; eschatology and, 122–23; Foessel on, 119–29; Hegel on, 127; Kant on, 120–21, 123, 129; Löwith on, 121; in science, 125; Spinoza on, 73n13
Prometheus myth, 60–61

Proudhon, Pierre-Joseph, 122, 167, 168, 185–86, 188, 189
Proust, Marcel, 210
providential-economic paradigm, 41
Puritans, 143, 145, 155n39, 183

Ratzinger, Joseph, 226n2
religion, 8–10, 67; afterlife of, 4–5, 71n1, 87, 88, 95; Egyptian, 220–24, 232–35; history of, 161–64, 239; myth and, 103–6, 109; philosophy of, 103, 107–8; "secular," 142; survival of, 5
religious speech, 161–64
Revelation, Book of, 162, 163, 174n24
Ricoeur, Paul, 127
Robespierre, Maximilien, 140, 142
Rohilla people, 138, 153n20
Romans, Letter to, 14, 103, 168, 195, 207–10, 215n77
Romanticism, 67, 72n4
Rousseau, Jean-Jacques, 166, 168–70, 182, 189

Sabbatai Sevi, 77n42
Sarug, Israel, 56
Schelling, F. W. J., 62–63, 74n27, 120
Schiller, Friedrich von, 55
Schlegel, Friedrich von, 80n60, 126
Schmitt, Carl, 220–24; Agamben on, 38–39; Arendt and, 7, 131–50; Benjamin and, 7, 195, 206–7, 215n72; Blumenberg and, 86–88; *The Concept of the Political*, 169; on democracy, 171; on Donoso Cortés, 169; Habermas on, 26–29, 46n10; Hobbes and, 118n27, 162; National Socialism and, 159–61, 169, 189, 190; on political theology, 86–87, 118n27, 131–33, 231–32, 240; *Roman Catholicism and Political Form*, 170; on secularization, 2, 3, 241n4; Taubes and, 13, 155n42, 159–73, 204–7; on US revolution, 139; Weber and, 26–29, 46n10; Weinreich on, 152n19
Scholem, Gershom, 52–55, 76n42, 193, 202–4, 206; Benjamin and, 214n68
Schulte, Christoph, 72n8

Schulz, Wolfgang, 203
secularization, 1–8, 30–39, 219–25; Arendt on, 12, 131–50; Assmann on, 219–25, 231–34; Blumenberg on, 3, 6–7, 24; critics of, 15; definitions of, 2–4; of eschatology, 121–24; genealogy and, 2–8, 15–16; as historical development, 83–97; metaphorical history of, 6; political theology and, 15–16; revolution as, 137; Schmitt on, 2, 3, 241n4; theologization and, 219–25, 231–34; theories of, 21–44. *See also* *Verweltlichung*
Sloterdijk, Peter, 173n5
Smith, William Robertson, 181
Sombart, Nicolaus, 46n10, 159
Sophocles, 163
Spinoza, Benedict de, 72n13
Steding, Christoph, 204
Steinmetz-Jenkins, Daniel, 14, 17n5, 219–25, 244
Stern, William, 101
Stoicism, 111–13, 121–23
Strauss, Leo, 72n13, 76n42
Styfhals, Willem, 1–16, 71n1, 245
surrealism, 195; Gnosticism and, 14, 196–201
Symons, Stéphane, 1–16, 71n1, 245
Szondi, Léopold, 39

Taubes, Jacob, 12–13, 67–70, 245; Arendt and, 194; Assmann, 228n23; Benjamin and, 13–14, 193–210; on Bosch, 172–73; "Culture and Ideology," 201, 204; emigration of, 161; existentialism and, 164; on Gnosticism, 172, 196–200; Löwith and, 78n46; *Occidental Eschatology*, 12, 67–68, 74n21; "On the Symbolic Order of Modern Democracy," 13, 164–73, 179–91; plagiarism charges against, 169–70; *Poetik und Hermeneutik*, 195, 196, 198, 200; Schmitt and, 13, 155n42, 159–73, 204–7
Taubes, Susan, 162, 193, 194
Taylor, Charles, 3, 15–16, 51–52, 225
theodicy, 33, 121, 122, 127

theologization, 7, 14–15; definition of, 221; secularization and, 219–25, 231–34
"theoretical curiosity," 32, 33
theosophy, 74n27
Thessalonians, letters to, 162–63
Tillich, Paul, 66, 194
Tocqueville, Alexis de, 184
transcendence, 52–54, 56, 67, 186; Heidegger on, 107–8; Schlegel on, 80n60, 126
translation, 67, 83–86, 92–93, 97, 98n5
Treml, Martin, 13, 159–73, 245
Troeltsch, Ernst, 107
*tsimtsum* (withdrawal), 54–58, 60, 72n7; as "perfect gift," 70, 73n16
Turgenev, Ivan, 166, 181

*Umbesetzung*, 88
*Unbehagen* (uneasiness), 32, 33
United States Revolution, 136–37, 139–47, 184, 191
*univocatio entis*, principle of, 58, 72n7

values, transvaluation of, 169
*Vergangenheitsbewaltigung*, 159
*Verweltlichung*, 64–66, 86–88, 90; Hegel on, 127; Löwith on, 122. *See also* secularization
Virgil (Roman poet), 145–46, 150, 155n38
Voegelin, Eric, 5, 142
Voltaire, 180, 188
voluntarism, 12, 112–14, 152n19

*Wahl* versus *Entscheidung* (choice versus decision), 95–96
Waldron, Jeremy, 154n34
Warburg, Aby, 4–5
Weber, Max, 43, 241n6; Adorno on, 21–22; Blumenberg and, 24, 32, 33; on disenchantment, 4, 7, 25, 43, 129; genealogy of, 22–26; Habermas on, 26–29, 46n10, 47n15; Parsons and, 26–27; *The Protestant Ethic and the Spirit of Capitalism*, 3, 4, 23, 24; on rationalization, 4, 25, 31–32, 43–44;

Weber, Max *(cont'd)*
  Schmitt and, 26–29, 46n10; *Science as Vocation*, 128
Weber, Samuel, 170
Weidner, Daniel, 16
Weigel, Sigrid, 11, 13–14, 75n27, 83–97, 177n67, 193–210, 245–46
Weil, Simone, 194
Weinreich, Max, 152n19
Weir, David A., 155n39
Wetters, Kirk, 10, 21–44, 78n46, 246

Winckelmann, Johann Joachim, 114
Wisdom of Solomon, 236
Wolfson, Elliot R., 73n16
Wolin, Richard, 45n9, 228n23

Yesenin, Sergei, 210

Ziolkowski, Theodore, 145–46
Žižek, Slavoj, 53, 60
Zwingli, Huldrych, 105

www.ingramcontent.com/pod-product-compliance
Lightning Source LLC
Chambersburg PA
CBHW030536230426
43665CB00010B/919